WHY I PREACH THAT THE BIBLE IS LITERALLY TRUE

WHY I PREACH THAT THE BIBLE IS LITERALLY TRUE

FOREWORD BY O.S. HAWKINS
TIMOTHY AND DENISE GEORGE, EDITORS

BROADMAN
& HOLMAN
PUBLISHERS

Nashville, Tennessee

4212-60
0-8054-1260-3

Dewey Decimal Classification: 286
Subject Heading:Biblical Inerrancy\Bible—Evidences, Authority, Etc.
Library of Congress Card Catalog Number:94-47061

Unless otherwise stated all Scripture quotations are from the King James Version.

Interior design by Leslie Joslin
Cover design by Steve Diggs & Friends

Library of Congress Cataloging-in-Publication Data
Criswell, W. A. (Wallie A.), 1909
    Why I preach that the Bible is literally true/ W. A. Criswell;/ Timo-
thy George, editor: Denise George, editor.
        p. cm.
    ISBN 0-8054-1260-3
    1.Bible—Evidences, authority, etc. 2. Bible Inspiration.
I. George, Timothy. II. George, Denise. III. Title. IV. Series.
    BS480.C71995
    220.1'3—dc-20   94-47061
                                                         CIP

*To that man
who stands anywhere in the earth
with an open Bible
and preaches to the people
God's infallible Word.*

Contents

General Editors' Introduction

The Baptist movement as we know it today began as a small persecuted sect in pre-Revolutionary England. One critic labeled them as "miscreants begat in rebellion, born in sedition, and nursed in faction." Excluded by law from the English universities, Baptists developed their own structures for pastoral training. They also wrote hymns, preached sermons, published confessions, and defended their beliefs against skeptics, detractors, and rival religious groups of all kinds. From the popular works of John Bunyan and Benjamin Keach to the learned theology of John Gill and Andrew Fuller, Baptists wrote with a passion and with a purpose. In time a large body of Baptist literature was developed, writings that both reflected and contributed to the emerging sense of Baptist identity.

The Southern Baptist Convention was organized in 1845 for the purpose of "eliciting, combining, and directing the energies of the whole denomination in one sacred effort, for the propagation of the Gospel." This was an ambitious undertaking for the 293 "delegates," as they were then called, who gathered in Augusta, Georgia, and embraced this far-reaching vision at the founding meeting of the convention. Through the years the SBC has suffered numerous setbacks and distractions—the Civil War, Reconstruction, the Great Depression, social unrest, denominational strife, and much more. But through it all God has graciously blessed Southern Baptists in ways that future historians will surely record as remarkable. By the end of the twentieth century, Southern Baptists had grown into America's largest Protestant denomination, a fellowship of some fifteen million members in nearly forty thousand congregations supporting more than nine thousand missionaries.

Drawing on this rich heritage, the Library of Baptist Classics presents a series of books reflecting the faith and vision of Southern Baptists over the past 150 years. We are republishing in fresh editions and with new introductions a collection of seminal writings. These works have proven their worth as classics among Southern Baptists in the past and still speak powerfully to Baptist and other evangelical Christians today.

The Library of Baptist Classics includes writings of pastors, theologians, missionary statesmen, and denominational leaders from the past. Some of them are popular, others scholarly in form. They include sermons, doctrinal treatises, missionary biographies, and an anthology of Baptist confessions, covenants, and catechisms. Most of these writings have long been out of print. We present them now in the fervent hope that the Lord will see fit to use them again, as He has in the past, not only to remind us of the great legacy we have received, but also to inspire us to be faithful shapers of the future under the lordship of Jesus Christ.

Timothy George and Denise George,
General Editors

Foreword

O. S. HAWKINS

No series on Baptist classics from the past 150 years would be complete without Dr. W. A. Criswell's volume *Why I Preach That the Bible is Literally True*. Dr. Criswell has lived in every decade of the twentieth century and has ministered here at the First Baptist Church in Dallas for fifty golden years. His thundering voice and prolific pen have reached to the ends of the earth. Instinctively, he has always risen to the occasion to address particular needs at particular times along our evangelical way. When within our own Southern Baptist Zion we were struggling with professors at certain seminaries who were advocating the evolutionary process, Dr. Criswell's pen produced his classic work, *Did Man Just Happen?* Thousands of people found in this apologetic the biblical basis to stand upon the inerrant Word of God in this field of study resting in the confidence that God is indeed the Creator of everything. When Baptists were wrestling in recent decades with a response to the charismatic phenomenon that was making inroads throughout much of the western world, once again it was Dr. Criswell who addressed the subject in his volume, *The Holy Spirit in Today's World*. When the battle for the Bible was raging in Baptist life, perhaps his most poignant and profitable contribution was made in this volume which you hold in your hand. Dr. Criswell's very name is synonymous with the Bible. We will always remember him "with a Bible in his hand."

It is my joy to serve as pastor of this great church where for fifty years he ministered with such effective power. Perhaps only one who has seen it from the inside can know the true genius of this great warrior saint. First Baptist in Dallas has been a ministry built upon the Word of God through proclamation as week after week, month after month, year after year, Dr. Criswell preached throughout the Bible to the world from our pulpit here. He has built it as a ministry of the Word not only in proclamation but in education. His vision, which came to fruition, includes not only a thousand-student academy but a fully accredited college, the Criswell College, offering bachelor's and master's degrees to hundreds of young men and women preparing for ministry. Its beautiful campus near downtown Dallas will carry his name into the next century and until Jesus returns as we continue his dream of educating young men and women to hold fast to the Word of God. Our First Baptist Church in Dallas has also been built upon the ministry of the Word through confrontation as people have been trained to confront a secular culture and engage a world with the message of hope and the good news of the gospel of Jesus Christ our Lord.

For many years in my own personal devotional life I've read Oswald Chambers' *My Utmost for His Highest*. Chambers says that giants dwindle into ordinary men when you really get to know them. Oswald Chambers never met W. A. Criswell. He is a giant among us and a role model for all of us. He is the prince of preachers and coupled with that is a sincere pastoral heart. Like David, he "shepherds his people with the integrity of his heart and the skill of his hands." Had the Lord led him into politics, he would have been president of the United States. Had the Lord led him into law, he would have been the chief justice of the Supreme Court. Had the Lord led him into business, he would have undoubtedly built a Fortune 500 company. It was our church's great joy and the Christian world's great joy that God called him as a young boy to preach the unsearchable riches of Christ which he has faithfully done throughout a lifetime.

As I write this preface, he is in his eighty-fifth year. He is like Caleb at eighty-five who said, "I am as strong this day as on the day Moses sent me. Now therefore give me that mountain where the milk and honey flow, where the grapes of Eschol grow." As I pray for him daily, I'm often reminded of the passage in 2 Kings 23:25 wherein is said of good King Josiah, "Now before him was no king like him who turned to the Lord with all his heart, with all his soul, and with all his might . . . nor after him did any arise like him."

Yes, Oswald Chambers never met W. A. Criswell. He is to our century what Charles Hadden Spurgeon was to the previous and much more. I am confident there will never arise another like him.

Introduction

TIMOTHY GEORGE

Criswell is an old English family name that can be traced to the early Middle Ages when Christianity was first introduced to the British Isles. When missionaries, such as Patrick, won people to the Christian faith in places where there was no natural body of water, they would dig a well, calling it "Christ's well," and proceed to baptize the new believers in it. In the 1720s a family of Irish Protestant Criswells immigrated from Dublin to Chester County, Pennsylvania. One of their sons, John Y. Criswell, moved his family by wagon train to a settlement near what is now Austin, Texas in 1786, three years before George Washington was inaugurated as the first president of the United States. Some seven generations later, Wallie Amos Criswell would be born in the dust bowl town of Eldorado, Oklahoma to a cowboy-barber and his beautiful wife. This little boy, born in obscurity and raised in poverty, would

1

become in time the most famous Baptist pastor in the world. Known far and wide as a passionate preacher, a powerful evangelist, and a redoubtable defender of the faith, W. A. Criswell will leave a legacy comparable in scope and influence only to that of Charles Haddon Spurgeon. Through seven decades of ministry, controversy, and phenomenal pulpit productivity, this "wellspring of Christ" has never run dry. More than anyone else before or since, he has fulfilled the promise of his family name.

Criswell sometimes refers to himself as a "Texahoman" because, although born in the Sooner state, he moved as a young boy to the Texas Panhandle, to the small railroad town of Texline, a place "with beautiful sunrises and beautiful sunsets and nothing much in between." Here in the little "cracker-box" Baptist church, he was converted to Christ during a revival meeting led by evangelist John Hicks. A few years later he was called to preach in a similar meeting, this one led by John R. Rice, a young music evangelist who boasted that he was from Baylor University, "where the best Baptist preachers in the world are trained." Rice knelt beside Criswell and prayed, "Father, this is W. A. Criswell, Jr., and he feels called to preach. Bless him, Lord. Guide his steps. Go before him in a cloud by day and a pillar of fire by night. Make sure his call is true and use him in building Your Kingdom. Amen."

Young Criswell was a voracious reader. He loved the poetry of Shakespeare and Browning, the classic biographies of Julius Caesar, Alexander the Great, and Napoleon, as well as the folksy stories of Zane Grey and Will Rogers. But above all, the Holy Scriptures became his constant companion and his daily bread. Criswell read, studied, and memorized the Bible. As John Bunyan once said of his early Christian experience, "The Word of the Lord was precious to me in those days." As a young preacher Criswell attended the great cowboy roundups and open encampments on the Texas prairies where he listened entranced to the great pulpit masters of the day. L. R. Scarborough, Wallace Bassett, J. Frank Norris, and above all, George W. Truett were all preachers Criswell heard and admired. Although they differed from one another in many respects, these great preachers all loved the Lord, believed His Word, and preached it with power.

Augustine once said of his mother Monica, "She loved to have me with her, as is the custom with most mothers, but much more than most mothers." Anna Currie Criswell felt something of this kind of overweening devotion for her precocious preacher son. Not that she was happy with his desire to enter the ministry. She wanted him to be a doctor, as her father had been, realizing no doubt that physicians of the soul were seldom spared the pinching poverty she had known for all of her married life. Still she sacrificed much, even leaving her husband temporarily in order to accompany her son to Amarillo, where he graduated from high school, and then to Waco, where he enrolled in Baylor University.

Criswell brought to Baylor an unquenchable zeal for preaching the gospel. At the end of his freshman year he was ordained by his home church in Amarillo, the ordaining council finding him "unusually sound and well posted in all the Baptist doctrines." Back in Waco he was called to exercise his ministerial gifts in student pastorates in such places of renown as Devil's Bend and Pulltight, Texas. During these years he was probably known more for his pulpit exuberance than his sermonic content. On a clear night, it was said, you could hear Criswell preaching five miles away! But his zeal was not without knowledge. This Spurgeon of the Plains graduated from Baylor in 1931, magna cum laude.

That fall, Criswell began a six-year stint of study at the Southern Baptist Theological Seminary in Louisville, Kentucky. There he earned the Th. M. (1934) and the Ph.D. (1937) degrees, writing a learned dissertation on "The John the Baptist Movement in its Relation to the Christian Movement." At Southern Criswell studied under such scholarly giants as A. T. Robertson, John R. Sampey, William Hersey Davis, and Kyle M. Yates. They instilled in Criswell a love for the study of the Scriptures in the original languages of Greek and Hebrew. From that time on Criswell's preaching was marked by a careful exegetical engagement with the biblical text. Criswell would later claim that the doctrine of biblical inerrancy with its correlary of verbal, plenary inspiration was the very teaching espoused and championed by his professors at Southern Seminary. While still in seminary Criswell gained a life partner when he married the church pianist, the lovely Betty Mae

Harris, at his part-time pastorate in Mount Washington, Kentucky. Married on Valentine's Day in 1935, they have recently celebrated sixty years of life together in the service of God.

When Criswell received his Ph.D. during a colorful ceremony at Crescent Hill Baptist Church in Louisville in the spring of 1937, the congregation stood to sing, "The Son of God goes forth to war, a kingly crown to gain, His blood-red banner streams afar: Who follows in his train?" Already the storm clouds of war were gathering across Europe, and soon America would be drawn into a global holocaust more horrible than the one Criswell had heard and read about as a boy in Texline. But at the time Criswell was facing a more personal crisis, namely, what church he should go to as pastor. He and Betty had promised the Lord that they would accept the first pastoral call which they received after graduation. A Baptist church in the little-known town of Chickasha, Oklahoma had indeed issued such a call to Criswell just shortly before a similar summons arrived from the much larger and more prestigious First Baptist Church of Birmingham, Alabama. Criswell was certain that God was calling him to Birmingham and his wife had no desire to head for Chickasha. "That's wilderness, desert sand, coyotes, and cactus," she said. But together they agreed to remain true to the covenant they had made with God and headed west. "I'm going to preach God's Word," Criswell said to Betty, "and let the chips fall where they may."

For seven years Criswell served as pastor of two Baptist churches in Oklahoma, first at Chickasha (1937–1940), and then at Muskogee (1941–1944). During these years of depression and world war, Criswell "learned the ropes" of pastoral ministry. Building on the excellent foundation he had received through years of preparation and study, he developed the homiletical approach of preaching expository sermons through specific books of the Bible. This approach transformed his preaching and became the hallmark of his later ministry. In retrospect, the Birmingham-Chickasha dilemma was one of the turning points in Criswell's life. Had he taken the larger, plusher congregation his subsequent usefulness might have come to naught. While such second-guessing is best left to "the imponderables of God," as Criswell is wont to say, he remains convinced that he was sovereignly led by divine providence from Kentucky to Oklahoma, and from there to the center of his life's work in the heart of Dallas, Texas.

In 1994 Criswell celebrated fifty years of pastoral ministry at the First Baptist Church of Dallas, a congregation of more than 28,000 members. Criswell succeeded the inimitable George W. Truett, who was pastor of this same congregation for forty-seven years. While this is not the world's record for tag-team pastoral longevity—the famous John Gill served Horsleydown, London for fifty-two years while his successor, John Rippon, stayed on for sixty-three more—it comes close! In some ways, however, one can hardly think of two more contrasting figures in Southern Baptist life: Truett, with his roots in the mountains of North Carolina, Criswell, wind-swept son of the Texas prairies; Truett, the self-educated denominational insider, Criswell, the highly educated mainstream maverick; Truett, the model of pulpit decorum and pastoral gentility, Criswell, a tornado from Sinai, "a Holy Roller with a Ph.D." How was is that W. A. Criswell became the successor of George W. Truett?

Criswell was not the first choice of the pulpit committee. His lifelong friend, Duke K. McCall, along with other prominent preachers throughout the Southern Baptist Convention, were held to be more likely successors to the great Truett. However, before the church had ever contacted him about the position, Criswell had an unusual dream. He dreamed that he was seated in the balcony of First Baptist, Dallas during the funeral of Dr. Truett. He had only visited the church once before, as a delegate to a BSU convention during his student days at Baylor. In his dream Criswell was seated in the same spot he had occupied on that previous visit. As Criswell tells it, he whispered to the man on his left:

"Why are they all crying?"

"The great pastor is gone," he answered, his own eyes filled with tears. "Dr. Truett is dead."

As I sat staring at that lone casket in the wilderness of flowers, I felt a hand on my knee and I heard a quiet voice say, "You must now go down and preach for my people."

Quickly, I turned to see who had spoken those strange words. It was Dr. Truett himself.

"Oh, sir, not I, " I answered him. "I could never do that."

Then he tapped my knee again and smiled.

"Yes, yes," he said, "You must go down now and preach for my people."

The pastor's eyes looked deep into mine. I felt a chill, and at that moment I awakened.

In time the church did extend a call to Criswell, and he accepted. In his first sermon as pastor he relayed the story of the Truett dream. While some critics have doubted Criswell's account of the dream, no one who knows Criswell can doubt that he sincerely believes it. Indeed, Truett himself experienced a dream and vision of the risen Christ following a great crisis in his early ministry at First Baptist, Dallas. Neither Truett or Criswell are know as mystics or clairvoyants, but both were transformed by these special disclosures from beyond.

Criswell honored the memory of Truett and built upon his legacy. During his inaugural sermon to the church, Criswell set forth his vision:

> We'll go on and up with our various works. We'll give to missions more money than ever before. We'll have a Sunday School with five thousand in attendance every Sunday and the services in the church will be in the eyes of God not because of an eloquent tongue and a magnificent personality, but because of prayer, love and labor.

It is beyond the scope of this essay to chronicle the phenomenal growth, evangelistic outreach, and multi-faceted ministries of First Baptist, Dallas during the five decades of Criswell's pastoral leadership there. When asked to give advice to young preachers, he simply replies, "Prepare your message, study, pray, pour over it, and then pour your whole life into it. Love the people; be good to them."

Through the years Criswell's ministry has been marked by his genuine love for people. While he always kept his mornings free for study and prayer, and never neglected his pastoral duties of vis-

itation and administration, he also reserved time to meet with anyone who cared to see him. Some years ago a teenage preacher-boy
from a nearby city who had experienced a call to the ministry came
to Dallas and boldly made an appointment to visit with Dr.
Criswell in his study. At the appointed hour, the secretary ushered
the young man into Dr. Criswell's private suite. The great pastor
listened with empathy and interest as the young preacher
recounted his call to the ministry and the difficulties he was facing.
He encouraged him to remain faithful to the Word of God, to seek
further training, and never to turn back from his calling. When
their conference was ended, Criswell knelt beside the young
preacher with his arm around his shoulder invoking the presence
of the Lord with such power and intensity that the antique furni-
ture in the office seemed aglow with supernatural fire. When he
returned home, the young preacher told his pastor what he had
done. "What?" shouted the surprised cleric, "you really prayed
with Dr. Criswell? Man, you have seen the pope!" Today that
young man is a seasoned pastor in Florida, but he still remembers
his encounter with Criswell as a major turning point in his ministry. No doubt many hundreds, perhaps thousands, of others could
tell a similar story.

When all is said and done, however, it is not Criswell's magnani-
mous personality, nor his great skill as an organizer and strategist,
nor yet his prodigious learning and prolific writing which has been
his greatest contribution to the work of God's Kingdom. Without
doubt Criswell's greatest legacy is his faithful, unfaltering, passionate, persuasive preaching of the Word of God. In 1946, soon after
coming to Dallas, he announced to the congregation his plan to
preach through the entire Bible. Seventeen years and eight months
later, this monumental project was completed. Many of Criswell's
books are slightly edited transcripts of these expository messages.
He preached for one entire year on the ninth chapter of Hebrews,
and for three years on the book of Revelation. During his long
walk through the Bible, members of First Baptist, Dallas would
mark pivotal events in their family life by reference to their pastor's
exegetical sojourns: Baby Jane was born in Chronicles, Aunt Ruth

got married in Mark, Billy Joe was baptized in Daniel, and deacon Smith died in Deuteronomy!

In pursuing a continuous expository pattern of preaching, Criswell modeled a homiletical style very different from that of Truett, who nearly always preached topical sermons. In this respect he also differed from Spurgeon, in so many other ways his hero, who preferred to develop great doctrinal sermons around isolated texts drawn from various portions of Scripture. In reality, Criswell recaptured a pattern of preaching first modeled in a definitive way by the great reformers of the sixteenth century, men like Huldrych Zwingli and John Calvin who discarded the "canned sermons" of the medieval lectionary in favor of verse by verse, chapter by chapter explication of Holy Writ. In turn Criswell's approach has encouraged countless other pastors to abandon their "Simple Sermons for Southern Baptists" and commit themselves to the difficult but joyous task of proclaiming the whole counsel of God. Criswell commends to others what he has practiced himself as the lifelong rule of his pulpit work: "Our preaching needs depth, force, and doctrinal content, and the only way to get it is by long hours of study and prayer."

It has been said that Criswell was "a fundamentalist when fundamentalism wasn't cool." Criswell has sometimes used this word to describe himself and it seems entirely appropriate if "fundamentalist" is used in the classic sense to refer to one who affirms unflinchingly the fundamentals of the faith. But if fundamentalist is defined pejoratively to mean narrow-minded, inflexible, obscurantist, then this is not an apt description of the real Criswell. Although his basic theology has remained consistent throughout his long ministry, Criswell has shown a remarkable ability to learn, grow, and adapt through the years. His most famous about-face came on the issue of racial reconciliation. After many years of advocating the policy of segregation, in 1968 Criswell preached a sermon on "The Church of the Open Door." In this message he announced a change of heart on this explosive issue. "I came to the profound conclusion that to separate by coercion the body of Christ on the basis of skin pigmentation was unthinkable, unchristian, and unacceptable to God." More recently, he has spoken out on behalf of the biblical call to peacemaking. "Just because a man is fundamental and believes in the whole Bible doesn't mean he doesn't believe in world peace. That is just a crazy idea of the left wing liberals." In 1971 Criswell scandalized some of his own Baptist brethren when Pope Paul VI received him in a papal audience. Criswell declared, "I'm not a Catholic. . . and I couldn't be, but I thank God for what they have done to name the Name of Christ in the world. I would be more comfortable praying with a Catholic priest who believes in the virgin birth, the blood atonement, and the deity of Christ than with a liberal Protestant who doesn't." Because of his openness and flexibility on these and other controverted matters, Criswell has been accused by some ultra-traditionalist Christians of being "involved in apostasy or compromise with it."

Since coming to First Baptist, Dallas in 1944, Criswell has never sought a higher office or a wider arena of ministry. Still, like Truett before him, Criswell has been a world Christian. A loyal Southern Baptist, he has led his congregation in major commitments to missions giving through the Cooperative Program. He has circled the globe numerous times on behalf of world evangelization, preaching the gospel in every continent on earth. One of his early mission trips, made with Duke McCall, is chronicled in their fascinating book, *Passport to the World*. He has also invested himself in the wider work of the Kingdom by serving as a trustee on numerous denominational boards, agencies, and missionary endeavors. In 1969 he was elected to the first of two terms as president of the Southern Baptist Convention.

Why I Preach That the Bible is Literally True is one of fifty-four books which Criswell has published. We are including it in the Library of Baptist Classics not only because it is his most famous book, but also because it is one of very few of his volumes that did not originate as a series of sermons. *Why I Preach That the Bible is Literally True* was written with a deliberate purpose and strategy in mind, namely, to encourage pastors to remain faithful to the truth of God's written Word and to make it central in their pulpit ministry. It is not coincidental that the book's title begins not with "Why I Believe" but rather "Why I Preach."

Why I Preach That the Bible is Literally True was first published in 1969, during Criswell's first term as president of the SBC, and it fell like a bombshell on the theological landscape of the day. The Association of Baptist Professors of Religion passed a formal resolution blasting the book and excoriating the Baptist Sunday School Board for publishing and promoting it. A spokesman for Broadman Press quickly pointed out that Criswell's book did not represent any "official" theological viewpoint, although he acknowledged, in what now appears as an understatement, that it "probably reflects the position of the majority of our folk." One of the critics, Robert Alley, professor of religion at the University of Richmond, declared: "Our greatest concern is the image of the ministry cast by preachers like Criswell. His example is detrimental to the first-rate education our best students are looking for." In the following year William Smith, one of Alley's colleagues at the University of Richmond, offered himself as an opposition candidate to thwart Criswell's second term as SBC president. Criswell, however, was re-elected overwhelmingly by a vote of 7,483 to 450. In the meantime, *Why I Preach That the Bible is Literally True* continued to sell at a phenomenal rate. It seemed that the more the critics denounced the book, the more others were buying, reading, and profiting from it.

Criswell himself was surprised at the vehement reaction elicited by his book. But in fact the storm over biblical authority had been brewing in the SBC for many years. In 1950 a young professor at Southern Seminary named Clyde Francisco had published his *Introducing the Old Testament* in which he reviewed fairly the results of contemporary biblical scholarship while also pointing out that many of the "higher critics" had dismembered the Old Testament by "tearing its contents into meaningless fragments." Francisco reminded his readers that Jesus always regarded the Scriptures as a unity rather than a compilation, and he warned against a wholesale acceptance of any approach to the study of the Bible which denied its unique character as a special revelation of God or downplayed the supernatural dimension of miracles and prophecy.

Francisco himself used critical methodologies judiciously, but one of his students, Ralph Elliott, proceeded with far less caution.

Elliott's 1961 Broadman book, *The Message of Genesis*, created a firestorm of controversy leading eventually to his dismissal from the faculty of Midwestern Seminary. In 1963 the Convention responded to the crisis by adopting, under the guidance of Herschel H. Hobbs, *The Baptist Faith and Message*. Article I of this confessional standard declared:

> The Holy Bible was written by men divinely inspired and is the record of God's revelation of Himself to man. It is a perfect treasure of divine instruction. It has God for its author, salvation for its end, and truth, without any mixture of error, for its matter. It reveals the principles by which God judges us; and therefore is, and will remain until the end of the world, the true center of Christian union, and the supreme standard by which all human conduct, creeds, and religious opinions should be tried. The criterion by which the Bible is to be interpreted is Jesus Christ.

Although Criswell nowhere mentioned Elliott by name, he clearly believed that certain teachers and scholars in the denomination had gone beyond the bounds of acceptable diversity by calling into question the total truthfulness of the biblical record. His book was a clarion call for his denomination, and by inference for all evangelical Christians, to return to an unbroken doctrine of Holy Scripture. Those who criticized the book for its truncated literalism, as though Criswell believed that God has feathers (Ps. 91:4) or that the trees clapped their hands (Isa. 55:12), had clearly not read what he had written about the poetical, rhetorical, figurative, and metaphorical uses of language in the Bible. Nowhere does Criswell eschew the legitimate use of historical and critical techniques for elucidating the biblical text. What he does deplore is the kind of unbelieving criticism and hypothetical reconstructions which deny the divine authorship of Scripture and detract from its total truthfulness.

What Criswell means when he says that he preaches the Bible "literally" is that he affirms without reservation the verbal, plenary inspiration of the biblical text as given by God, a text which he seeks to understand, under the illumination of the Holy Spirit, through careful grammatical and historical study. Otherwise put: What the Bible says, God says. What the Bible says happened, really happened. Every miracle, every event, in every book of the Old and New Testaments is altogether true and trustworthy.

In all honesty it should be stated that Criswell's book was never intended to be a scholarly treatise drafted for the benefit of academic technicians. It was written as a tract for the times, a passionate manifesto from the heart of a preaching pastor who week by week was required to face a congregation hungry for a word from the Lord. In the twenty-five years since the book was first published, evangelical biblical scholarship has continued to make advances, bringing ever new insights to the unchanging truth of God's written Word. *The Chicago Statement on Biblical Inerrancy* (1978) and *The Chicago Statement of Biblical Hermeneutics* (1982) have been widely recognized as helpful guides in setting forth a balanced doctrine of biblical inerrancy. In 1994 the SBC adopted a resolution commending these statements to the boards, agencies, and churches of the denomination.

In the meantime, of course, the SBC has undergone a major change in direction and leadership. This reorientation is called by those who dislike it a "take-over," and by those who look on it with favor a "turn-around." Whatever perspective one takes, no one can deny that W. A. Criswell has played a major role in the conservative resurgence within America's largest Protestant denomination. Criswell frankly sees the redirection of the SBC as the providential work of God, shielding the denomination from, to quote his beloved Spurgeon, "the boiling mud showers of modern heresy," and calling it back to biblical fidelity and evangelistic and missionary advance. At the same time, he recognizes the harsh turns the controversy has sometimes taken and speaks with remorse about ruptured relationships along the way: "I wish that the people who believed the most about the Bible had the most loving spirit about what they believe, me included. But so many times the opposite is true. The war of words must have grieved our loving Father, for it certainly broke my heart." As the SBC moves on toward a new era of rebuilding and reconciliation, it is important to remember that the legacy of biblical faithfulness must be owned afresh in every new generation. The price of spiritual and theological integrity, like that of liberty, is eternal vigilance.

After all these years, W. A. Criswell is still going strong—stronger than ever! His ability to outlive and outlast his contemporaries in minisry, to weather the storms of controversy with unflappable poise, is truly amazing. A former ministerial associate who knows him well once remarked: "If the whole world were one game of musical chairs with all four billion people involved and only one chair, when the music stopped no one would have to guess who would be in the chair: it would be W. A. Criswell."

Criswell is a survivor, but he is more than that. He is a patriarch who has been given a vision of the Promised Land and likes what he sees. The secret of his life and ministry is his combustible confidence in Almighty God, the God who spoke and still speaks through his Word which cannot be broken. Significantly, Criswell entitled his autobiography *Standing on the Promises*. Near the end of this memoir, he offered the following prayer which sums up his life and spirituality as well as anything I know:

> Thank you, Father, for allowing me a lifetime in your Word. Thank you for standing beside my desk all these decades, informing, correcting, inspiring, and directing me.
>
> For my blunders along the way, I ask your forgiveness. The errors, Lord, were mine. Sometimes I got in a hurry. Other times I let my mind wonder and my brain rest. Yet other times, I was tired, lonely, or afraid. Still, Lord, you never failed me.

As this millennium rushes toward its close, W. A. Criswell is still at his desk, still on his knees, and still in the Word. And he is still preaching that the Bible is literally true. As one scholar put it, you can still hear him five miles away!

Sources:

Bush, L. Russ. "W. A. Criswell," In *Baptist Theologians*, eds. Timothy George and David S. Dockery. Nashville: Broadman Press, 1990.

Criswell, W. A. *Look Up Brother!* Nashville: Broadman Press, 1970.

———. *Standing on the Promises.* Dallas: Word Publishing, 1990.

Patterson, Paige."The Imponderables of God," *Criswell Theological Review* 1 (1987).

Russell, C. Allyn. "W. A. Criswell: A Case Study in Fundamentalism," *Review and Expositor* 81 (1984).

1969 Preface

W. A. CRISWELL

The invitation to write this book "from the top of my head and from the bottom of my heart" was accepted with the earnest and prayerful hope that it might encourage other ministers to preach the Bible as the literal, inspired, God-breathed truth of heaven. The Lord has so greatly blessed me in preaching from this conviction that I covet for every pastor a like supernal experience.

The volume is my testimony, not a documented textbook on biblical theology. It is written with my words, with the words of others, and with the words of God taken from the Holy Scriptures. No need exists for me to publish a textbook on the inspiration of the Bible. A library of volumes can be found on the character and composition of the Bible, books that are fully and meticulously documented. There are scholarly works such as L. Gaussen, *The Inspiration of the Holy Scriptures*; Arthur W. Pink, *The Divine Inspiration of the Bible*; B. B. Warfield, *Inspiration and Authority of the Bible*; John Urquhart, *The Inspiration and Accuracy of the Holy Scriptures*, and a multitude of others. If you seek an in-depth, detailed study of the Word of God, read these books and the countless references upon which their conclusions are based. But this present volume I have written is a testimony from my heart, how I feel about God's Word; and from my best judgment, what I have factually observed in my own extended ministry and in the ministries of others concerning the preaching of the Bible.

Even though I wrote the book in a time of tremendous pressure—busy in my own pastorate, busy with evangelistic Encounter Crusades and, of all things, elected president of the Southern Baptist Convention!—yet when I had done the writing, the pages numbered several hundred, in fact, so many that the volume printed would have been excessively expensive. I had the assignment, therefore, of cutting out and lopping off half of what I had said. Believe me, it was a task hard to do. So much I wanted to explain and so much I wanted to illustrate I have had to take away. I regret this, for it robs the book of a thousand experiences with which I so wanted to present the ministry God has given me in my dear church. Maybe, some day, I can write another book in my old age and include in it all these things I have seen and heard, things that sometimes sound like a twenty-ninth chapter to the book of Acts.

Let me thank Mrs. Maxine Dudley for typing the manuscript and Howard Laing for checking the grammatical construction of the sentences, and all who have had a part in helping me meet the publisher's deadline. And let me conclude this "Foreword" as I conclude my "Pastor's Pen" written each week for our little paper, *The First Baptist Reminder*: "See you Sunday with a Bible in my hand and with a message from God in my heart."

God bless you forever.

PART I

Why I Believe that the Bible Is Literally True

THE PRECIOUS BIBLE

Though the cover is worn
And the pages are torn,
And though places bear traces of tears,
Yet more precious than gold
Is the Book, worn and old,
That can shatter and scatter my fears.
When I prayerfully look
In the precious old Book,
Many pleasures and treasures I see;
Many tokens of love
From the Father above,
Who is nearest and dearest to me.
This old Book is my guide,
'Tis a friend by my side,
It will lighten and brighten my way;
And each promise I find
Soothes and gladdens my mind
As I read it and heed it today.

—Anonymous

CHAPTER 1

God's Quickening Word

In the providence of God, an older man was wondrously saved in one of the services of our church. He had been a great sinner. For the years of his life he had known no other thing than the wayward ways of the world. But he happened to marry a devout Christian woman who brought him to our congregation, where, listening to the Word of God, he found the Lord. The change was instantaneous. He became a new and a different man. He loved to come to church where we read the Holy Scriptures together and where I preach the Bible. Both at home and in his business office he constantly read the Book as though seeking to redeem the years he had wasted in the world.

Then that day of sorrow came. He was stricken with a heart attack and died immediately. I went to the memorial service to lay his body away and to thank God for his Christian conversion. With hundreds of other friends, I looked at the sleeping figure in the casket. To my great surprise, his right hand pressed his Bible against his heart. I turned to his wife in astonishment.

"What an unusual thing," I exclaimed, "that he holds his Bible in his hand! Why have you done this?"

"For the compelling reason," she replied, "that he loved it so. We read the Bible at church; we read it together at home. He read it at his business office. It seemed appropriate that his Bible be in his hand as his last testimony to the saving power of the Word of God."

And thus he was buried with that Bible in the casket where his body awaits the great resurrection day of the Lord when the God of the Book will bring to fulfilment every promise written on every page. Believing the Bible, "Surely goodness and mercy shall follow me all the days of my life; and I will dwell in the house of the Lord for ever." The Bible is a book to live by and to die by. It is worthy to be received as an infallible guide to heaven. It is true and trustworthy in every way. It is the veritable Word of God.

While writing these words a postman placed in my hands a letter from a young man in which he thanked me for conducting the funeral service for his beloved father. He closed the letter of appreciation with this paragraph: "Father loved to hear you preach the Bible and would have been comforted to know that you were there with words of assurance and peace when we needed you. God bless you for being a pastor who feeds his flock on the Word of God."

This is one of the reasons why I believe that the Bible is literally true: namely, because of the marvelous effect it has upon those who hear it and read it. It contains the gospel which is the power of God unto salvation.

The Power of the Word to Convert

The Bible works. Its truths transform the hearts and lives of men and women. It converts to a better life the small and the great. The beggar on the street and the king on his throne, the poor woman weeping in an attic room and the philosopher in his endowed chair, the profoundest thinker and the uncultured savage, are all changed by the power of this Book. The drunkard, the thief, the libertine leave their sin to walk in the light of God's precepts. The proud atheist becomes a humble believer in Christ by the truths of the Bible.

A Christian missionary will land on a savage island. The inhabitants of the place have no written language and they possess no literature. They regard this stranger as an enemy. In their savage hostilities they have no desire to change their way of life. They are cannibals in background and more like beasts than human beings in their daily life. But this Christian man, who has come ashore without money and without an army, works a remarkable miracle in the lives of those people. His only weapon is the Bible. His only possession is the salvation of Christ. He preaches the gospel. He gives an invitation. Then the miracle happens. In a few short years the naked savages of the island wear the raiment of godliness. Their murderous immorality is transformed into Christian brotherhood. Their tragic cruelty is now wondrous kindness. All of this has been accomplished with no other instrument but the Word of God.

The Miracle

This miracle is being repeated in every part of the earth. It was my illimitable joy to visit the work of the missionary among the Auca Indians in the Amazon jungle of South America. For generations these Stone Age Indians had bathed their hands in human blood. They had murdered even the five white missionaries who had landed in a little airplane to bring them God's message. In nothing disheartened, two dedicated missionary women gambled their lives to enter the boundaries of the jungles over which roamed these savage Aucas. Within a matter of months they had won them to Christ, and the savage cruelty of these naked, Stone Age Indians had been changed into humble, loving disciples of Christ.

Such a transformation I could not imagine. I went to the Amazon to look upon it with my own eyes. This truly is one of the greatest miracles in modern history. Our airplanes are miraculous, our radios are miraculous, but nothing is as miraculous as the glorious, Christian transformation demonstrated in the lives of these savage Aucas of South America.

The Wonderful Change by Conversion

This story of wonderful change by conversion can be repeated throughout the earth. One time in a rural church I pastored, a godly deacon and farmer in the community was given a Bible in Spanish. He could not read it and wondered what to do with it. Then it occurred to him that he could give it to a Spanish-speaking family that lived a few miles distant from his homeplace. He made the journey over to the Mexican home and placed in their hands that Spanish Bible. It was not long until the father in that Mexican home came to see my godly deacon. He said he and his family had been reading the Book, they had found the Lord, and, in obedience to Christ's commands, they wished to be baptized. I baptized them "in the name of the Father and of the Son and of the Holy Spirit." They were truly changed and truly saved.

In the passing of time, their home burned. When I went out to see them and to help them in their destitution, they laid in my hands a Bible. It had been partly burned, and it was completely soaked with water. The Mexican father in the home said to me: "This is the only thing that we rescued from our burning house. The Word of God meant so much to us that we sought to save it first." Oh, the amazing power of God's Book!

The testimony of transformed lives to the literal truths of the living Word spans the centuries. From Saul of Tarsus to Justin Martyr to Augustine to John Bunyan to John Newton to John Wesley to B. H. Carroll to Jerry McCauley—to the host of God's glorious witnesses today, the testimony is ever the same. There is power in the Word of God to convert.

A doctor was won to Christ under the preaching of Dwight L. Moody. Someone asked him how it happened and he said: "I went to hear Mr. Moody preach with no other idea than to have something to laugh at. I knew he was no scholar and I felt sure I could find many flaws in his argument. But I found I could not get at the man. He stood there hiding behind the Bible and just fired one Bible Scripture after the other at me until they went home to my heart straight as a bullet from a rifle, and I was converted." Moody's power was in the way he had his Bible at the tip of his tongue and the way God blessed his preaching of the everlasting Word.

Centuries of Preachers

It has been thus with the preachers of the Word of God through the centuries. Charles Haddon Spurgeon, the far-famed London pastor, was a Bible preacher. He believed every part of the Book. He delivered over four thousand sermons covering the Bible from Genesis to Revelation. One can take those sermons in textual order and have an almost complete commentary on the Bible. He believed every syllable in the Book. He preached from the Old Testament. He preached from the New Testament. He preached from Genesis. He preached from Revelation. He preached from Leviticus. He preached from Ephesians. He preached from Esther. He preached from the Book of Acts. What was the result? Not since the days of the apostle Paul were so many people turned to the Lord.

But what else followed? These blessings were added: homes for widows, orphanages for destitute children, societies that bring the Word of God to those who do not possess it, and missionaries to preach the message of salvation beyond the seas. From that one man's preaching of the Bible, marvelous influences flowed out over the world. A man was found frozen to death in the Alps. He had one of Spurgeon's sermons in his hand. When David Livingstone died, he had one of Spurgeon's sermons in the top of his hat. The influence of the preaching of the Bible by Spurgeon in the Metropolitan Tabernacle in London literally moved the whole world toward God.

The Bible is a book which reveals to us truth able to bring us into living union with God. Scientific knowledge and the words in which that knowledge is conveyed have no power to change our character or to give us a living hope of heaven. But the Word of God has in it that vital power. When received with meekness into our hearts with spiritual understanding, it is able to save us to the uttermost. It is the instrument of the Holy Spirit wherewith God accomplishes in us the regeneration of our souls. The Word of God is a living message containing within itself God's own life (John 5:24).

The life of God is in His Word; the Word is quick and living (Heb. 4:12–13). The Word of God is a mirror (James 1:23); it reveals to us our true selves. The Word of God is a seed (Luke 8:11); it contains the life and the vitality of the Lord. The Word of God is a sword (Eph. 6:17); it pierces the heart and lays bare and naked our sinful souls before Him who only can save us from death. The Bible is a life-giving word (1 Pet. 1:23); it is the vehicle for imparting that life to us which is in Christ Jesus the Incarnate Word. Eternal life for the individual soul begins through believing the testimony of God.

The Universal Appeal of the Bible

The appeal of the Bible is universal. Truly it is without a parallel in literature. All races claim it as their very own. I heard of a missionary from Africa who said that a Hottentot had come up to him and told him that he felt sorry for the missionary because he could not read John 3:16 in Hottentot. The black man said there was nothing so beautiful in the world as the story of Christ in Hottentot.

The appeal of the Bible is truly to all people through all ages and throughout every place and status in life. The Bible has a wondrous interest to every age group from the lisping child to the white-haired saint. Our boys and girls read and study it in myriads of homes and Sunday Schools; and great scholars like Newton and Faraday, great statesmen like Gladstone and Lincoln, and great soldiers like Robert E. Lee and Douglas MacArthur have taken this Book as the pride and guide of their lives.

A missionary traveling in the Near East stopped for the night in the tent of a shepherd whom he had visited several years before. The old nomad greeted him with a question, "Did you bring back the 'sheep book'?" For a moment the missionary was at a loss to understand the meaning of the question. Then it occurred to him that when he had last seen the old shepherd he had read to him in his own language Psalm 23. To this ignorant, unlearned keeper of the flocks the Bible was "the sheep book." He understood its language.

If We Had No Bible

If we were to take from the world the comfort of this blessed Bible, our loss would be indescribable. When the Baptist World Alliance met in London, England, in 1955, I was present to lead the prayer preceding the sermon delivered by Dr. João Soren, pastor of the First Baptist Church of Rio de Janeiro, Brazil. In that message I was moved by a story he told of his experience while a chaplain in World War II. Dr. Soren described in unforgettable words a cold morning on February 23, 1945. The Brazilian infantry serving in Italy with the American Fifth Army had just fought its bloodiest battle in the foothills of the Italian Apennine Mountains where the snows of that severe winter had begun to fall.

As chaplain of the Brazilian Division, he set out to search the area for the bodies of soldiers who had fallen in battle and had remained buried under the snow in no man's land during the winter months. He eventually came upon the body of a young sergeant who had grown up in the Sunday School of the First Baptist Church in Rio de Janeiro. Since the ice and snow were just beginning to thaw, the body of that soldier, who had disappeared in combat two months earlier, was perfectly preserved. He had used up all his ammunition. It appeared that, as he was about to charge in the final assault upon his objective, an enemy missile had pierced his chest. He did not die immediately. He had time to reach into his pocket and take out his New Testament and Psalms which the chaplain had given him. He had opened it to the Shepherd's Psalm. He had evidently read, as his life slowly ebbed away, "The Lord is my shepherd; I shall not want." His head had fallen forward, and the flowing blood had glued the pages to his frozen face. In that crucial moment the dying soldier had turned to the Word of God, whose precious comfort never fails.

The Bible's Perennial Freshness

The Bible never grows old. While it is an ancient Book, century after century it renews its youth. It is as up-to-date as tomorrow's newspaper. What book is there written that does not seem trite after repeated readings? But the Holy Scriptures, read constantly, by the affirmation of thousands of the most gifted and talented people in the world, grow richer, more majestic, more celestial, and more unfathomable.

The perennial freshness of the Word of God is a miracle in itself. In this the Bible radically differs from all other books of the world. The Bible never becomes exhausted. It never diminishes. It is a well that never runs dry, a fountain of infinite wisdom springing up into everlasting life. The Bible does not become obsolete. One of the characteristics of books written by secular authors is that they very quickly become outdated. This is particularly true with our textbooks on science and other related subjects. But the Word of God endures forever. Although the Bible treats the greatest and most serious subjects that face us, its revelation concerning these subjects is ever new and ever pertinent. Centuries of so-called progress and advancement have added nothing to the truths of the Scriptures that move our souls. What God has revealed to us can be trusted yesterday, today, and forever.

The Bible is like a gold mine in which one finds one inexhaustible vein of treasure after another. Like a diver in the sea who, having brought up many jewels from the depths of the ocean, still finds greater riches of gems lying on the floor, the reader discovers inexhaustible treasures in the Bible. Like the widow's oil and the widow's meal which nourished Elijah, and which never wasted or ran dry, so the contents of the Bible are never exhausted. Just as a fresh supply of manna was given each day to the Israelites in the wilderness, so the spirit of God ever breaks anew the Bread of Life to those who hunger or thirst after righteousness. Just as the loaves and the fishes in the hands of our Lord were more than enough to feed the famished multitude with a surplus still remaining, so the honey and milk of the

Word of God are more than sufficient to satisfy the hunger of every human soul. The supply still remains undiminished for every new generation.

The Influence of the Bible upon Human Life

The mighty influence of the Bible affects every facet of human life. The contents of the Scriptures have supplied themes for the greatest poets, artists, and musicians which the world has ever produced. Destroy such sublime oratorios as *Elijah* and the *Messiah* and you have taken out of the realm of music something which could never be replaced. Obliterate the sweet hymns which have drawn their inspiration from the Scripture and you have left our hearts empty. Delete from the literature created by Dante, Milton, Tennyson, Wordsworth, and Carlyle every reference to the moral and spiritual truths taught in God's Word and you have stripped them of their glory and robbed them of their beauty. Take down from the walls of our best galleries the incomparable paintings which portray scenes and incidents in the life of Israel and in the life of our Lord and you have removed the richest gems from the crowns of human genius.

The Bible has been the mightiest factor in shaping the moral progress of the entire race. Remove from our statute books every law which is founded upon the Ten Commandments and the Sermon on the Mount and you have removed the very cornerstone of modern civilization. Rob our libraries of every book which is written against the background of the precepts and concepts of Holy Writ and you have taken from us no small part of the treasured wisdom of the world. The transformation of modern civilization can be traced to the Bible.

The Bible's Creative Power

The creative power of the Bible is one of the miracles of history. John Bunyan was locked up for twelve years in a Bedford jail with his Bible for his constant companion. In that jail he composed an immortal dream written in the beauty of style and in the simple manner of the King James Version of the Bible. So matchless was the intellectual and spiritual culture of this unlearned tinker of Bedford that the scholarly John Owen testified before the king, "Your majesty, if I could write as does that tinker in Bedford jail, I would gladly lay down my learning." *Pilgrim's Progress* is truly one of the greatest classics in human literature. Where did John Bunyan get his culture? He obtained it in glorious fellowship with Moses and the Law, with David and the psalms, with Isaiah and the prophets, and with Jesus and the apostles. Living with them, he came to speak, like them, the language of the Bible.

God's Quickening Power

This beauty of language gained from reading the Bible has been confirmed by my own observation through the years of my pastoral ministry. Some people I have known who spoke most beautifully have been untaught, unlearned people who had absorbed the language of the Bible. We can read Homer and Virgil, Shakespeare and Dante; yea, we can pore through the best literature of all the ages, but it will all fall infinitely short of the purity, beauty, and grandeur of the thought and expression found in the Word of God.

Some time ago an enterprising newspaperman wrote to a hundred men representing various positions and offices in England, such as the House of Lords, members of the House of Commons, professional men, bankers, merchants, and others. In his letter he asked this question: "Suppose you were condemned to three years solitary imprisonment and could only take with you three books. Which three would you select? Please state them in the order of your preference." To the amazement of the newspaperman, 98 of the 100 put the Bible first of the three. This is all the more remarkable because quite a number of those men were not Christians. They were not only not churchgoers but some of them had actually worked against the Christian faith. Nevertheless, as they thought of the possibility of three years' solitary confinement, the Bible was the most coveted of companions.

This but reflected the studied and learned attitude of the finest men in modern civilization. Everywhere men of letters, eminent statesmen, and men of science have testified to the value and inestimable importance of God's Holy Word.

Benjamin Franklin said, "Young man, my advice to you is that you cultivate an acquaintance with the Holy Scriptures."

Thomas Jefferson said, "I have said and always will say that the studious perusal of the sacred volume will make better citizens, better fathers, and better husbands."

Daniel Webster one time said, "From the time that at my mother's knee I learned to lisp the sacred writings they have been my daily study."

Truly, God's Book is God's quickening power, to the saving of the soul, and to the regeneration of the human race.

CHAPTER 2

The Infallible Authority of Christ

Why do I believe that the Bible is literally true? One reason is the testimony of Jesus Christ, our Lord. The teachings of Jesus are the highest authority to which a Christian can make direct appeal. Christ's view of the Scriptures must be the view of His servants. There is no more reliable witness to the nature of the Scriptures than the One who died and rose again from the dead. If we accept the teachings of Jesus Christ, we must accept the teachings of our Lord concerning the Bible.

The evidence is clearly and plainly stated in the New Testament. There, according to Jesus, divine revelation is mediated in a written record. What the Scriptures say, God says. This can be easily seen in such passages as Matthew 5:18; 19:4; and John 10:35. Whether or not we receive His testimony to the Scriptures

31

is a commentary on the consistency of our Christian discipleship. It is not difficult to understand a Biblical critic who cares nothing for its divine Saviour, doubting the veracity of the Scriptures, but it is strange to find a believer professing his faith in the Lord and then disregarding Christ's doctrine of the inspiration of the Book. The authority of the Scriptures rests upon the deity of Christ. When a person receives in faith the Son of God, the question of authority is settled. If we accept the teaching of Jesus Christ, we must accept the whole Bible, for Jesus Christ has set His stamp of authority upon the entire Book.

Jesus and His Bible

The most convincing of all the proofs and arguments for the verbal inspiration of the Bible is the fact that the Lord Jesus Christ regarded it and treated it as such. Look at such passages as Matthew 19:4–5; 22:29; 23:35; Mark 7:13; Luke 24:44; John 5:39; 10:35. Jesus believed and taught the infallibility of Scripture. He regarded it as divine authority and as the final court of appeal concerning all questions. The way in which He quotes the Scriptures plainly shows this. Constantly, His questions were, "Have you never read?" and "It is written," and "Search the Scriptures." He sets His seal to its historicity and its revelation from God. He supplements it, but He never supplants it. He amplifies it, but He never nullifies it. He modifies it according to His own divine prerogative, He fulfils it according to His divine mission, but He never lessens its divine authority.

Jesus never set aside the Scriptures in favor of an encounter with God. (Compare the discussion in part 3, chap. 3.) To Him, the Scriptures were the medium and the test of the encounter. His attitude towards the Scriptures was one of total trust. It was the first written Word of God to human beings. What is written we are to believe and obey, not what we suppose the writer might have intended. Thus Jesus in Matthew 4:4 directly quotes Deuteronomy 8:3 to show us God's will for our lives.

Jesus was not bound by human tradition. He claimed direct, divine inspiration for His own teachings (John 7:16; 12:49). In many respects He was alien to the religious life of His day, yet at the point of Scripture Jesus Himself bowed to its inviolable authority. In the Bible He heard the voice of God (Matt. 5:18; John 10:35). His arguments are clinched with a Biblical text. His foes are rebuked for not knowing the Scriptures better. Satan is rebuffed with a simple appeal to the written Word of God. Jesus' ministry was governed down to the smallest detail by what the Bible predicted the Messiah would do and be. He must die upon the cross because it was written of Him. His entire message about the Kingdom of God is grounded on the Old Testament revelation. He never dreamed of separating revelation from the Scriptures. Such a breach could only lead to the morass of subjectivity.

Jesus Himself was inspired as to His words. In the earliest reference to His prophetic office in Deuteronomy 18:18, Jehovah God says, "[I] will put My words in His mouth." Jesus thus spoke under the guidance of heaven (John 6:63; 8:26,28,40; 12:49,50). In Revelation we read, "He that hath an ear, let him hear what the Spirit saith unto the churches." But it is Jesus delivering the message. The message of Christ is the Spirit of God speaking (Luke 4:18).

Jesus' use of the Holy Scriptures is a marvelous revelation in itself. At twelve years of age, in the Temple of Jerusalem, He showed an exceptional, astonishing knowledge of their contents. Throughout the story of His life and ministry we are introduced to this same marvelous acquaintance with the Word of God. In the story of the temptation of Jesus we read that three times He used the Word of God from the book of Deuteronomy. It is remarkable that the Lord Jesus refused to overwhelm Satan with the force of His superior wisdom. He scorned to crush him with a display of His almighty power. His defense for each assault plainly and simply was, "It is written."

We see Jesus in Matthew 4 overcoming the tempter in the wilderness by three quotations from Deuteronomy without note or comment except the word, "It is written." There is nothing in the whole history of humanity or even in the field of divine revelation that proves more clearly than this the inspiration of the

Scriptures. Jesus, who spoke from heaven, fortified Himself against the temptations of hell by the Word of God.

When Jesus Spoke

After the terrible ordeal of the temptation of Christ by Satan, the Lord began His public ministry in Nazareth. How did He begin it? He began it by reading from the prophet Isaiah. The story is found in Luke 4:16–21. As the Lord's ministry continued, we find Him again and again vindicating His deity before the Jews by the Word of God (John 5:39).

In Mark 7:13 the Lord Jesus Himself distinctly asserted that the Law of Moses is the Word of God. It is ofttimes said that the Bible nowhere claims to be the Word of God. Here Jesus distinctly avowed that it is. Christ taught that the Scriptures are inspired as to their words (Matt. 5:17,18). Christ affirmed here the indestructibility of the law, not its substance only but its very form, not the thought but the Word itself. He says that one jot or one tittle shall in no wise pass from the law. Every Hebrew scholar knows that a "jot" is the Hebrew character yodh, the smallest character in the Hebrew alphabet, less than half the size of any other character in the list. Every scholar knows that a "tittle" is a little horn that the Hebrews placed on their consonants. In referring to these small characters in the Scripture text, no stronger words could be employed by our Lord to affirm the divine authority of every part of the Old Testament, both the law and the prophets.

In John 10:34–36, Christ vindicated Himself from the charge of blasphemy by claiming to be the Son of God on the basis that the Old Testament Scripture could not be broken. This is verbal inspiration in its plainest and most vivid form. When He defended Himself against the charge of blasphemy, He used the specific and written words of the Old Testament.

In Matthew 22:31–32, Christ used the very tense of the verb in the Scriptures to affirm one of the greatest doctrines of the Christian faith. He substantiates the doctrine of the resurrection against the skepticism of the Sadducees by emphasizing the present tense of the verb "to be." The word "Am" in the language of Jehovah to Moses at the burning bush was the basis of the Lord's doctrine of the resurrection and of the life of the saints beyond the grave.

In Matthew 22:44–45, the Lord made reference to Psalm 110 and said that David was completely under the Spirit's influence and the production of the psalm was such that the words were absolutely authoritative.

In Matthew 22:42–44, we find our Lord defending His own deity by alluding to the second use of the word "Lord," in Psalm 110.

Jesus After His Resurrection from the Dead

If some critic says that the Master in the days of His flesh had only partial knowledge of the whole truth and was limited, therefore, in His understanding of the Scriptures, there can certainly be no question of His partial knowledge after His resurrection. Then our Lord was manifestly free of all limitations of earthly conditions. Yet it was after His resurrection that He set His seal on the whole Old Testament (Luke 24:27,44,46).

The Jews divided their Bible, our present Old Testament Scriptures, into three parts. The first part was the "Law," the five books of Moses. The next part was the "Prophets," most of the books which we call prophetic and some of those which we call historical. The remaining books, including the Psalms, the Hebrews called "the sacred writings." Jesus Christ, after His resurrection, takes up each one of these three recognized divisions of the Old Testament Scriptures and sets His stamp of authority upon each one. If, then, we accept the authority of Jesus Christ, we are logically driven to accept the entire Old Testament Scriptures.

When Christ makes reference to Old Testament narratives and records, He receives them as authentic and historically true. He does not give or suggest in any case a mythical or allegorical interpretation of them. The accounts of the Creation, the Flood, the overthrow of Sodom and Gomorrah, as well as other incidents and events of later date, are taken as authentic. It is abundantly evident that the Jewish Scriptures are the veritable Word of God.

No word of Jesus ever calls in question the genuineness of any book, and He distinctly assigns the Scriptures to the writers whose names they bear. The Law is ascribed to Moses; David is connected with the Psalms; the prophecies of Isaiah are attributed to Isaiah; the prophecies of Daniel are attributed to Daniel. The Lord reproaches His countrymen with ignorance of the Scriptures and with making the Law void through their tradition, but He never suggests that they have forged any book in the canon nor does He hint that they have rejected any book which deserved a place.

Christ and the New Testament

Our Lord's authority not only included the Old Testament Scriptures but He set the seal of His authority upon the New Testament also. How was this possible when there was not a book of the New Testament written when Jesus departed from the earth? The answer lies in the fact that Jesus placed His stamp of authority upon the writings of the apostles by anticipation. "But the Comforter, which is the Holy Ghost, whom the Father will send in My name, He shall teach you all things, and bring all things to your remembrance, whatsoever I have said unto you" (John 14:26).

We have Christ's own authority for it that in the apostolic records we have not the apostolic recollection of what Jesus said but the Holy Spirit's recollection of what Jesus said.

While the apostles might forget and report inaccurately, the Holy Spirit could not forget. We see from this that the New Testament Scriptures are the product of the inspiration and direction of the Holy Spirit of God. This affirmation is repeated in John 16:12–13: "I have yet many things to say unto you, but ye cannot bear them now. Howbeit when He, the Spirit of Truth, is come, He will guide you into all truth: for He shall not speak of Himself; but whatsoever He shall hear, that shall He speak; and He will shew you things to come."

If we accept then the authority of Jesus Christ, we must accept the apostolic teachings and New Testament writings as being given by the Holy Spirit. They contain the truth that Jesus would have us know after He left this earth. The cry "Back to Christ" is not a bad one. But when you get back to Christ you hear Christ Himself saying: "On to the apostles. They have further truth which My Holy spirit will reveal."

Did Jesus think of the Bible as being full of errors? While the teaching of Jesus with respect to the Scripture was expressed in positive terms, it is most unusual and singular that He never, on the other hand, uttered a word or syllable to indicate that He supposed them to be otherwise than true from beginning to end. How shall we account for this?

A Threefold Possibility

We face a threefold possibility:

1. First, that there are no errors in the Scriptures.

2. Second, that the errors were there but Christ was not aware of them.

3. Third, that He was aware of these errors but did not choose to tell the people of them.

What shall we think of these three alternatives? If the errors were in the Bible and Christ did not tell us, then He hid from our eyes the full truth of God. Again, if the errors were in the Bible and Christ was not aware of them, He is certainly not the divine Son of God which He claimed to be. There is left, then, no other conclusion than the one that there are no errors in the Scriptures. If this Book was true enough for Christ, it is true enough for every Christian.

Our Final Court of Appeal

The Bible is our final court of appeal. It is not a question of what I think or what anyone else thinks. The question is always, "What saith the Scriptures?" It is even as the psalmist wrote,

"For ever, O Lord, Thy word is settled in heaven" (Ps. 119:89). Therefore, it is for me to bow to God's authority, to submit to His Word, and to obey His teachings. Because the Bible is God's Word, it is the final court of appeal in all things pertaining to doctrine, duty, and deportment. For us who love the Lord and who have received Him as our Saviour, His Word concerning the infallibility of the Holy Scriptures is full, final, and complete.

The authority of Christ settles for us forever the question of the inspiration of the Bible. It is wholly inspired and is our medium of God's power in this life and of God's salvation in the world that is yet to come.

CHAPTER 3

The Internal Witness
of the Holy Scriptures

The attitude of Jesus towards the Scriptures is no different from that of the entire self-attestation of the Book. His words are confirmed by the startling claims which the Bible makes for itself, claims which are true about the Bible, but which are not true, and could not be true, about any other book (Exod. 31:18; Ps. 119:152,160; Prov. 30:5; Isa. 40:8; 1 Pet. 1:23-25).

The idea of the authority of the Scriptures is a conception which lies in the Scriptures themselves. The Bible itself claims to be an authoritative Book and an infallible guide to the true knowledge of God and to the way of salvation. The Word of God is its own tremendous witness to its own inspiration. The Scriptures so often quote, "And God said," or "The Word of

God came, saying." This kind of formula is said by some to occur no less than 3,808 times in the Old Testament.

Look at the emphatic way the formula is used. The prophets, for example, habitually introduced their message with the avowal, "And the Word of the Lord came unto. . . ." The prophet does not regard himself as a speculative theologian; rather, he delivers a message which he understands to have originated from heaven.

The Bible Is the Word Of God

The Bible is the Word of God, not merely contains it. The Bible calls itself the Word of God and by that very title it is distinguished from all other books. The Bible consistently claims divine authorship. Woven into the warp and woof of the Scriptures is the repeated assertion that this is true. In the Bible, God speaks. When we listen to God, we are born again by God's Word (1 Pet. 1:23–25).

Notice how the utterances of the Old Testament writers are introduced into the New. Take Matthew 1:22 as an illustration: "Now all this was done, that it might be fulfilled which was spoken of the Lord by the prophet." It was not the prophet who spake, but the Lord who spake by the prophet. Notice also how Hebrews 3:7 quotes Psalm 95:7–8, saying that the Holy Spirit is the Author of the Scriptures.

The Verbal Theory

Second Timothy 3:16, "All scripture is given by inspiration of God." Two words used in this text present to us the apostolic view concerning the inspiration of the Holy Scriptures. One word is *graphe*, which means "writing," and the other is *theopneustos*, which means "God-breathed." It is the "writing," the Scriptures, that is "God-breathed," that is inspired. On the original parchment every sentence, word, line, mark, point, pen stroke, jot, and tittle were put there by inspiration of God. There is no question of anything else. Men may destroy the parchment, time may waste it, but the writing remains. Some of the speakers of the Bible, like Balaam and Caiaphas, are made to speak in spite of themselves, but what is written is inspired by God Himself.

Paul plainly states in this text in 2 Timothy 3:16 that *all the Scriptures* are "God-breathed." The inspiration of the Scriptures includes the whole and every part. There are many who deny this and say that the Scriptures are inspired in spots, in portions, in pieces, in sections. However, no such doctrine as this is found in the Bible. The historical books, the books of Mosaic legislation, the poetical books, the prophets, the Gospels, the Epistles, the apocalypses all are inspired in every detail. The inspiration includes the form as well as the substance, the word as well as the thought. This is called the verbal theory of inspiration, which is vehemently denied by many modern theologians. They say it is too mechanical. They say it degrades the writers to the level of machines. They say it has a tendency to make skeptics and unbelievers, and they say many other things. But I am insisting upon, and presenting, no theory except that which is found in the Bible. God used the human personality and the human mind to deliver His divine revelation.

The Prophets and the Words They Wrote

I now consider 1 Peter 1:10,11: "Of which salvation the prophets have inquired and searched diligently, who prophesied of the grace the should come unto you: searching what, or what manner of time the Spirit of Christ which was in them did signify, when it testified beforehand the sufferings of Christ, and the glory that should follow."

What is Peter saying? He is saying that the prophets wrote down what they were told to write, whether they understood it or not. They did not originate their message. If we were to see a student, who, after taking down the lecture of a profound philosopher, was now studying diligently to comprehend the sense of the discourse which he had written, we would have the meaning of the passage. The prophets of the Old Testament studied the meaning of what they themselves had written. They were reporters of what they heard rather than formulators of that which they delivered. They were voices and echoes. They did not originate their message. The message came from God.

Examples from the Bible

When Moses would excuse himself from the service of the Lord because he was not eloquent, God said that He had made the mouth of Moses and He would tell him what to say. Look at Exodus 4:10–12. God did not say, "I will be with your mind and teach you what you shall think," but, "I will be with your mouth and teach you what you shall say." This explains why, forty years afterwards, Moses said to Israel: "Ye shall not add unto the word which I command you, neither shall ye diminish aught from it, that ye may keep the commandments of the Lord your God which I command you" (Deut. 4:2). Several times Moses will thus emphasize that the commandments are the work of God and the writing is the writing of God.

When we pass from the Pentateuch to the poetical books, we find that same degree of inspiration. "Now these be the last words of David. David the son of Jesse said, and the man who was raised up on high, the anointed of the God of Jacob, and the sweet psalmist of Israel, said, The Spirit of the Lord spake by me, and His word was in my tongue" (2 Sam. 23:1–2). Here, too, God does not say that the thought was inspired but that the very words were given the psalmist by the Lord.

When we come to the prophets, the same avowal is made on the part of the prophets that we find in Moses and in the Psalms. Look at Jeremiah, for example. Jeremiah declared that he is but a child and cannot bear the assignment of appearing before Israel, but God says that He will put the words in the mouth of Jeremiah that the prophet is to speak (1:6–9).

Look at Daniel 12:8–9. Here we find Daniel writing words given him by divine inspiration which he could not understand. Surely, if the will of man had nothing to do with the prophecy, he could not have been at liberty in the selection of the words. God gave him the words to speak. This lifts the Bible from human hands and places it back in God's hands.

The Remarkable Fact

A remarkable fact regarding the revelations of the Bible is that oftentimes there are two seemingly contradictory lines of prophecy, so much so until it would seem that if one line of prophecy were fulfilled, the other could not be. For example, in the Old Testament we have two lines of prophecy concerning the Messiah. One line predicts a suffering Messiah, despised and rejected of men, a man of sorrows and acquainted with grief, a Messiah whose earthly mission would end in death, ignominy, and shame. The other line of prophecy predicts with equal clearness and emphasis the coming of an all-conquering Messiah who will rule the nations with a rod of iron.

How can both of these prophetic lines be true? The best answer the ancient Jew had before the fulfilment of both lines in Christ was that there were to be two Messiahs. This was behind the question John the Baptist sent to Jesus in Matthew 11. Jesus seemed to be the Suffering Servant, but was He also the Conquering Prince who was to burn up His enemies with unquenchable fire? Were they to look for yet another Messiah, a second one?

In actual fulfilment both lines of prophecy meet in the one Person, Jesus of Nazareth. At His first coming, He is the Suffering Servant making atonement for our sins by His death on the cross. At His second coming, He will be a conquering King to rule over the nations of the earth. It is plainly evident that the prophets did not understand this. The message they received from God was one thing, but their understanding of the words in that message was another thing. It was only until the fulfilment of the following centuries that we came to see what the words of God meant.

Men Moved by the Holy Spirit

I turn now to the Scripture in 2 Peter 1:21: "For the prophecy came not in old time by the will of man: but holy men of God spake as they were moved by the Holy Ghost." The Holy Spirit, the active and working force of the divine Trinity, inspired the authors of the Bible to produce the Book. God used many methods in originating the message: the voice of God, the revelation of Jesus Christ, the word of angels, the writing of apostles; yea, in many ways and in many manners God spoke to the people and the speaking we have is our Bible (Heb. 1:1–2). Over a period of many centuries the Holy Spirit used the divergent traits of many individuals to create this holy Book. But however God used the differing traits of men. Peter declared in this passage that the will of man had nothing to do with any part of the revelation, but that the whole of it from Genesis to Malachi was inspired by the Lord.

In the Bible we find a number of passages where the divine Author and the human instrument are mentioned.

Matthew 1:22 is an apt example. "Now all this was done, that it might be fulfilled which was spoken of the Lord by the prophet." Here is the divine source and the human instrument.

In Acts 1:16 the Holy Spirit spoke by the mouth of David. Peter then declares in 2 Peter 1:21 that the Holy Spirit spoke through the prophets. The instruments of the Spirit's work were the men who wrote the divine revelation.

Direct from God

I now turn to a passage in the Apocalypse: "The Revelation of Jesus Christ, which God gave unto him, to shew unto his servants things which must shortly come to pass; and He sent and signified it by His angel unto His servant John" (Rev. 1:1). John simply wrote what God revealed (vv. 18–19). Wherever the Bible writers allude to themselves, they invariably say that their words are not their own but that they come from God. God used their faculties, traits, and abilities.

- Some write that God put words in their mouths.

- Some write that God directed them to use their own words to convey what God had transmitted unto them.

- Some write that the Holy Spirit moved them in a special way and directed them just what to say.

But all are unanimous in declaring that their writings came direct from God and that God simply used them as agents to show His will for all humankind.

When reading the Bible in even a casual way, one will readily see that it was necessary for the Holy Spirit carefully to guard and to guide every step of the way so that a true and perfect message would be delivered. No one else other than the Holy Spirit could accomplish such a miracle. The Bible actually is that miracle. As the books of the Testaments were being written down through the centuries, different men spoke as they were moved by the Holy Spirit and, God being the Author of the Word through the generations, the words all attest to one great truth, point to one great God, and offer to us one marvelous way of salvation.

CHAPTER 4

The Literal Fulfillment of Prophecy

Why do I believe that the Bible is literally true? One cogent reason can be found in the literal fulfillment of its prophecies. The outstanding, differentiating characteristic of Israel's religion is predictive prophecy. Only in the Bible will you find the phenomenon of prophecy.

Where is there a god or gods; where is there a founder of religion such as Confucius, Buddha, Muhammad, or Zoroaster; or where is there any other who could with such certainty predict the future? Where is there a statesman who, in these times, can foretell what will be the condition of things in Europe or in America one hundred years from now or even ten years from now? Yea, I can tell any person how he can become a multimillionaire within a relatively short time. If he can predict what will happen even in the course of an hour, he can make himself fabulously rich by playing the market on the New York Stock Exchange. We do not know the future. It is the prerogative of God to know what tomorrow will bring. The fulfilled prophecies of the Bible bespeak the omniscience of its Author.

In Isaiah 41:21–23, we have what is probably the most remarkable challenge to be found in the Bible. "Produce your cause, saith the Lord; bring forth your strong reasons, saith the King of Jacob. Let them bring them forth, and shew us what shall happen: let them shew the former things, what they be, that we may consider them, and know the latter end of them; or declare us things for to come. Shew the things that are to come hereafter, that we may know that ye are gods: yea, do good, or do evil, that we may be dismayed, and behold it together." This Scripture reference has both a negative and a positive.

1. Negatively, it suggests an infallible criterion by which we may test the claims of religious impostors.

2. Positively, the passage calls attention to an unanswerable argument for the truthfulness of God's Word.

Jehovah bids the prophets of false faith to successfully predict events lying in the distant future; their success or failure will show whether or not they are true sages or merely pretenders and deceivers. On the other hand, the demonstrated fact that God alone knows the future and in His Word declares the end from the beginning, shows that He is God and that the Scriptures are His inspired revelations to humankind.

Detailed Prophecies in Scripture

To the finite mind, the future is filled with unknown uncertainties. How then can we explain the hundreds of detailed prophecies in the Scriptures which have been literally fulfilled to the letter hundreds of years after they were uttered? How can we account for the fact that the Bible successfully foretold hundreds, and in some instances, thousands of years beforehand, the history of the Jews, the course of the Gentiles, and the consummation of this age? Fulfilled prophecy, indeed, is a potent argument for the inspiration of the Bible.

The Lord God boldly states in Isaiah 46:9–11: "Remember the former things of old: for I am God, and there is none else; I am God, and there is none like me, declaring the end from the beginning, and from ancient times the things that are not yet done, saying, my counsel shall stand, and I will do all my pleasure: calling a ravenous bird from the east, the man that executeth my counsel from a far country: yea, I have spoken it, I will also bring it to pass; I have purposed it, I will also do it."

God alone can declare the end from the beginning. People are powerless to find out things to come. None of the sacred books of the nations contain predictions of the future. None of the books of other religions contain the phenomenon that is called prophecy. If the authors of these writings of other religions had attempted to foretell the future, they would have furnished the strongest evidence of their lack of inspiration and of their manifest deceptions.

But the Bible is preeminently a book of prophecy. One of the distinguishing characteristics of the living God is His capacity to announce the future beforehand. God's ability through His spokesmen to transcend the confines of human knowledge provides objective proof of His sovereignty over history. "Who hath declared this from ancient time? who hath told it from that time? have not I the Lord? and there is no God else beside me; a just God and Saviour; there is none beside me" (45:21).

The Tests of a True Prophet of God

The Bible is very bold in delineating the credentials of a true prophet of God. Observe Deuteronomy 18:21–22. "And if thou say in thine heart, How shall we know the word which the Lord hath not spoken? When a prophet speaketh in the name of the Lord, if the thing follow not, nor come to pass, that is the thing which the Lord hath not spoken, but the prophet hath spoken it presumptuously: thou shalt not be afraid of him."

The Old Testament prophet could be identified by the test of whether or not what he predicts actually comes to pass. This is also the test recorded in Jeremiah 28:9. But there is another test in the Old Testament in regard to this significant matter. The people were to know by the character of the thing prophesied whether or not it came from the Lord. If a prophecy did not honor the Lord, even though it came to pass, it was not a true prophecy. It might come to pass and yet not be a genuine word from God. That complementary test is found in Deuteronomy 13:1–3: "If there arise among you a prophet, or a dreamer of dreams, and giveth thee a sign or a wonder, and the sign or the wonder come to pass, whereof he spake unto thee, saying, Let us go after other gods, which thou hast not known, and let us serve them; thou shalt not hearken unto the words of that prophet, or that dreamer of dreams: for the Lord your God proveth you, to know whether ye love the Lord your God with all your heart and with all your soul" (see also vv. 4–5).

Fulfilled Prophecy in the Bible

As we look at fulfilled prophecy in the Bible, we are impressed with the fact that one of the most remarkable chapters in the Pentateuch is Deuteronomy 28. Here is prewritten the sad history of Israel. Though without a land, Israel through the centuries was still to be a nation. All this is written beforehand in the Bible (cf. Jer. 30:11). There have been great scholars who call the Jews the "enigma of history." What human mind could have foreseen that this peculiar people dwelling in so small a land would yet remain alive although scattered among the nations? Suffering? They have suffered as no other nation has suffered and yet they have been kept and marked out as the covenant people of a God whose gifts and calling are without repentance. Here indeed is an argument for the Word of God which no infidel can answer. The very fact that Israel is a nation today is in fulfilment of the Word of God. As long as the sun and the moon shall stand and as long as there shall be day and night, just so long will there be a nation of Israel to stand before the Lord. So declares Jeremiah 33:23–26. Jesus also said that the Jew will be here when He comes again. Read Matthew 24:34 where the Master declares that this kind—this race, shall not pass away until all these things that pertain to the consummation of the age have been fulfilled.

There were many ancient people cited in the Old Testament. There were the Hittites, the Hivites, the Jebusites, the Ammonites, the Moabites, but nobody today has ever seen anybody who ever saw anyone who ever heard of anyone who ever saw a Hittite or a Jebusite or a Hivite or a Moabite. But Jesus said the Jews will be here until He comes again. Are they? Do you know a Jew?

Into Their Own Land

God always says in Ezekiel 36 that they will return to their own land and God says that someday He will plant them in their own land where they shall remain forever. Read again Amos 9:15: "And I will plant them upon their land, they shall no more be pulled up out of their land which I have given them, saith the Lord thy God."

In addition to the many prophecies concerning the Jewish nation, there are many other prophecies in the Bible concerning other nations. These prophecies have been fulfilled to the letter and others are in the process of being fulfilled.

Literally have been fulfilled the prophecies respecting the destruction of those great ancient cities of Nineveh, Babylon, and Memphis.

Ezekiel's precise prophecies of the judgment of the nations in chapters 25 to 37 have been fulfilled to the letter.

Consider the prophecies of the judgment of Egypt in Isaiah 19:1–14. All these prophecies have been literally fulfilled.

Look at the prophecies concerning the once rich and flourishing land of Edom whose terrible end was prophesied in Jeremiah 49 and Ezekiel 35. Today one can travel for miles and miles through its appalling desolation without encountering any living person, without seeing even an animal or a bird. Not one trace of an Edomite can be found in all the earth.

Consider also the case of the three cities whose destruction was commented upon by Jesus Himself in Matthew 11. The ruins of these cities lay buried in the dust until archaeologists uncovered them.

The New Testament contains many prophecies which are now in the process of fulfilment. An example is the prophecy concerning the present apostasy from the historic faith as predicted in such passages as 1 Timothy 4:1–2; 2 Timothy 3:1–5; 4:1–3. Since, of the more than six thousand verses of prophecy in the Bible, about three thousand have already been fulfilled, we may conclude that the other three thousand verses of prophecy are going to be fulfilled in the years to come.

The Detailed Prophecies Concerning Christ

Of all the prophecies in the Bible none are so full and complete and none have been so marvelously fulfilled as the prophecies concerning the coming of Israel's Messiah. Christ is the center of the Bible. He is the burden of the prophet's message, the theme of the psalmist's song, the chief character of the Gospels, the fountainhead of inspiration of the Epistles, and the sublime and majestic central figure of the Revelation. The great burden of the prophecies concerns the first and the second coming of our Lord. Christ is the center of Old Testament prophecy as He is the center of New Testament history. From Genesis 3 to Malachi 4, the Lord Jesus Christ fills up the historic and prophetic profile.

The Portrait of Christ

The marvelous portrait of Jesus to be found in the Old Testament is a miracle of the omniscient God. Who could draw a picture of a man not yet born? Surely God and God alone. Nobody knew a thousand years ago that Milton was going to be born or five hundred years ago that Washington was to be born or two hundred years ago that Churchill was to be born. Yet here in the Bible we have the most striking and unmistakable likeness of a man portrayed, not by one, but by twenty or twenty-five artists, none of whom had even seen the man they were painting. The man was Jesus, the Christ. The painters were the Bible writers. The canvas is the Bible.

Beginning with faint touches in the books of Moses, Christ's whole career is described through the following pages of the Old Testament. The picture becomes more and more precise as the time of fulfilment draws near. Radical and destructive critics deny this. They take the position that there are no predictions concerning Christ in the Old Testament. But such denials are a reflection upon the men who utter them.

The messianic prophecies and their fulfilments in Christ are simply amazing in their number and in their detail. Let us consider just a few of them:

1. Genesis 3:15 says He is to be born the seed of the woman.

2. Isaiah 7:14; 49:1; Micah 5:3 tell us He is to be born of a virgin.

3. Genesis 9:18, 27 says He is to be a descendant of Shem.

4. Genesis 12:3; 18:18; 22:18 tell us He is to be a descendant of Abraham.

5. Genesis 17:19; 21:12; 26:4 tell us He is to be a descendant of Isaac.

6. Genesis 28:4–14; Numbers 24:17; Isaiah 49:3 tell us He is to be a descendant of Israel, that is, of Jacob.

7. Genesis 49:9–10; 1 Chronicles 5:2; Micah 5:2 tell us He is to be born of the tribe of Judah.

8. Second Samuel 7:12–15; 23:1–5, and other passages too numerous to mention, tell us that He is to be born of the house of David.

9. Micah 5:2 tells us that He is to be born in Bethlehem, the City of David.

10. The passages in the Bible that describe the characteristics of His life and work are too numerous even to mention.

11. Isaiah 62:11 and Zechariah 9:9 describe His triumphal entry into Jerusalem.

12. Psalm 41:9 and Zechariah 11:12–13 describe His betrayal by a friend and disciple even at the cost of thirty pieces of silver.

13. Genesis 3:15; Psalm 22:1–21; Isaiah 50:6; 53:1–12; and Zechariah 13:7 describe His sufferings on the cross and His death for our sins.

14. Psalm 22:16 and Zechariah 13:6–7 describe the piercing of His hands and feet.

15. Psalm 22:16 and Isaiah 53:8–12 describe His death on the cross.

16. Psalm 22:18 describes the lots cast for His vesture.

17. Psalm 16:10 and Isaiah 53:9 describe His being embalmed and His being entombed.

18. Psalm 16:10; 17:15; and Jonah 1:17 portray His resurrection on the third day.

19. Psalm 8:5–6 and 110:1 describe His ascension into heaven.

Prophecies Found in the Types

In the Old Testament there are two kinds of prophecies. The first refers to explicit verbal prophecies. The second concerns the types and the symbols. These prophecies are even more conclusive. They comprise unquestionable foreshadowings of the truth concerning Jesus, for we can find the Christ in the lives of Abraham, Isaac, Joseph, David, and Solomon.

Every sacrifice and offering, every feast and institution in the tabernacle pictures the Holy One of Israel. When we look at the outer court, the brazen altar, the holy place, the most holy place, the golden altar, the seven-branched lampstand, the table of shewbread, the veil that hung between the holy place and the most holy place, the ark of the covenant, the mercy seat, and, in fact, when we look at any part of the tabernacle, we see it all clearly setting forth a great truth about Christ. These types portray His person, His nature, His character, His atoning death, His resurrection, His ascension, and His coming again.

Modern critical theories regarding the construction of Exodus, Leviticus, Numbers, and Deuteronomy fall to pieces when considered in the light of the meaning of the types of the Old Testament. There never has been a destructive critic who would acknowledge the types of the Old Testament. The critic necessarily dismisses them with scorn and contempt because if he considered them in the light of God's true meaning, he would no longer be a destructive critic. One cannot study the types thoroughly without being profoundly convinced that the real Author of the Old Testament inspiring the human authors is none other than God Himself.

The Lord God who gave us the Old Testament wrote in it the language of heaven in order that we might understand the atonement for our sins in Jesus Christ. Having been taught the nomenclature of heaven, we can understand what it means when Christ is referred to as "the Lamb of God." From the types of the Old Testament we know what is meant by the word "altar," by the word "sacrifice," by the word "atonement," by the word "propitiation," by the word "expiation," by the words "sin offering." All of these matters that pertain to the ministry of Christ have been clearly delineated before our very eyes by the construction of the tabernacle and by the Levitical offerings and worship services. God had a profound purpose in writing beforehand concerning these marvelous types and symbols. They were fulfilled in Christ. They clearly picture before us the meaning of Christ's death and His atoning grace in bringing us forgiveness of sins and the gift of life everlasting.

No person with a fair and open mind could read the prophecies in the Old Testament and follow the types and symbols of the worship of the Hebrews without seeing that it all was inspired by the Lord of heaven and recorded according to the dictation of the Holy Spirit.

CHAPTER 5

The Confirmation of Archaeology

Why do I believe that the Bible is literally true? The testimony of archaeology to the Scriptures is another sure and certain reason. This chapter could well have been called "What the Spade Has Done for the Bible" or "What the Pick and Shovel Have Revealed Concerning the Word of God." The confirmation of archaeology to the truthfulness of Scripture is one of the amazing developments of modern times.

One of the great facts of life is this: no one has intelligence enough to insert a hypothetical fact into circumstances not belonging to it and make it fit perfectly and exactly. This only infinite intelligence can do. A successful forgery, therefore, is impossible if we have a sufficient sample of the original circumstances. This can be easily seen in the hoaxes of anthropology, such as the Piltdown Man, and in other ingenious methods by which pseudoscience has sought to find the missing link between the ape and the man.

Consider the examination of witnesses. If a witness is truthful, the more he is questioned the more accurately will his testimony be seen to accord with the framework of circumstances into which it is fitted. If he is false, the more he is questioned the more will his falsehood become apparent. It is this principle, applied in the field of archaeology, which has confirmed the Word of God. A thousand silent witnesses have been brought to life to testify to the truth of the record we find in God's Book.

The writers of the Scriptures have been charged with resorting to folklore or legend in order to prove certain spiritual lessons. Critics have said that certain statements, particularly in the Old Testament, were utterly without historical confirmation. Should this be true, then a thousand circumstances would conspire to confirm the unreliability of the Bible. The Bible would be demonstrably shorn of its credibility.

The Records of Archaeology

What literally has happened? The records of archaeology are clear and distinct. When the faith of many was waning and many heralds of truth were tempted to speak with uncertain sounds, the very stones have cried out with a voice that only the deaf could fail to hear. Both in the writing and in the preservation of the Bible we behold the handiwork of Almighty God.

It is well known that during the last one hundred years a vast number of archaelogical discoveries have been made in Egypt, Palestine, Babylonia, and Assyria. Many of these have shed remarkable light on the historical features of the Old Testament. A great number of persons and habits and periods have been illuminated by these discoveries. Ancient ways, habits, and historical records that once seemed so far away are now seen with a clarity which was before impossible. It is a simple and yet striking fact that not one of these discoveries during the whole of this time has given any support to the distinctive features and principles of the higher critical position. On the other hand, every stone that has been turned and every spade of dirt that has been lifted has been in confirmation of the truth of the Word of God. There has been no shred of archaeological evidence yet discovered that contradicts the Word of God. Rather, the discoveries of the archaeologist have put to shame the critics who before have laughed and scoffed at the Bible.

What the Spade Has Done to the Book of Genesis

In recent years the book of Genesis has been considered a hopeless collection of unsubstantiated myths. Moses, they said, could not write. The Hittites never existed. The cities and the people mentioned in the early record of the Scriptures were all mythological places and characters in legendary stories. The very literature of the Old Testament was considered to have been put together with scissors and paste at the hands of fairly unintelligent ancient bookmakers. Then came the avalanche of these discoveries in the Near East as archaeologists dug into the records of past civilizations. Endless confirmations of the stories, characters, cities, countries, and civilizations of the Bible world have come to light. Archaeology has confirmed the antiquity of writing, the historicity of the account of the campaign of the kings in Genesis 14, the puzzling story of Sarah and Hagar, the Egypt of Joseph and Moses, the historicity of Sargon and Belshazzar, the nature of the Aramaic language of Daniel and Ezra, and a thousand other things all and everyone of which at one time and in other days the higher critics had scoffed.

Several Instances

Let us take several of these instances that come from the confirmations of archaeology. Formerly it was thought incredible that Moses could have written the Pentateuch since he lived before the days of the invention of writing. This was one of the assured results of modern criticism. We know now, however, that writing in the Near East was a well-established art over two thousand years before Christ. Instead of writing being unknown in the days of Moses, we have discovered that centuries and centuries before the time of Moses writing was a most extended, well-developed art, far antedating the time of the great lawgiver.

Another one of the assured results of criticism has been their avowal that the book of Deuteronomy was a forgery composed in the sixth century before Christ. The critics said it was written at the time that the book was supposed to have been discovered in the days of good King Josiah. On such a view, of course, the book is clearly fraudulent. What has archaeology done to the book of Deuteronomy? Without exception, everything that has been discovered emphasizes the antiquity and authenticity of this great volume. Its entire historical and theological outlook has been confirmed by what has been discovered in the life and literature of the people of that time. The more we study these archaeological discoveries of the ancient peoples who lived in the days of Moses the more we are compelled to recognize that the origin of Deuteronomy lies in the days of Moses himself.

Early in the book of Genesis we find one of God's heroes, Abraham, living in a city called Ur of the Chaldees. From this city God called Abraham to go out to the Promised Land. However, the critics had a field day here. No one had ever heard of an Ur of the Chaldeans. Where was it? It seemed most certainly to have been a mythological city and was a part of a fable that was woven by some romanticist. But what of it now? Did the writer of Genesis just pull its name out of the air? Is it a mythological place like the Land of Oz? The critics of the Bible said so.

But they no longer are able so to avow, thanks to the labors of the archaeologists. Today a great portion of the ancient city of Ur has been discovered. It was a city with wide streets and lovely homes containing spacious patios and sanitary systems. As an added touch the name itself "Abram" has been found inscribed on some of the columns in the ancient city.

Another archaeological witness to the truth of the Bible is found in the treasure city of Pithom which was built for Rameses II by the Hebrews during the time of their hard bondage in Egypt. This city has recently been unearthed, and the walls of the houses were found to be of sunbaked bricks, some with straw and some without straw, exactly in accordance with Exodus 5:7, written thirty-five hundred years ago.

The Scriptures intimate that there was a city called "Petra" built out of solid rock. Infidelity scoffed at the idea. The critics cried, "Where is your city of Petra?" Then the archaeologists went forth in their explorations and came upon that very city. The mountains stand round about like great giants guarding the tomb where the city is buried. A street six miles long once knew imperial pomp and the laughter of lighthearted maidens on the way to the theater or to temples fashioned out of colored stone. Some of the stones have blushed into the crimson of the rose and some have paled into the whiteness of the lily; yes, on column and pediment, in tablement and statuary God has written the truth of His Word.

The Walls of Jericho and the Empire of the Hittites

World without end, the critics and the infidels have scoffed at the story of the fall of Jericho. The record in the Bible states that as Joshua was leading the children of Israel into their own land, a warlike city by the name of Jericho stood in the way. Acting under instructions from God, Joshua had his army perform a very unmilitary-like maneuver. They merely marched around the city once a day for six days, and on the seventh day they marched around it seven times. Then, according to the Biblical record, trumpets were sounded and the walls came tumbling down. Joshua's army then clamored up, easily took the city and burned it. It was easy and inviting for the critics to ridicule this story. They classified it with *Alice in Wonderland* and *Jack and the Beanstalk*.

These Bible critics do not smile so confidently nor scoff so contemptuously today. The walls of Jericho have been carefully excavated. There is abundant proof that these walls tumbled down in the exact manner that the Bible narrative relates. One can go to these excavations and look upon them for himself.

Furthermore, as the dust of succeeding centuries is cleared away, the city is shown to have received a very severe fire which was sudden and evidently unpremeditated. Today it is quite safe to rest your entire confidence on the complete credibility of the Biblical story of the fall of Jericho.

The Hittites

Up until the century in which we live, the critics laughed at the Biblical presentation of a people called the Hittites. They scoffed at the Bible delineation of such an ancient empire. Over fifty times in the Scriptures this name "Hittite" is used, and the people are described as rich, powerful, warlike, and industrious. But the Bible critics claimed that this entire story was a figment of the imagination. In no uncertain terms they claimed that a people as the Hittites never existed. The Biblical accounts dealing with this nation were nothing more than legendary. None of their inscriptions had ever been discovered. None of their cities had ever been seen.

Here again, however, the "miner-prophets," the diggers called "archaelogists," came to the rescue. The Hittites are now shown to be everything that the Bible had predicted and more. The uncovering of the Hittite empire and the Hittite civilization is one of the miracles of modern archaelogy. As a result of the labors of a number of scholars on Hittite inscriptions, a people and an empire scarcely less important than the Egyptian or the Assyrian has emerged. One of the great magazines of America put out an issue wholly devoted to the fabulous capital and conquests of these ancient Hittites. Once again Bible history has proved to be accurate, while the scoffing of the critics has proved to be ridiculous and absurd.

Daniel

It would be impossible for me in this brief space to go into what the critics have said about Daniel. Daniel, in the minds of the critics, has been nothing other than a thinly disguised forgery, purporting to describe the events of the sixth and fifth centuries, B.C., while actually it was written in the second century B.C. and reflects the background and events of the Maccabees. Historical blunders and linguistic anachronisms were referred to as proof of its pseudepigraphy.

But what has archaeology done to the book of Daniel? I have written a book upon these discoveries, published in the fall of 1968. The discoveries of the archaeologists, without exception, have confirmed the historicity and the authenticity of the book of Daniel.

Belshazzar

We can take just one instance. The critics scoffed at the idea that there was such a person as Belshazzar. From the historical records of the kings and from the writings of profane historians there was no place for any such ruler as Belshazzar. The critics made their case watertight, then laughed at the Bible believer. No such person as Belshazzar could have existed because there was no place for him in the records.

But once again the archaeologists have come to the rescue. Not only was there a Belshazzar whose name is written on the tablets of Babylonia, but also he now stands before us as one of the greatest figures of that period. We know the names of his secretaries. We are introduced to his sisters. We know him to be the son and coregent of Nabonidus, his father, and we know that the two reigned together in Babylon when the city fell to King Cyrus. Thus, once again, what was a subject for ridicule on the part of the critics has been discovered to be one of the great, historical facts of the Bible. It is a marvelous thing that this Belshazzar whose very name fell out of human history should have been introduced to the world by the Holy Scriptures which have been once again proved to be correct.

Archaeological Confirmation of the New Testament

In the last century it was taken for granted on the part of the higher critics that the story of the book of Acts was nothing but a second-century fabrication and that with a definite purpose. The critics saw in the Bible a conflict between Simon Peter and the apostle Paul. They found in the Book of Acts, therefore, nothing but a romance and a legend designed to cover over this Petro-Pauline rift in the primitive church.

But the Critics Were Wrong!

This theory was not constructed on factual evidence but on the Hegelian interpretation of history as thesis, antithesis, and synthesis. One of the men who was a believer in this hypothesis concerning the Book of Acts was a scholar named Sir William Ramsay. He decided, however, to test it out on the fields of archaeology in the Near East. He went out to the Mediterranean convinced that the Acts of the Apostles was not genuine. But he was openminded and for years studied the archaeological evidence as it was brought to life in Eastern Europe and in Asia Minor.

The facts that he discovered utterly changed all of his presuppositions. His research into the archaeological data convinced him of Luke's reliability and converted him to the authenticity of the volume that Luke wrote. He came back convinced that the Book of Acts dates from the first century and that it is the work of the beloved physician, Luke, who was the companion of the apostle Paul.

Confirmed by Archaeology

I mention just two other things by way of illustration of what archaeology has done to the New Testament. In Acts 13:7, Luke speaks of a deputy, or more accurately, a proconsul who was the ruler of Cyprus. Now the Roman provinces were of two classes: imperial and senatorial. The ruler of the imperial provinces was called a "propraetor" and the ruler of a senatorial province was called a "proconsul." Now, until a comparatively recent date, according to the best information we had, Cyprus was an imperial province and therefore its ruler would be a "propraetor." But Luke calls him a "proconsul," and for years and years this was

thought to be a mistake on the part of Luke. But, as the archaeologists dug into the ground and as the historians continued
their research, there was brought to light the fact that at the time
of which Luke wrote, the senate had made an exchange with the
emperor whereby Cyprus had become a senatorial province and
therefore its ruler was a "proconsul." Luke was right after all,
and the scoffing critics were themselves in error.

Another instance of the historicity of the New Testament can
be seen in the case of the Roman proconsul Gallio. He is mentioned in Acts 18:12–17. The critics said that there was no such
man and that certainly he was not the ruler of Corinth. However, the spade of the archaeologist has uncovered the record of
this man and an inscription has been found with his name written on it.

Thus, the Word of God is confirmed by every stone and every
spade of earth that is brought to light by the archaeologist. The
very stones themselves cry out, proclaiming the factual historicity of God's Holy Word.

CHAPTER 6

Is the Bible Full of Errors and Contradictions?

Can I believe in a literal Bible when it is said to be filled with errors and contradictions? To begin with, let me protest vigorously against the false impression left by so many modern critics to the effect that the Book is error-ridden. In recent years there was published in one of the popular magazines of America a long and spacious article entitled "Twenty Thousand Errors in the Bible." If the destructive critics were to be taken at their word, then the Bible is full of monstrous mistakes. Its prophecies have failed, its history is not historical, its science is unscientific, its stories are myths, its facts are fables, and there is practically nothing trustworthy in it. For many people, even church people, infallibility seems to die the death of a thousand agonies before the sheer rate and number of errors alleged to exist in the Scriptures.

We must remember that only a very small proportion of the so-called errors currently being proposed against the infallible Word of God are of recent vintage. Most have been mouthed by ancient infidels. Certainly, all have been dealt with long ago by the classical commentators on the Holy Scriptures, men who offered for the most part satisfying solutions to the difficulties. In fact, I have the temerity to affirm that as yet the destructive critics have not been able to produce a single error or discrepancy which cannot be reasonably explained. As a result of factual truths that are being unearthed concerning the Book, a critic with the rash misjudgment to announce an indubitable error in the Word of God ought to leave himself plenty of room to retreat. He had better be infallible himself or face certain humiliation.

So-called Biblical Errors Are an Elusive Lot

The so-called errors of the Bible are a very slippery lot. Just when you think you have your hands on one it evades you and disappears. In essence, these are not errors but difficulties which can be solved or explained. I read one time that in A.D. 1800 the French Institute in Paris had issued a list of eighty-two errors in the Bible which they believed would destroy Christianity. Today not one of these so-called errors is received as such, for with new discoveries the difficulties have been cleared away. It is imperative to distinguish between a difficulty not yet solved and an error. Errors are inconsistent with an infallible Bible, but difficulties are not.

One of the most unusual things that I have read has been the testimony of two scholarly men of God concerning errors in the Bible. One came from B. H. Carroll and the other from R. A. Torrey. Dr. Carroll said that he had seen so many contradictions and errors in the Bible melt away that he had lost all confidence in their existence. As a boy he had thought he had discovered a thousand more contradictions than as a man he now saw. Dr. Carroll avowed that there are perhaps half a dozen difficulties in the Bible that he could not satisfactorily explain to himself, but that since he had seen 994 out of one thousand harmonize with the truth of God, he was disposed to think that if he had more understanding of the facts, he could harmonize those other six.

The word of R. A. Torrey has been no less pertinent. Dr. Torrey said that he found that all of his difficulties were disappearing as he studied the Bible more intimately. At first, he avowed, they disappeared one by one, then two by two, then by scores, ever disappearing more and more. It is thus with all so-called errors and seeming difficulties. As we study them, they increasingly disappear. As we draw nearer to God, the Bible becomes more inevitably the veritable truth of heaven.

Difficulties in the Bible

Difficulties in the Bible are generally scientific, historical, or ethical. Scientific difficulties, for the most part, turn upon interpretation. There is not so much a difference between what the Bible says and what science says as between men's views of the Bible and men's views of so-called science. Both views may be wrong; our interpretations of either may not be correct. The difficulties of history have to be tested one by one. As yet we have not found any statement in the Bible relevant to history that has proved to be unhistorical. With regard to moral and ethical difficulties, we must remember that even Moses, because of the hardness of the hearts of his people, allowed them to follow a course that fell short of the full expectations of God (Matt. 19:3–8). In the next chapter we shall discuss the morality of the Bible.

We are not to be afraid of any criticism of the Bible. We are not to be frightened when we find a difficulty, no matter how unanswerable or how insurmountable it first appears to be. Thousands saw these same difficulties before we were born. The Bible has been God's rock upon which His people could stand through centuries of rigid examination and it is not likely to go down before that which we might be able to discover today. To one who is at all familiar with the history of the critical attacks on the Bible, the confidence of the modern destructive critic who thinks he is going to annihilate this Gibraltar seems simply amusing.

Mountains Yet to Be Scaled

Difficulties in the Scriptures do not overthrow their infallible nature. The difficulties are but mountains yet to be scaled and lands yet to be conquered. For example, 2 Peter 3:16 speaks of some things hard to be understood which they that are unlearned and unstable wrest to their own destruction. This is especially true in our modern day. When our finite mind tries to understand the infinite mind, there is bound to be difficulty. It never seems to occur to the rationalist that God can have a good reason for saying or doing a thing even though he, the rationalist, cannot see the reason. One of the greatest discoveries that a man could ever make is to discover that God might possibly know more than he does, that God might possibly be right and he, the man, might be wrong.

The time spent in some areas of ecclesiastical scholarship regarding the difficulties and the supposed inaccuracies in the Bible is an astonishment to behold. When men ought to be taught to proclaim the message of Christ and the truths of the Holy Book, the time of instruction seems to be spent in pointing to inconsequentials. What would we think of any one who, in studying some great masterpiece of art, concentrated his whole attention upon what looks like a flyspeck in a corner? So a large proportion of our much-vaunted critical study of the Bible is a laborious and empty investigation of supposed flyspecks.

Yet, the man who is not willing to squander the major portion of his time in this erudite and profitless investigation of flyspecks but prefers to devote his efforts to the study of the unrivaled splendors of the holy revelation is counted in some quarters as not being scholarly and up-to-date.

Applying Standards to the Scriptures

As we confront the difficulties of the Bible, we are ever to remember that we are not to apply standards to the Scriptures which do not suit them. The Scriptures were not written to give us a course in mathematics or in biology; nor were the Scriptures written to recount a full history of the chosen people of God or to narrate a full biography of Jesus. God speaks to us through the Scriptures, not in order to make us mathematicians or biologists or historians but in order to make us children of our heavenly Father.

We are also to remember that difficulties sometimes arise in our understanding of the Bible due to the remoteness of our day from the events that are recorded. This is especially true when we seek to harmonize different descriptions of a historical event. If our knowledge were greater, all of our seeming difficulties would be swept away. So we can read the books of 1 and 2 Samuel, 1 and 2 Kings, 1 and 2 Chronicles, and the four Gospels with a perfect assurance that the authors had infallible direction concerning what they wrote, even though the events are so far away and there are so many details that are not given that we are sometimes unable to put it all together perfectly.

We must remember that there are fashions in scholarship as there are in such things as sex, clothes, sports, philosophical thought, fiction, poetry, and in literature generally. The fashions change. The approaches change. But the truth of God stands forever.

There are two forms of criticism. "Lower criticism" is a technical term descriptive of that study which seeks to discover the exact text written by the original author. "Higher criticism" refers to the effort to ascertain the authorship, date, and character of the book. While an erudite and scholarly pursuit that is perfectly legitimate and vital, higher criticism is often turned into channels of blasphemy and defamation because of the presuppositions of the men who are thus studying the Word of God.

Difficulties that Arise from Our Stupidity

As we enter into the study of the difficulties of the Bible, we are certainly being truthful when we say that no small part of our problem lies in our stupidity. One of the first difficulties that will be raised in any group of people will be the question, "Where did Cain get his wife?" The answer to that is very simple. In Genesis 5:3–4 we learn that Adam in his long life of 930 years begat many sons and daughters. There can be but little doubt that Cain married one of the numerous offspring of Adam and Eve. In the beginning of the race, of course, one of the male children of Adam married his own sister. If the whole Adamic race was to descend from a single pair, the sons and daughters of that first couple had to intermarry. But, as the race continued the offspring would greatly multiply. One time I read where a man figured out that in the lifetime of Adam, as he begat sons and daughters, Cain could have chosen among more than thirty-five thousand descendants of Adam when he married his wife!

We have arranged another tremendous difficulty for ourselves in the chronology that we place in many of our Bibles. Ofttimes we read these dates at the top of the pages of the Scriptures as though they were printed there by the Almighty. Now, in many such chronologies it is thought that God created the world in 4,000 B.C. and that the story from Adam begins then. But we know from many, many archaeological discoveries that the race is older than six thousand years and civilization antedates by many centuries 4,000 B.C. Our trouble, therefore, lies not in the Bible but in what man has done to the Bible.

The age of the human race by some of these chronologists has been largely calculated by means of the names that are given in the genealogies in Genesis. But the genealogical tables are following a line of descent and by no means propose to include all the names of any generation. For example, the New Testament begins the story of Jesus with the genealogy of our Lord as being the Son of David, the Son of Abraham. "Son" here literally means descendant. In following these genealogical tables, many centuries have intervened between the name of one person in the list and the name of the next person. No chronology is intended to be formulated by these figures, much less would their purpose be to show the age of the world. The genealogies are merely recounting the lines of descent and it is only our stupidity that would make it do other than what God has purposed for it to do.

The ridiculous ends to which people will go to find fault with the Word of God is almost unbelievable. For example, in Numbers 11:31–32, there is the story of the quail sent by the Lord to the children of Israel in the wilderness in order that they might have meat to eat. A man who scoffed at the Bible read this story and with his own mathematical figures came to the conclusion that the record in the Bible spoke of a composite of quail about four feet deep, covering all the surface of the earth for 3,136 square miles. He said the content of this mass would be approximately 300,500,258,522,448 cubic feet of quail. The total number of quail, he surmised, would be 19,538,468,306,672. That was what he had fully figured out as one of the ridiculous things to be found in the Word of God.

There was one defect, however, in his calculations. He did not know the Hebrew language. Actually, the Holy Scriptures say that God blew the quail into the wilderness from the Nile Valley, and the birds, having lost their sense of direction, were flying above the face of the earth about two cubits high. The Bible in no way intimates that they were pressed down and packed together like sardines in a can but that they were flying close to the earth. It was easy, therefore, for the people to catch them with their hands or knock them down with a stick. This is all God said in His Book.

Fault-finding

Another example of the carping criticism of those who have set for themselves the task of finding fault with the Word of God can be seen in their objection to the language in which way God will describe an event. Note, for example, the story of the battle of Gibeon in Joshua 10:12–14. The battle was described in the way that it appeared to those who saw it and the Lord wrote it in such a way that those who read it could understand it. In speaking of the sun in the sky, there is no talk about the fraction of the sun's rays or the revolving of the earth or any other thing, but the sun is said to have stood still or to have tarried in the heaven.

It is one of the perfections of the Bible that it was not written in the terminology of material science. If it had been, it would never have been understood, nor would it even be understood in the present day. Science with its terminology is constantly changing and if the Bible had been written in the terminology of science yesterday, it would be outmoded today and if it were written in the terminology of science today, it would be out of date a few years hence. But being written in the nontechnical language of the people, it has a message for all and is always contemporary.

The language used in the Bible to describe the natural world is the language of simple observation, not scientific empiricism. The expressions employed in popular speech have not changed much over the centuries. For example, we still speak of sunrise; we still refer to the four corners of the earth; the North Pole is "on top" of the earth and Australia is "down under."

There is no contradiction in the Bible to any fact of science. The physical universe, the mystery of planetary and stellar movements, the constitution of man, the world of plant and animal life, the mystery of life itself, and the constitution of the earth in material forms and forces—all of these things that we know in science are in perfect harmony with what is presented in the Bible. There is topographical, geographical, chronological, and historical trustworthiness in the Word of God that is according to His infallible knowledge.

Difficulties We Make for Ourselves

We also make difficulties for ourselves when we receive the emendations in the original text of the Bible as being the Word of God itself. One of those texts, for example, which is found in our Authorized English Bible (the King James Version) is the story told in John 5:4. Now this statement regarding the angel disturbing the water seems improbable for many reasons. Upon thorough investigation through textual study we find that the whole thing is a mistake of an unknown copyist. Some early scribe, reading John's account, added in the margin his explanation of the healing properties of this intermittent, medicinal spring. A later copyist, thinking that the original scribe had left the text out and had put it in the margin, later embodied this marginal note in the body of the text itself; hence, it came to be handed down and got into our Authorized Version. These instances of copyist's errors are very few and they are very plainly and distinctly seen in the text. In our modern versions of the Bible they are appropriately omitted.

Errors and Contradictions Melting Away

As we turn to so-called errors in the Holy Record, I have not space to begin to answer all the castigations. As examples only, I have chosen to write of one in the Old Testament and one in the New Testament.

For many years there were great questionings as to the accuracy of 2 Kings 18:14, where the Holy Spirit records that the king of Assyria made Hezekiah, king of Judah, pay a tribute of three hundred talents of silver and three hundred talents of gold. When the archaeologists discovered the Assyrian record of this transaction, the accuracy of which no one questions since it was Sennacherib's own account, the amount of the tribute there was stated as being eight hundred talents of silver, not three hundred talents as in 2 Kings 18:14. The number of talents of gold was the same in the Sennacherib inscriptions as in the Biblical records, namely thirty. For a long time it was felt that there was no way of reconciling the different figures; therefore, one of them must certainly be wrong, and, of course and as usual, the record of the Bible was condemned.

Actually, nothing but a little time was needed to discover the answer. We have recently found from archaeological testimony that the difference in those figures, far from proving the existence of a mistake in either record, constitutes a most remarkable testimony to the accuracy of both. The standard of calculating talents of gold was the same in Judea and Assyria, but the standard for calculating the talent of silver was altogether different in each country. In fact, it took exactly eight hundred Assyrian talents of silver to equal three hundred Hebrew talents. Thus, in what was supposed to be a mistake, the minute accuracy of the Word of God was once more demonstrated.

The New Testament

Turning to the New Testament, we find the critics attacking a passage in Acts 5:36. The order Luke follows in this text is first Theudas, then Judas. But Josephus dates a Theudas in A.D. 65, a full decade after Gamaliel speaks in the Book of Acts. The critics point out that here Luke made a double mistake: he was guilty of a gross anachronism and he was guilty of a false and faulty order. Such a conclusion, however, does not correspond with our knowledge of Luke's historical trustworthiness throughout his two volumes of history, Luke and Acts. It is far more probable that Luke is referring to another insurrectionist named Theudas otherwise unknown to us and who lived before Judas. His order, then, would be correct; first Theudas, unknown to us, and then Judas. Withal, these carping criticisms seem small and insignificant when compared with the infinite wonder and glory of God's revelation.

Biblical Contradictions?

We come now to a discussion of so-called contradictions in the Bible. Here, again, we have not space to discuss all that the enemies of God's Word unnervingly say. We choose as typical of them only these few.

Many times have I heard it said that the Bible contradicts itself as to the number of animals taken into the ark, saying in one place there were two of a kind and in another place seven of a kind. All of this is due to our lack of reading what the Bible says. When we turn to Genesis 7:2 it is manifestly and plainly resolved. "Of every clean beast thou shalt take to thee by sevens, the male and his female: and of beasts that are not clean by two, the male and his female."

Another contradiction that is pointed out by the critic is supposed to be found in the superscription of the words which were placed above the cross of Christ. Matthew records it one way, Mark records it another way, Luke records it a third way and John records it still another way. Since no two of these absolutely agree in the words, the objector asks how all four can possibly be right? He says that at least three must be wrong. However, the answer to this is very plain. John tells us in John 19:20 that in order that all the different nationalities might read it the superscription was written in Hebrew, in Latin, and in Greek. It was written in Hebrew for the common people of Judea; it was written in Latin for the Roman people; it was written in Greek, the universal language, for all the strangers who were present. The inscription, being written in three languages, was quoted in different ways as each one of the gospel writers used a particular language or a part of the language. One of them doubtless included the entire inscription. There is no contradiction in the testimony of the Gospel writers at all.

Another passage that is used as a flagrant contradiction in the Bible is to be found in James' discussion of faith and works. James, in his letter (2:21), refers to Abraham as being justified by works whereas Paul in Romans 4 speaks of Abraham as being justified by faith. So deep is this apparent contradiction of doctrine that even Luther called the Epistle of James an epistle of straw. When we look carefully at the two authors, we find a perfect reason for their presentation of this doctrine of justification. When Paul writes, he refers to the fifteenth chapter of Genesis where it is recorded that Abraham, by faith, believed God and his faith was counted for righteousness. The illustration used in James, however, refers to Genesis 22 where it is described how Abraham offered up Isaac as a sacrifice on Mount Moriah. The illustration used by James in Genesis 22 is a confirmation of what Paul was speaking in Genesis 15.

There is no contradiction between the two; together they present the entire, full, rich life of a Christian. In our salvation we are justified by faith, having trusted in the Lord Jesus, and in our devoted works we give evidence of that commitment of faith that we have made to Christ. Faith without works is dead. That is true. If I am regenerated, I have a new heart and I will want to do good works for Jesus because of my love and gratitude to Him.

Miracles in the Bible

There are many who profess a disbelief in Biblical revelation because of the miracles recorded in the Book. There is absolutely no question but that the Scriptures teach and present the fact of miracles. This is interwoven into the very fabric of the Bible's sixty-six books. Miracles assume a place of great prominence. But what is wrong with miracles if there is a living God?

A miracle in a scriptural sense is simply a wonder and a sign. Its use is for the purpose that God may give a tremendous verification to His words and to His reality in a world that people can observe. "Miracle" is a signature of God. Wherever there is God, there is miracle. In a certain sense the Bible as a vehicle of God's revelation would lose its uniqueness were it not for its miraculous element. It is to be expected that when God speaks as the Master of the universe, those signs which would attend the message of God would be supernatural. A Bible without miracles would be a Bible without God.

One miracle, already referred to, is found in the book of Joshua and tells the story of God's lengthening the day in the battle of Gideon. The critic is quick to reply that if such a thing had been done, the machinery of the earth and of the universe would disintegrate. Not taking away from the ability of God to do anything that He pleases with our vast solar system, we must be careful to observe, however, that the story in Joshua merely tells us that the sun tarried above the visible horizon. This means that an event occurred on the day in the Valley of Ajalon that occurs many days every year at the North Pole: namely, that the sun remains visible beyond a certain length of time such as a twelve-or thirteen-hour period.

Now the method by which God accomplished this tarrying of the sun above the horizon we are not told. It might have been a slight dip of the pole, it could have been a fraction of the rays of light, or it could have been in other ways concerning which we could only conjecture. The miracle certainly would not necessitate such a crash of the physical universe as objectors have imagined.

It is a remarkable fact that we have a suggestion of this same thing in history outside the Bible. Herodotus, the great Greek historian, tells us that the priests of Egypt showed him a record of a long day. Chinese writings state that there was such a day in the reign of a long-ago emperor, a man who is supposed to have been a contemporary of Joshua. The Mexicans also have a record that the sun one time tarried above the horizon far beyond the regular length of day. There is nothing of real weight to prove that there was no such event in the history of the world.

Once again, there are those who look upon the story of Jonah and the miraculous fish as being something that is altogether impossible. The critic has ridiculed such a story almost out of court. Now, one of the first things we must be careful of is our use of words. In Matthew 12:40 Jonah is spoken of as being in the stomach of a "whale," but this is not a true translation. The word used in the Greek refers to a "sea monster," while the Hebrew story expressly states that God "prepared a great fish" for His purpose. The word "whale" is not used either in the Greek New Testament story or in the Hebrew Old Testament story. God prepared a fish for the reception of Jonah, and if we believe in God at all, we could believe that God is able to prepare a whole suite of rooms in that ocean monster to take care of Jonah until God had taught him his unforgettable lesson.

Where the Difficulty Really Lies

However, there is something more to this story of Jonah and the so-called whale than just the ability of God to have done such a miracle. One time there came home from Sunday School a little boy who said to his father that he did not believe the Sunday School lesson that day. When the father asked the lad what the lesson was about, the little boy replied that it concerned Jonah and the whale and that he did not believe the story. The father took the little boy on his knee and said: "Son, I also have difficulty with that story. You tell me your difficulty and I will tell you mine." The little boy replied: "Well, Daddy, my difficulty is that I just do not believe such a thing ever happened. I do not believe that a man could live in the stomach of a whale for three days and come out alive." The father then replied, "Son, my difficulty with the story is not quite what yours is. My difficulty is this: I cannot understand how God could make a man and I cannot understand how God could make a whale. If I could understand those two things, it would be very easy for me to understand how God could put the two together."

That is as it is in my own heart. My problem is not the miracle but my problem is the realization in personal life of the illimitable magnitude of the Great Jehovah of heaven. We are not to limit God. We are to believe His matchless work and to adore and to praise Him for all that He has done to reveal Himself and His truth to humanity.

CHAPTER 7

Is the Bible an Immoral Book?

Do I condone unethical teachings if I believe that the Bible is literally true? Some want me to think so. One of the castigations on the part of those who scoff and ridicule the Book is to the effect that the Holy Scriptures are full of moral blemishes. These scoffers purport to be greatly shocked at what they find in the Bible! Nevertheless, this is one of the darts that is plunged into the body of God's Holy Word.

One immorality that they refer to concerns God's command to exterminate the ancient Canaanites. Such a command is found in Joshua 6:17. There is no doubt about it: the holy war conducted by the Israelites at the command of the Lord was truly aimed at the total annihilation of these ancient people.

The reason for this command from God is most apparent. It is found in the hopeless depravity of Canaanite life. The religious culture of the land of Palestine during the second millennium B.C. was by any reckoning polluted, corrupt, and perverted. This is increasingly revealed by archaeological discoveries of the practices of Canaanitish religion. The destruction of that religion and culture is presented in the Old Testament as a display of God's righteous anger. The moral degradation in which the Canaanites lived before Israel invaded the land required not a revelation of the love of God but a manifestation of His holiness and severity. In certain diseases surgery is the only key to healing. Therefore, the destruction of the Canaanites might well have been essential for the survival of the true religion of the Hebrews.

The God of Wrath and Judgment

All of this but brings up again and anew the doctrine of the judgments of Almighty God. Is God a God of wrath as well as a God of love? The latter is certainly true according to the Holy Scriptures. God is love. But is God also a Judge who condemns sin? He is. If the justice of God is vindicated in condemning sinners to an external exclusion from Himself, such as found in Romans 3:5,19, and 2 Thessalonians 1:5–10, it would be petty to protest against a temporal judgment of sinners in the Old Testament. After all, is human sentimentality the yardstick for divine truth? From what source, therefore, are we to draw the picture of deity with whose character the judgments of God are inconsistent? The destruction of the Canaanites was a visitation from heaven upon the sins of the people.

There is no evidence that Jesus found difficulty in identifying the God of wrath of the Old Testament with the God whom He claimed to reveal. The Father God of the New Testament is a God of judgment. Christ would have repudiated the idea that the Old Testament view of God and of His wrath is at variance with the views of the God of love in the New Testament. In any event, even after the fuller revelation of God's person and being in Christ, we will find in the New Testament that the wrath of

God is even more fully evident in the New Covenant than it is in the Old. We have but to read the words of Christ in Matthew 23 and the words of the Apocalypse to see that the true God of heaven and earth is one whose righteous dealings with men necessitate judgment upon unrighteousness.

Another criticism of the morality of the Bible is found in Exodus regarding the hardening of Pharaoh's heart. It is said in criticism that if God hardened Pharaoh's heart, in consequence of this act on the part of God, then God Himself was responsible for Pharaoh's sin and that it was unjust to hold Pharaoh accountable for his rebellion and to punish him for it. If God did it, they say, then God is responsible and should be held accountable. For God to take a man who desires to know and do God's will, harden his heart, and thus incline him not to do God's will, would indeed be an action on God's part that would be impossible to justify.

However, when we read this story we are in an altogether different world from what the critics avow. To begin with, Pharaoh was not a man who wished to obey God. The whole account begins not with God's hardening Pharaoh's heart but with Pharaoh hardening his own heart. In Exodus 5:1–2 we are told that Moses and Aaron appeared in the presence of Pharaoh with Jehovah's message and Pharaoh definitely and defiantly refused to recognize or obey God. In response to the appeals for mercy from Moses, Pharaoh gave himself over to even more cruel and terrible oppression of the Israelites (vv. 5–14). In Exodus 7:10 and the following verses we see Moses and Aaron doing signs in the presence of Pharaoh to prove that they were messengers from God. Pharaoh would not listen, but, rather, hardened his heart against the Lord, as the Revised Standard Version in Exodus 7:13 correctly translates.

God did not do the hardening but Pharaoh did. God gave Pharaoh up to his recalcitrant will. This is God's universal message. If a person chooses error, God gives him up to that error (2 Thess. 2:9–12). If, with a hard heart and an obstreperous will, people choose sin, then God finally gives them over to that sin with its accompanying judgment (Rom. 1:24–26).

The Imprecatory Psalms

In the same vein and in the same category the critics of the Bible are greatly offended by the morality of what they call the imprecatory Psalms. They point out as examples Psalms 58–59, 69, 79, 109, and 137. They say that they see in these psalms a spirit of revenge and a desire to see one's enemies crushed in a way contradictory to the teachings of our Lord.

Here again, however, we come into the discussion of the doctrine of the wrath and judgment of God. Give attention to Romans 3:10–18. There Paul himself employs the language of these psalms to indict the enemies of God whose sins have rendered them liable to His wrath.

We must remember that sometimes in the Psalms we have what God says to man and sometimes what man says to God. In the imprecatory Psalms all of the passages are what men have said to God. To God they breathe out the agony of their hearts and to God they cry for vengeance upon their enemies. This example is exactly what the New Testament commands us to do regarding those who wrong us: we are to cry to God and to lay before the Lord our case. Vengeance belongs to the Almighty and He will repay (Rom. 12:19).

In these imprecatory Psalms, in most cases if not in all, while the tense in our English translation is in the imperative, making the language look like an imprecation pure and simple, yet the tense in the Hebrew is in the future. This indicates that the words contain prophetic warnings regarding the various kinds of judgment that certainly will one day fall upon the wicked, whether individuals or nations, unless they repent. The whole tone of the Psalms runs in this direction. The imprecatory Psalms announce the fate of all the godless when final judgment comes.

This can be seen easily in Psalm 137:8–9. These words sound like cruel bitterness against the enemies of Israel. The utterance actually is a prophecy that will someday fall upon the nations that rejoiced in their destruction of Israel. Especially is the psalm a declaration of an awesome visitation that will come upon Babylon because of the way Babyon had treated the people of God. Babylon as well as Edom was to reap what it had sown. They were to be served by others as they had served downtrodden Israel. It was a way of prophecy of what actually occurred afterwards in Babylon. We find a similar but even more awesome prophecy of the coming doom of Babylon in Isaiah 13:13–18. Observe Revelation 18:1–24!

The critics are quick to point out another supposed moral blemish in the Bible in the story of Saul and especially in 1 Samuel 16:14 where the Bible says that "the spirit of the Lord departed from Saul, and an evil spirit from the Lord troubled him."

What is meant by this "evil spirit" from the Lord? The context clearly shows that it was a spirit of discontent, unrest, and depression. The context of the narrative is very clear in presenting this judgment upon the king of Israel. Saul had proved untrue to God. He had deliberately disobeyed God (1 Sam. 15:4–26). As a consequence of this disobedience God withdrew His Spirit from him, and a spirit of tragic discontent and unrest cursed him. When we compare this with what we know of human life, we find that there is nothing truer when men turn away from God.

It is one of the judgments of the Almighty that when we disobey God's laws and refuse His will, we become unhappy, discontented, dejected, and full of despair in our sin. Like pain in our bodies the judgment warns us that something is wrong. Now, if we make right use of this spirit of unrest and depression, repentance will follow and bring us back to God and to the joy of the Holy Spirit.

There are many today who once knew something of the Spirit of the Lord and the gladness of serving Christ but who have fallen into sin. Now they bitterly know the truth of the biblical word that an evil spirit of unrest, dissatisfaction, and discontent plunges them into abject misery. When we disobey God, we face certain judgment. When we obey God and in repentance come back to God, we are filled with the joy of God's holy presence.

Moral Blemishes in Bible Characters

There are those who purport to be greatly offended by the so-called immoralities that are found in the characters of the Bible. As we look at these criticisms, we are certainly correct in saying that the Bible presents its heroes exactly as they are. The Bible does not embellish any of the men who cross the stage of scriptural history. Noah's drunkenness, Abraham's deception, Lot's disgraceful conduct, Jacob cheating his brother, Moses' outburst of temper, David's adultery, Peter's cursing and swearing, and even Paul and Barnabas' quarreling about Mark are fearlessly and publicly presented in God's Word. God does not attempt falsely to glorify the heroes of the faith.

The Bible condemns sin wherever it is found (1 John 2:15–17); Rom. 3:10–12). This includes the mighty men of the Bible. Men may regard sin as a misfortune, as a stumbling upward, as a drag of our animal ancestry, but God does not look upon it as such. God looks upon sin as a denial of His law in the universe. Men seek to minimize the enormity of their transgressions. God does not do so. God pronounces swift and immediate judgment upon our iniquities, whether upon an Adam or a Moses or a David. Unlike all other books, the Bible strips man of every excuse and emphasizes his responsibility and culpability.

The delineation of the characters that walk across the stage of Biblical history is faithful and true in every respect. God does not seek to hide away their imperfections and blemishes. A man, of course, in exaltation of his kind seeks to cover his shortcomings, but God does not. Hannibal, the mighty Carthaginian general who lived about 200 B.C., lost an eye in one of his perilous campaigns for which he was so famous. When later in life two artists were engaged to paint his portrait, they were so anxious to hide the physical defects of their hero that neither of them gave a true representation of the man. One of the artists painted him full-faced but gave him two good eyes; the other artist produced a side view picture and was more careful to select the side which had the good eye. The intention was kind but the result was, in both cases, a deception.

You will not find that in God's Word. God presents the characters who move in Biblical history exactly as they really were.

In final discussion of the charges of the critics concerning the moral blemishes in the Word of God the question finally resolves down to this. Shall we expurgate the Bible? Shall we add our human embellishments to the Word of God? Shall we touch up places that we think ought to be touched up, take out things that we think ought to be taken out, and add to things that which we think ought to be added?

One might as well go to the old picture galleries in Bresden or in Paris or in Rome and improve upon the old masterpieces. Perhaps one could find a foot of Michelangelo's *Last Judgment* that ought to be improved.

Perhaps one could throw more expression into Raphael's *Madonna*.

Perhaps one could put more pathos into Rubens' *Descent from the Cross*.

Perhaps one could change the crest of the waves in Turner's *Slaveship*.

Perhaps one could go into the old galleries of sculpture and change the forms and postures of the statues of Phidias and Praxiteles.

Such a one would be a brave soul indeed. What he did would be worse than vandalism. No less so would it be a piece of folly to try to remake the portraits God has drawn of the giants in the stories of the Bible.

The most apparent and simple denial of the critics' thrust against the Bible in saying that it is an immoral Book is just to look around you and see the power of the Bible and the influence of the Holy Scriptures to lift people up to God. A stream cannot rise higher than its source, and a book cannot lift men up beyond that moral station it itself possesses. This Book has power to lift people up to God in a way that no other book possesses in all the literature of humankind. In literally millions of cases the Bible has demonstrated its power to reach down to men and women in deepest depths of iniquity and degradation and to lift them up, up, up until they find a place beside Christ on the very throne of glory.

The Bible is truly the celestial book of heaven as can be witnessed by the character of those who believe it, love it, and accept it. The godliest men and women I have known were men and women living in the spirit of God's precious Scriptures. On the other hand, men who live in sin, selfishness, smallness, and sordidness are for the most part men who live far from God and who would never think of accepting the Bible as the Word of God for their lives. The fact that a man who is living upon the plains of evil refuses to accept the revelation and appeal of God is a testimony in itself that the Bible has in it the spirit of holiness. Where is the stronghold of the Bible? It is in the pure, happy, and godly home. Where is the stronghold of infidelity? It is in the dens of iniquity and in homes that curse God. God's Book is like God Himself, holy and pure, sinless and undefiled; and God's true people reflect the purity and holiness of that Book.

CHAPTER 8

Words: The Media of the Divine Revelation

The media of the divine revelation of God to man are words. God speaks and has recorded for us His words in the Bible. We read in Exodus 32:16, "The writing was the writing of God." We read in Revelation 19:9, "These are the true sayings of God." These passages are but typical of the witness of the Holy Scriptures from first to last, from beginning to end. Notice Luke 1:70 where the text plainly says that God spoke by the mouth of His holy prophets. Look at 1 Corinthians 2:13. The American Standard Version ends the verse with this translation, "combining spiritual things with spiritual words." Paul distinguishes between the thoughts which God gave him and the words in which he expressed them, and he insists upon the divinity of both. The text avows that not only is the Bible a divine revelation but also it asserts that the messages from heaven were written, not in words which man's wisdom teaches, but in words the Holy Spirit teaches. God inspired the words that the men used in writing down His revelation.

Sometimes the Bible writers understood the meaning of the words and sometimes they did not. Let us read again 1 Peter 1:10–11. This passage clearly teaches that the contents of the Word of God are so infinitely beyond what men would have understood and would have written that we can only say that they wrote God's truth with words which God Himself gave them. The inspiration of the Holy Scriptures, therefore, concerns not only the minds of the writers but also and more pertinently the writings themselves because the writers in many instances did not understand what they wrote.

Words are vital in any self-disclosure of God. Truth which is to be communicated must be related in language. If the Bible had nothing to do with words it would be nonexistent. Divine truth demands divine revelation and infallible language. What the Scriptures say and what God says are the same thing. The Scriptures can be so personified as if it were God Himself speaking. Look at Galatians 3:8. In this test it was God who gave the great promise to Abraham, but the passage speaks as though the Scriptures gave that promise. Look at Romans 9:17. In this passage it is said that the Scriptures spoke to Pharaoh, yet it was God speaking. In both instances the Scriptures and God are so close together in the minds of the writers of the New Testament that they could naturally speak of the Scriptures doing what the Scriptures record God as doing. The human word stands in the service of God and participates in the authority and infallibility of God's self-disclosure.

Men who have been dead for ages speak to us God's message through their words. If we are to know the revelation of truth that came to the prophets and the apostles, it must be through their words. If we are to be sure of their message from God, then we must be sure of their written words, for they are not here to speak for themselves. Thus, John will write in John 20:30–31 that these words are written in order that we might believe that

Jesus is the Christ, the Son of God. The words of the apostle take the place of Christ's personal presence and are the media of His revelation. We have no record of Jesus Christ and what He did and said except in the Bible. When we study the New Testament stories of our Lord, we study Christ Himself. Any rejection of the Bible is a rejection of Jesus our Lord.

When we refer to the inspiration of the Bible, we refer to the fact that the collection of words in the Holy Scriptures is veracious and conveys the divine truth effectively to the human mind. The very existence of revealed truth calls for the creation of infallible Scriptures to preserve and conserve it. It is verbal inspiration which assures us that the truth delivered from God is trustworthy because the Lord communicated it to us without error.

The Inspiration of Ideas and of Words

There are those who speak of the inspiration of ideas as though the words were not particularly significant. They speak of the inspiration of ideas instead of the inspiration of words. But we cannot escape the equally vital significance of words. Jesus said, "Heaven and earth shall pass away, but my words shall not pass away" (Matt. 24:35). This stresses the importance of words. On the basis of words we will be justified or condemned (Matt. 12:37). There is a prediction of Jesus that He would be killed, which is followed by this observation, "And they understood none of these things" (Luke 18:34). The self-disclosure and the revelation was made in words. It was not in the general realm of ideas. We are told specifically that the disciples did not grasp it, but the revelation is there because the precise words are recorded. The same comment can be made about Simon Peter's confession in Caesarea Philippi (Matt. 16:16). Peter said what he said by divine revelation but afterwards was rebuked because he did not comprehend the meaning of what he said (v. 23). Although the proposition had been revealed and Peter could repeat the words, yet at that time he did not really understand their meaning.

Thoughts Wedded to Words

Thoughts are wedded to words as necessarily as soul to body. As for thoughts being inspired apart from the words which give them expression, you might as well talk of a tune without notes or a sum without figures. No such theory of inspiration is intelligible. It is as illogical as it is worthless. We cannot have geology without rocks or anthropology without numbers. Neither can we have a divine record of God without words, and if that divine record is to be a true revelation of God, it must be without error. It must be infallibly correct.

If God had any message for us it had to be written in words. Words are mere signs of ideas, and it would be impossible for us to know how to get an idea except through words. If the words do not tell us how to get the idea, it is impossible for us to achieve any understanding. Can even God Himself give a thought to man without the words to clothe it? The two are inseparable.

To say that the inspiration of the Scriptures applies to their concepts and not to their words, to declare that one part of the Bible was written with one kind or degree of inspiration and another part with another kind or degree of inspiration, is not only destitute of any foundation or support from the Scriptures themselves but is repudiated by every statement in the Bible which bears upon the subject. The apostle Paul plainly writes in 2 Timothy 3:16 that "All scripture is given by inspiration of God."

The Media of the Bible

Inspiration extends to the form as well as to the substance, to the words as well as to the thoughts. How can we know God's thoughts if we do not know God's words? This is what is meant by the words being the media of the Bible. First Corinthians 14:37 declares, "If any man think himself to be a prophet, or spiritual, let him acknowledge that the things that I write unto you are the commandments of the Lord." Paul's words are the words of the Lord. They are the commandments of the Lord.

They are divinely inspired and carry with them the authority of Almighty God.

There are those who make much of the inspiration of events and of experiences, but who discount the inspiration of the words that describe the meaning of those events and experiences. The doctrine of verbal inspiration is for the most part discounted in our day. The modern, academic approach to the Bible takes almost as axiomatic that the revelation came not in words but in events. Modern theologians say that God performed certain mighty acts in history, in the process He revealed Himself, but all that the prophets did was to give an interpretation the best they humanly could of those historical events. We are informed by the modern theologian this revelation of God is not in the form of propositions, but in the circle of those mighty deeds. Is this what we find in the Bible? No. In making a contrast between the inspiration of deeds and the inspiration of words, we have in the Bible situations in which the deeds are almost nonexistent but where it is impossible to deny the revelation. For example, in the making of the covenant between God and His people on Mount Sinai (Exod. 24) we have a revelation made in words. What did God actually do on this occasion? It is difficult to see any objective deed at all; but the revelation at that time, with God entering into covenant relationship with Israel, was of the most profound importance and proved to be such in all the subsequent history of the nation. Indeed, there are vast sections of the Bible that have nothing to do with deeds whatsoever. The book of Psalms, much of the writings of the prophets, and Paul's epistles have very few deeds. The story of the creation of the universe in the beginning, the prophecies of the consummation at the end, the revelation of the coming judgments and the realities of heaven and hell—all make up an extensive part of the Bible. If the modern contention concerning the Scriptures is correct (that God inspired the deeds and not the words), then a vast portion of the Bible is not revelation at all.

Experience Judged by the Word

It is not experience that is to judge the Book but the Book that is to judge all human experiences. We have in the Word of God a standard by which we are to interpret all human history. There is no such thing as a God of the gaps. There were divine interpretations of events in the Old Testament and in the New Testament, and there are infallible words from God written in the Bible by which we are to judge and to test all experience and all events. In the archives at Washington there are weights and measures which are the finest that human genius can perfect. They are our standards for all weights and measurements. There is a perfect inch, a perfect foot, a perfect yard. Other rulers and yardsticks may go wrong, but in Washington there is a perfect paragon by which these may be corrected again and again. So it is with our clocks. They may lose time or gain time. Our watches and our clocks may be slightly off standard time, but there is a naval observatory which corrects time, puts it on the wires, and lets us know that the frailties and failures of our clocks and watches can always be righted. This is what we ought to do with human experience. We are to judge our human experience and the events in history by the infallible Word of God (Ps. 119:89, 160). Revelation is not an ecstatic experience, a wordless encounter with the Other; rather it is a gift of grace in which language is employed in all its rich functions to inform, to evoke, to rebuke, to summons, to bless, to heal, to save. The words bear the weight of personal instruction, guidance, fellowship, and exchange between God and humankind.

When we speak of the inspired authors of the Bible, we refer to the inspiration of the words and not of the men. The inspiration terminates upon the record. It is what the man has written that is inspired, not that the man himself is always inspired. Moses, David, Paul, John were not always and everywhere inspired, for then always and everywhere they would have been infallible and inerrant. This, of course, was not the case. As men they sometimes made mistakes in thought, and as human beings they erred in conduct. But however fallible and errant they may have been as men, and however they may have been encompassed with infirmities like ourselves, yet by inspiration from the Holy Spirit of God their fallibility and errancy was never under any circumstances communicated to their sacred writings.

For example, the inspiration of the book of Ecclesiastes does not mean that Solomon was inspired as he tried this or that experiment to find out what no one had been able to find outside of God. The inspiration of the book means that his language was inspired as he records the various feelings and opinions which possessed him in his pursuit. God has so ruled over these human authors that they excluded nothing that He willed to be included in the Scriptures and included nothing that He willed to exclude. As men hoist their sails against the wind, so each Biblical author yielded up his entire personality to the will and to the employment of the Holy Spirit. Therefore, what they wrote was inspired by God. This, by the way, was certainly Jesus' conviction concerning the Old Testament. No inspired writer was gifted with plenary knowledge; it was quite unnecessary for communicating the message he had to deliver. Inspiration did not make Paul a physicist or a physician. It did not even make David entirely sanctified. The truth of inspiration concerns only the miracle by which the Spirit of God produced a document in human language which could function as a truthful instrument of God's self-revelation.

The Bible Is the Word of God

Frequently we hear discussions concerning whether the Bible is the Word of God or only contains the Word of God. If, by the former, it is meant that God spoke every word in the Bible, the answer, of course, is no. But if it is meant that God caused every word in the Bible, true or false, to be recorded, the answer is, yes. There are words of Satan in the Bible; there are words of false prophets; there are words of the enemies of Christ; yet they are inspired as being in the Bible, not in the sense that God uttered them, but in the sense that God caused them to be recorded infallibly, inerrantly, and for our profit. In this sense the Bible does not merely contain the Word of God; it *is* the Word of God.

The object of inspiration is to put correctly in human words the ideas that come from God. If the words are not inspired, how would we know how much to reject and how to find out anything about God? It is insane talk that the Bible contains the Word of God but is not the Word of God. There can be no inspiration of the Bible without the inspiration of the words of the Bible. This inspiration includes accuracy of record. What the devil speaks is sometimes recorded in the Bible. It is there because God is giving us an infallibly true record of what Satan is like. There are many words of the enemies of God that are recorded in the Bible. But the inspiration of the Bible concerns the fact that they are perfectly and infallibly recorded. To say that the Bible is not the Word of God but merely contains the Word of God is a figment of an ill-employed ingenuity and an unholy attempt to deprecate and to invalidate the supreme authority of the Words of the Almighty.

Concerning this doctrine of the inspiration of words in the Bible, there are those who say that there is no such phenomenon witnessed in the Scriptures since different words are used in describing the same events. Critics bolster this argument by pointing out that the quotations of passages from the Old Testament by New Testament writers are not always in the exact words. It must be remembered, however, that there is a principle in ordinary literature that an author may quote himself as he pleases and give turn to an expression here and there as a changed condition of affairs renders it necessary or desirable. This is the principle used by the Holy Spirit in the Bible. In the New Testament, different words by which authors quote the Old Testament, the different recordings to be found concerning the institution of the Lord's Supper, and the different words used in the Lord's Prayer as found in Matthew and Luke are examples of the freedom of the Spirit. We must allow the Spirit to speak as He speaks. We must allow the Holy Spirit of God freedom to choose His words and to define His words as the Holy Spirit of God would choose to employ nomenclature.

The Certainty of the Exact Scriptural Text

We now turn to a brief discussion of the text of the Holy Bible. Do we possess the exact words that were inspired of God in the Old Testament and in the New Testament? The autographs, of course, have been lost, but God has seen to it that there is no fundamental doctrine that has been changed by the repeated copying of God's revelation through the centuries and the centuries. A comparison of the Isaiah scroll discovered in the Qumran library agrees almost verbatim with the Massoretic text from which we have our modern Hebrew Bible and which comes down to us after a full thousand years of copying. The ancient manuscripts go back literally hundreds and hundreds of years, and the number and variety of these manuscripts render it comparatively easy to arrive at an exact knowledge of the text.

A copyist might make a mistake, but when we have these thousands of manuscripts of the Bible, each many centuries old, it is very easy to recognize a mistake because the older manuscripts will not have that change or error. It is thus that from every part of the ancient world—from the tomb, from the rubbish heaps, from the ancient libraries, from the writings of the fathers, from the versions—there comes evidence piled upon top of evidence for the authenticity of the text of the Word of God. The multiplication of these ancient manuscripts is unbelievable. They come from every part of the ancient world and witness to every part of the New Testament and of the whole Bible. One scholar estimates that there are 4,105 ancient Greek manuscripts of the New Testament. It has also been variously estimated that there are as many as fifteen thousand to thirty thousand Latin versions of the Holy Scriptures. Besides these there are at least one thousand other early versions of the sacred Word. When all of these thousands of documents are checked, compared, combined, grouped, studied, we have a certain and final answer regarding the original and ultimate text.

When we remember that there is but a single manuscript that preserves the annals of Tacitus; when we remember that there is but a single manuscript that preserves the Greek anthology;

when we remember that the manuscripts of Sophocles, of Thucydides, of Euripides, of Virgil, of Cicero are most rare and that the very few which are in existence are for the most part late, then we can see with what profusion of evidence God supported the truth of the transcription of His sacred Word. Indeed, for all practical purposes, the original text is settled. There is not one important doctrine that hangs upon any doubtful reading of any text. The respect for the Old Testament text which Jesus and the apostles held expressed their confidence in the providence of God which assured them that their copies and translations were indeed substantially identical to the inspired original.

It is because of the inspiration of the infallible Word that we have the reason for our exegesis of God's Holy Scriptures. The method of exegesis, the science of the exposition of the words of the Bible, is based upon the doctrine of the inspiration of each word. If the Bible is not inspired in its words, there would be no reason for Biblical exegesis. We examine minutely every Scripture text and look closely at the history and the meaning of every single word. We look at the delicate coloring of mood, tense, and accent. This is because we believe that the divine Word is divinely inspired.

We can see the extent of the inspiration of the Holy Scriptures by looking at the use the Bible will make of a single word. In Galatians 3:16 Paul will make an argument for a great doctrine on the basis not only of a single word in the Scripture but also of a single letter. The entire doctrinal discussion turns on one letter of one word, the difference in the Scriptures' use of "seeds" and "seed." In doing this Paul was but following the example of his Master and our Lord Jesus Christ, who based the doctrine of the resurrection from the dead on the use of a certain tense of a verb in the Old Testament (see Matt. 22:31–33).

Who is the author of the Bible? Who spoke these words? Undoubtedly the Author is God, and it is God who speaks these words. When we open the Scriptures, we find that sometimes the penman is Moses, sometimes it is David, sometimes it is Amos, or Hosea. When we turn further through the pages of the

Holy Book, we see that sometimes the penman will be Matthew, Luke, John, or Paul. But did these men claim to be the authors of the Bible? Did they compose this tremendous Volume? Do they divide the honors among themselves? No! For this Volume is the writing of the living God. Each sentence was dictated by God's Holy Spirit. If Moses was employed to write, God guided the pen. If the prophet delivered a message to the people, it was God who formulated that message. If we find a description of the Lord Jesus Christ and a publication of His deeds and words, it will be according to the elective purpose and choice of the Holy Spirit. Everywhere in the Bible we find God speaking. It is God's voice, not man's. The words are God's words, the words of the eternal, invisible, Almighty Jehovah of heaven and earth.

The Bible rightly read, read as a whole, read Christo-centrically, read humbly and under the guidance of the Holy Spirit will lead us to life everlasting. In the open fellowship of the church and in our personal commitment to the Lord, we shall find that those words can never deceive us as to what God is like or as to what man is like or as to what God would have us to be like. All of the true discoveries of scholarship and all that we know of the Holy Scriptures have tended to raise, not lower, the status of the Bible as a true document inspired by the great God Himself.

CHAPTER 9

The Wonder of the World Is the Word

I believe that the Bible is literally true because of the miraculous wonder working of God in the Book. The Bible is an amazing phenomenon in the earth. Anyone who has studied the history and origin of the divine Word must be overwhelmed at the mysterious methods of its formation. That it ever was a book and is today *the* Book of the modern world is really a literary miracle.

Just think of this: There never was any order given to anyone to plan the Bible. Nor was there any concerted plan on the part of men to write the Bible. The way in which the Bible gradually developed through the centuries is one of the mysteries of time. Little by little, part by part, century after century, it came out in disconnected fragments and unrelated portions written by various men without any intention of anything like concerted arrangement.

The Bible was written on two continents, in countries hundreds of miles apart. One man wrote one part of the Bible in Syria; another man wrote another part in Arabia; a third man wrote another portion in Italy and in Greece. They wrote in the desert of Sinai, in the wilderness of Judea, in the cave of Adullam, in the public prison of Rome, on the Isle of Patmos, in the palaces of Mount Zion and Shushan, by the rivers of Babylon and on the banks of the Chebar. Such a variety of places and circumstances were the various bits of this strange mosaic created! No literary phenomenon in the world can be compared with it.

The Bible was written in three different languages: namely, Hebrew, Aramaic, and Greek. Some writers wrote hundreds of years after or before the others. The first part was written about fifteen hundred years before the man who wrote the last part was born. The authorship of the books of the Bible extends through the slow progress of nearly sixteen centuries. It is almost unbelievable that the authorship of the Bible covered nearly sixteen centuries.

The Bible was written by men upon every level of political and social life, from the king upon his throne down to the herdsmen, shepherds, fishermen, and petty politicians. Here are words written by princes, by poets, by philosophers, by fishermen, by statesmen, by prophets, by priests, by publicans, by physicians, by men learned in the wisdom of Egypt, by men educated in the school of Babylon, by men trained at the feet of rabbis like Gamaliel. Men of every grade and class are represented in this miraculous Volume. The circumstances under which the Book was written were sometimes most difficult and always most varying. Parts of it were written in tents, deserts, cities, palaces, and dungeons. Some of it was written in times of imminent danger and other portions of it were written in seasons of ecstatic joy.

Not only in background and in circumstances do the authors differ who wrote the Word of God, but they also display in their writings every form of literary structure. In the Bible we will find all kinds of poetry such as epic poetry, lyric poetry, didactic poetry, elegiac, and rhapsodic poetry. Also we find every kind of prose. There is historic prose, didactic prose, theological prose. The Bible will be partly in the form of letters, in the form of proverbs, in the form of parable, in the form of allegory, in the form of oration. Every kind of style and type of literature we will find in the Word of God.

In the light of even this brief review, is it thinkable that any book written in different places, languages, and literary genre by authors out of varying cultural levels and circumstances could ever come to be one volume, an organic whole? What would we naturally expect from such a background? We would expect whole areas of discord and all of it utterly lacking any basic or organic unity. In point of fact, what do we find? We find the most heavenly and marvelous unity of any book on the earth. Every part of the Bible fits every other part of the Bible. There is one ever-increasing, ever-growing, ever-developing plan pervading the whole.

The Organic Unity of the Word of God

Despite the varying circumstances, conditions, authors, and workmen who produced the Bible, the Bible is not many books but one Book. Behind its many parts there is an unmistakable organic unity. It contains one system of doctrine, one system of ethics, one plan of salvation, and one rule of faith. If forty different men were selected today from such varying stations and callings of life as to include clerks, rulers, politicians, judges, clergymen, doctors, laborers, fishermen, and many other types of workmen, and each was asked to contribute a chapter for some book on theology or church government, what kind of a collection do you think you would have when you bound it all together? It would be anything except one organic whole. It would be merely a heterogeneous mass and a miscellaneous collection of varying opinions. Yet we do not find this to be the case in connection with God's Book. Although the Bible is a volume of sixty-six books written by forty different men, treating such a large variety of themes as to cover nearly the whole range of human inquiry, yet we find the Book is one book. It is *the* Book, not the books. It is *the* Bible.

The phenomenon of the oneness of the Bible is one of the great miracles in the history of the human race. Let us illustrate this miraculous development. Pick out fragments of Augustine and the venerable Bede and Anselm; then as you pass through the centuries select parts of Dante, Milton, and Spencer, and add to it fragments of Bacon, Calvin, and Knox. When you have collected these fragments, add to them passages from Shakespeare, Bunyan, Newman, and Tennyson until you have the fragments of forty or fifty different writers. Bind all of this into one volume and you will have in a rough way a kind of literary parallel to the range of material used by the Holy Spirit in composing the Bible. It would be impossible for the man who wrote the first pages to have had the slightest knowledge of what the man would write fifteen hundred years after he was born. Yet his miscellaneous collection of heterogeneous writings is not only unified in one Book but so unified by God that no one ever thinks of it today as anything else than one Book, and indeed, one Book it is, the miracle of all literary unity. There is a perfect harmony throughout the Scriptures from the first verse in Genesis to the last verse in the Revelation. The profound ethical and spiritual values presented in the Bible agree. The more one really studies the Bible the more one is convinced that behind the many authors there is one overruling, controlling mind.

That there is one master-controlling mind behind the writings of the Bible can be most vividly illustrated in the construction of a great temple. Suppose there were built upon Mount Moriah a temple of stone, which stones were already cut and ready-made before they were brought together. During the building of the temple suppose there was heard neither the sound of hammer nor axe nor any other tool of iron. When all was completed, suppose the temple presented a glorious paragon of beauty, symmetry, and architectural perfection? What would you think? Would you not think that a mastermind had conceived it and directed its construction? You would. Without this mastermind there could be no such thing as the bringing of stones to the temple which, when they were placed together, would fit perfectly. It is even so that we are able to account for the structural unity of the Word of God. The structure was planned and wrought out in the mind of a divine Architect who superintended His own workmen at work. Over so long a period of time, through so many human authors and under so many different circumstances was the Bible written, yet every part fits every other part. Everything is in agreement with everything else because the whole Bible was built in the thought of God before one book was laid in order. The building rose steadily from cornerstone to capstone; foundations first, then story after story, until like a dome flashing the spendors of the noonday sun, the Apocalypse stands, to crown and complete the whole glorious volume with celestial visions. It is so with the Word of God.

The unity of the Bible is not superficial or peripheral but dynamic. It is not the unity of a dead thing like a stone but the unity of a living thing like a tree. The miracle of the unity of the Bible is the unity of one organic whole. The Decalogue demands the Sermon on the Mount; Isaiah's prophecies make necessary the narratives of the Gospel writers. Daniel fits into the Revelation as bone fits into socket. Leviticus explains and is explained by the epistle to the Hebrews. The Psalms express the highest anticipations and longings of a comfort we find in Christ Jesus. When we read the last chapters of the Revelation, we find ourselves mysteriously touching the first chapters of Genesis. As you survey the whole circle of the Bible, you find you have been following the perimeter of a golden ring. The extremities actually bend around, touch, and blend.

The Great Themes that Run Through the Bible

There are certain conceptions that run through the entire Bible like cords on which are strung many precious pearls. First and foremost among these conceptions is *the divine plan of redemption*. Just as the scarlet thread runs through all the ropes of the British Navy, so a crimson aura surrounds every page of

God's Word. Another one of the heavenly conceptions that run through the entire Bible is *the theme of Christ*.

There is one Personality that stands out above all others, pre-eminent, eternal, celestial. Just as in the scene unveiled in the fifth chapter of Revelation we find the Lamb in the center of the heavenly throne, so we find that in the Scriptures the Lord Jesus Christ is accorded a place which alone befits His unique and heavenly Person. Considered from one standpoint, the Scriptures are really the biography of the Son of God. All history is *His-story*. Christ is the great cohesive which holds all time together. He is the reason behind all events. He is the goal to which all life moves, and especially is this true on the pages of the Holy Scriptures. The face of Christ is the spiritual water-mark on every leaf of God's Holy Book. The Bible exists to reveal Him.

In type, figure, and simile He is everywhere presented.

The offering up of Isaac by Abraham is a picture of the offering up of Christ on Calvary.

The lifting up of the brazen serpent in the wilderness is a type of the lifting up of Christ for the healing of the people.

Joseph sold into Egypt is a type of the betrayal of the Son of God.

Bible characters present the fulness of the personality of our Lord.

As Adam is the federal head of the race, so Christ is the head of the new humanity.

As Melchizedek is a priest without beginning of days or end of ministry, so Christ is a priest forever after the order of Melchzedek.

As David is the king of his people, so the Lord Jesus is the King of His regenerated humanity.

As Aaron is the high priest of the church of Israel, so Christ is the High Priest of the church of the firstborn.

Bible institutions portray and present the wonderful work of our Lord.

The ark of Noah is a picture of the safety of the Christian in Christ.

The tabernacle in the wilderness exemplifies in its ministries the work of our atoning Saviour.

The water from the rock, the manna in the wilderness, the pillar of cloud by day and the pillar of fire by night, all point toward the glorious Person of Jesus our Lord.

Surely the Bible is one Book with one story, one revelation, one plan of redemption, and one offer of salvation to humanity. The story of the Bible is the story of Christ and the words of the Bible are the words of God.

As we hold the Bible in our hands, we are amazed at its logical order. The story of Christ is gradually unveiled throughout the Scriptures.

The Old Testament is the story of the preparation for the coming of Christ.

The Gospels record the manifestation of Christ.

The Acts recounts the propagation of the gospel of Christ. The Epistles comprise the explanation of the message of Christ.

The Revelation presents the consummation of the return of Christ.

One of the most beautiful and impressive tributes to the Bible ever written is that by Billy Sunday in one of his sermons. What Billy Sunday so effectively and eloquently said was this:

> Twenty-nine years ago, with the Holy Spirit as my Guide, I entered at the portico of Genesis, walked down the corridor of the Old Testament art-galleries, where pictures of Noah, Abraham, Moses, Joseph, Isaac, Jacob, and Daniel hang on the wall. I passed into the music room of the Psalms where the spirit sweeps the keyboard of nature until it seems that every reed and pipe in God's great organ responds to the harp of David the sweet singer of Israel.
>
> I entered the chamber of Ecclesiastes, where the voice of the preacher is heard, and into the conservatory of Sharon and the lily of the valley where sweet spices filled and perfumed my life.
>
> I entered the business office of Proverbs and on into the observatory of the prophets where I saw telescopes of various sizes pointing to far off events, concentrating on the bright and morning Star which was to rise above the moonlit hills of Judea for our salvation and redemption.

I entered the audience room of the King of kings, catching a vision written by Matthew, Mark, Luke, and John. Thence into the correspondence room with Paul, Peter, James, and John writing their Epistles.

I stepped into the throne room of Revelation where tower the glittering peaks, where sits the King of kings upon His throne of glory with the healing of the nations in His hand, and I cried out:

"All hail the power of Jesus' name!
Let angels prostrate fall;
Bring forth the royal diadem
And crown Him Lord of all."

CHAPTER 10

The Word of God Shall Stand Forever

I believe that the Bible is literally true because it partakes of the nature of God, who is eternal, who is the same yesterday, today, and forever. The Bible is not *a* book; it is *the* Book. It is the indestructible, undestroyable, ever-living, eternal, enduring Word of God.

Psalm 119:89 reads "For ever, O Lord, thy word is settled in heaven."

God says His Word is a sword and that it will pierce (Heb. 4:12).

God says His Word is a hammer and that it will break in pieces (Jer. 23:29).

God says His Word is a fire and that it will purge, purify, consume, and refine (Jer. 23:29).

God says His Word is a lamp and a light (Ps. 119:105). God's Word and God's Book is a living Word and a living Book.

God's Book is called the living oracles (Acts 7:38). It is impossible for God's Book to die.

The sacred Scriptures form the most remarkable Book the world has ever seen. They record profound events. The history of the influence of the Bible is the history of civilization itself. The wisest and best of humanity have borne witness to its power as an instrument of enlightenment and holiness.

Throughout the ages the Bible has been the central object of Satan's assault. Every available weapon in the devil's arsenal has been employed in his determined and ceaseless effort to destroy this temple of God's truth. But however hated, the Bible cannot be destroyed. However warred against, it continues to survive. It is omnipotent against all men's attacks. What man has made, man can destroy, the multiplied centuries of strenuous and determined assault have been unable to destroy or undermine intelligent faith in this Holy Book.

Generations of people have arisen with a determination to annihilate the Bible, but they have never succeeded. Celsus tried it with the brilliancy of genius and failed. Porphyry tried it with the hammer of philosophy and failed. Lucien tried it with the keenness of satire and failed. Then Diocletian came on the Roman stage of history and tried to destroy the Word with other weapons. He inaugurated the most terrific attack against a book that the world has ever known.

The Bible and Diocletian

While it is true that Diocletian attempted the destruction of the whole Christian community, he sought especially to destroy the Scriptures. He brought to bear against the Bible in 303 B.C. all the military and political power of the greatest empire the world had ever known. He brought this weaponry at the height of the strength and glory of the Roman goverment. Diocletian issued edicts that every Bible should be burned, but that failed. Stronger edicts were issued but they failed. The Imperial government then demanded that the Scriptures be given up or else those who possessed them would face execution. But that failed. Christians refused to give up the Bible. The emperor ordered the penalty of death if they were found with a copy of the Holy Scriptures. Myriads of Christians perished. At last when Diocletian had destroyed so many of them and had burned so many of their Holy Books that he thought he had won the victory, a column of triumph was erected over an exterminated Bible with the inscription, *Extincto Nomine Christianorium*, meaning, "The name of the Christians has been extinguished."

Was that so? Did Diocletian actually succeed? No! The Diocletian butcheries, like the torture of the later Inquisition, utterly failed. As Noah came forth from the ark to repeople the earth, so in a few years after Diocletian, the Bible came forth as a Book of resurrection and life. In the year A.D. 325, at the first general council, the Council of Nicea, Constantine enthroned the Bible as the infallible judge of truth.

The following centuries, after the conversion of the Roman empire to Christianity, have been no less a story of trouble and tribulation for those who love the Word of God. Through the years the attack upon the Bible has continued. Every engine of destruction that human wisdom, human science, human philosophy, human wit, human satire, human force, and human brutality could bring to bear against the Bible has been brought to bear against it. Yet the Bible still stands!

Pseudoscience has tried to laugh it out of court. The skeptics and the infidels have shouted their victory over the Word of God. Yet the Bible still stands. Over two hundred years ago the skeptic Voltaire said, "Fifty years from now the world will hear no more of the Bible." It is a strange commentary on this prophecy that in the very year the British Museum paid to the Russian government over $500,000 for a copy of a Greek Bible, the ancient Codex Aleph, a first edition of Voltaire's sold on a bookstore counter in Paris for less than eight cents!

The Age of Reason

About two centuries ago a book made its appearance in America which attracted wide attention, particularly in the upper circles of academic achievement and culture. It was attractively entitled, *The Age of Reason*. Its author, Thomas Paine, was probably without a superior in intelligence among all his contemporaries. So confident was Thomas Paine that his reasonings would prove beyond doubt the untrustworthiness of Scripture and that they would destroy forever the claims of the Bible upon the consciences of men that he jubilantly predicted that in a few years the Bible would be practically out of print. Not only that, but when Thomas Paine, returning to America, got off the ship to come ashore he boasted, "When I get through there will not be five Bibles left in America."

What of his boast? He said his *Age of Reason* would be read to the abandonment of the Bible. Is it? Actually, his *Age of Reason* is read more as a curiosity, while the Bible is read as a fountain of life unto salvation. Nearly two hundred years have passed since the boast of Thomas Paine was uttered. The boaster and his book have passed away and their very names are well nigh forgotten. But the Word of God has continued to be loved and read. It has maintained its place in God's grace and power. They who believe and cherish it are usually a feeble folk, but the Almighty God is with them.

The Attack of Modern Rationalism

Perhaps the most deadly persecution against the Bible of all time has materialized in the last 150 years. The German rationalistic host mounted against the Bible the fiercest and deadliest of all attacks. This assault has been taken up by the liberal theologians of England and America and continues unabated to this present day.

In the first days of the Christian era the attack of the unbelievers against the Bible was made openly and by the overt assault of men who were the antagonists of the Christian faith. The chief instrument of their destruction was the bonfire. But in these modern days the assault against the Bible is made in a more subtle manner and comes from a most unexpected quarter.

The divine origin of the Scriptures is now disputed in the name of scholarship, science, and religion. This is being done by those who profess to be friends and champions of the Word of God. Much of the learning and theological activity of the present hour is dedicated to the attempt to discredit and destroy the authenticity and authority of God's Word. The result of this is that thousands of nominal Christians are plunged into seas of doubt. Many of those who are paid to stand in our pulpits and defend the truth of God are now the very ones who are engaged in sowing the seeds of unbelief and destroying the faith of those to whom they minister.

The Word of God Still Lives!

But the Word of God still lives. We are challenged in our proud age no less than the children of Israel were challenged by Moses in Deuteronomy 4:32–33:

> Ask now of the days that are past, which were before thee, since the day that God created man upon the earth, and ask from the one side of heaven unto the other, whether there hath been any such thing as this great thing is, or hath been heard like it? Did ever people hear the voice of God speaking out of the midst of the fire, as thou hast heard, and live?

As I hold in my hands a copy of the divine, infallible, inerrant Word of God, I cannot but be overwhelmed by its miraculous preservation. Word for word, jot for jot, tittle for tittle, through the centuries, the saints possessed God's holy self-disclosure of Himself. We, too, can be assured that the Bible we hold in our hands is the Word of God as the Lord wrote it, and that it contains what God would have in it, and that it does not contain what God refuses to make a part of it.

Think of this. Fifteen hundred years after Herodotus wrote his history there was only one copy of it. Twelve hundred years after Plato wrote his books there was only one copy of it. But God was so careful to let us have the Bible in the exact way that He wrote it that we have thousands of ancient manuscripts of it. The Books of the Bible that we have in our present catalog are the same as they have been through all the centuries.

Though the volume has been assaulted, spit upon, torn to pieces, and burned, yet the catalog of the sixty-six books of the Old and New Testament is the same catalog that has obtained through the ages. Thirty-nine books of the Old Testament thousands of years ago, thirty nine now. Twenty-seven books of the New Testament hundreds of years ago, twenty-seven books of the New Testament now.

The Unchanging Bible

Not only have all attempts to detract from the Book failed but also all the attempts to add to it or to take away from it have failed. Many attempts have been made to add the apocryphal books to the Old Testament. The Council of Trent, the Synod of Jerusalem, the Bishops of Hippo, all decided that the apocryphal books must be added to the Old Testament. "They must stay in," said those learned men. But they stayed out. There is not an intelligent Christian today who would put the Second Book of Maccabees or the Book of Judith beside the book of Isaiah or the book of Romans.

Then a great many said that we must add books to the New Testament, and there were epistles, gospels, and apocalypses written and added to the New Testament. What has happened to these? They have all fallen out. You cannot add anything to the Bible. You cannot subtract anything. It is a divinely protected Book as we hold it in our hands today. Let no one dare to mutilate it with the intention of detracting from the Book or tearing out any of its holy pages.

The more I think upon it the more I am convinced that man, unaided by the Spirit of God, could neither have conceived, nor put together, nor preserved in its integrity the precious deposit we know as the sacred oracles of God, the Bible. God's Word has been an anvil for nineteen hundred years, and when other hammers today try to break God's eternal anvil of truth, we but remember the inscription on the monument to the Huguenots in Paris, France: "Hammer away, ye hostile hands. Your hammers break, God's anvil stands."

My favorite verse is still in the Book: "The grass withereth, the flower fadeth: but the word of our God shall stand for ever" (Isa. 40:8).

These are my reasons for believing that the Bible is literally true.

PART II

What I Preach, Believing that the Bible Is Literally True

GOD'S WORD OUR GUIDE TO HEAVEN

The heavens declare Thy glory, Lord,
In every star Thy wisdom shines;
But when our eyes behold Thy Word,
We read Thy Name in fairer lines.
The rolling sun, the changing light,
And nights and days Thy power confess;
But the blest Volume Thou didst write,
Reveals Thy justice and Thy grace.
Great Sun of Righteousness, arise,
Bless the dark world with heavenly light;
Thy gospel makes the simple wise,
Thy laws are pure, Thy judgment right.
Thy noblest wonders here we view
In souls renewed, and sins forgiven;
Lord, cleanse our sins, our souls renew,
And make Thy Word our guide to heaven.

—Isaac Watts

CHAPTER 11

Preaching Through the Bible

There is a plainly stated text in 2 Timothy 3:16 to 4:2 which reads like this:

All scripture is given by inspiration of God, and is profitable for doctrine, for reproof, for correction, for instruction in righteousness: that the man of God may be perfect, thoroughly furnished unto all good works. I charge thee therefore before God, and the Lord Jesus Christ, who shall judge the quick and the dead at his appearing and his kingdom; preach the word.

The text avows that *all* the Scriptures are inspired of God, that *all* the Scriptures are God-breathed, that the writing is the writing of God and contains the breath and the presence of God. The passage says that the Holy Bible is not inspired in places, spots, and sections, while other places, spots, and sections remain uninspired. All of it is God-breathed. On the basis of that statement Paul makes the appeal to his young son in the ministry that he "preach the word."

This, also, is our assignment. Our pulpit task is plainly stated and plainly outlined. We are to preach the whole Bible, all of it. It is unfortunate that there is a chapter heading between the close of chapter 3 in this passage in 2 Timothy and the beginning of chapter 4. It is all one passage. *All* Scripture, *all* the Bible is inspired of God and all of it is to be *preached.*

I have found that even in those sections and passages in the Bible that seem the least profitable are the seedbeds for some of the most profitable and precious sermons. One might use as an illustration the dull dreariness of the genealogical tables that are found in the Bible, yet out of those tables I delivered a message entitled, "The Family of God," which was unusually blessed of heaven. Insofar as God gives us wisdom and help, we are able to deliver to the people the whole message of God from the whole Bible.

Preaching the Whole Word of God

Soon after coming to the pastorate of the First Baptist Church in Dallas, Texas, I made an announcement that I would preach through the Bible. It was my first intention to go through the Book much faster than I finally did. In fact, at first I did preach rapidly through the books of the Old Testament. But as the days multiplied I found myself going slower and slower and slower. Finally, I came to the place where I preached for several years on some of the sections of the New Testament. In all, from Genesis to Revelation, I spent seventeen years and eight months going through the Book. Where I left off Sunday morning, I began Sunday night; where I left off the previous Sunday night, I began the following Sunday morning.

When I made the announcement that I was proposing to preach through the Bible, an obvious foreboding fell upon a part of the congregation. They were afraid that the church would be ruined. Some of them felt that no one would come to listen to long passages in the Bible that were not familiar and that had never been discussed or preached on. The whole outlook was one of gloom. The lugubrious prognostication would have made any church dark with the foreboding of inevitable failure.

What actually happened, however, was as if heaven came down to attend church with us. As I continued to preach through the Word of God, the congregation continued to grow. Finally, throngs and throngs came to wait unto the Word of the Lord. The auditorium in the First Baptist Church of Dallas is one of the largest in America. We filled it to capacity and the people kept coming in increasing numbers. The people grew to esteem Bible preaching. Their every comment was one of love and appreciation. Many times have I heard our new members in talking to one another facetiously say, "You know, I joined the church in Isaiah!" Another would add, "I joined in 2 Timothy!"

People Are Hungry for the Word

To this present hour our people hunger and thirst for the Living Word of the Living God. We fill the spacious auditorium three times every Lord's Day. The congregation is still growing as I continue to preach the Bible. And everything else grows. The teaching ministry of the church through the Sunday School grows. The training ministry through Church Training grows. The financial program is vastly expanding. The whole life of the congregation is quickened. God seems to bless every part of our endeavor.

A few years ago, when New Year's Eve fell on a Sunday, I announced that I would begin at 7:30 and continue until after midnight preaching through the whole Bible in that one evening. I entitled the message "The Scarlet Thread Through the Bible." I presumed that I would begin with the congregation that usually filled the auditorium in the evening. I also presumed that as I continued preaching through the hours until midnight that the congregation would gradually thin out.

What actually happened was just the opposite. Not only was the house of the Lord filled at 7:30 o'clock when the service began, but, also, the people were standing around the walls on the lower floor and around the walls of the balconies. Nor did their interest abate. When I closed the message after midnight, the throngs were still in the auditorium with the people jammed and standing around the walls downstairs and upstairs. It was one of the most phenomenal preaching experiences of my life.

Now let me say a word concerning what I preach as I preach through the Bible. Some of these messages delivered during those seventeen years and eight months have been published. For example, the book, *The Gospel According to Moses*, is a selection of some of the sermons that I preached from the Pentateuch. These are typical of many, many others that I delivered. Again, there have been published five volumes of the sermons that I preached on the Revelation. They are entitled *Expository Sermons on the Revelation*. Looking at these sermons one can gain a clear idea of what I did as I preached through the entire Word of God.

One Great Theme in the Bible

There is one great theme in the Bible. That theme never varies from beginning to end. The Scriptures present the Lord Messiah through every event, type, paragraph, chapter, and verse. Christ is in and through it all. Someone came up to Charles Haddon Spurgeon, pastor of the world-famed Metropolitan Tabernacle in London, England, and said to him, "Your sermons all sound alike." To which Mr. Spurgeon replied: "Yes. I take a text anywhere in the Bible and make a beeline to the cross." What Spurgeon did is certainly a true reflection of the spirit and message of the Word of God. All of it speaks of Christ, whether it is the story of Noah's ark or the construction of the tabernacle in the wilderness or the messianic prophecies of Isaiah. The whole Bible either points to Christ in His first coming or to Christ in His second coming. The entire Bible presents Jesus our Saviour.

Speaking of Mr. Spurgeon, I am reminded of a story that I heard of him long ago. At one time he was in Scotland and while visiting in a home, he came across a very old and much-worn Bible. He lifted it up and held it reverently in his hands, turning it this way and that way as he looked upon it. It was then that he observed a small hole where a worm had eaten its way through the Book from cover to cover. Upon seeing it, the great London preacher exclaimed: "O Lord, make me a bookworm like that. From Genesis to Revelation it has gone clear through the Bible." That is the way that I have felt. "O Lord, guide my mind and my heart as I study clear through this Holy Book and as I seek to make its message known to the people."

Now let us speak of the effect such a preaching ministry has had upon the habits of the members of the church. One of the most noticeable changes that has taken place in the people is the increasing disposition to bring Bibles to the worship services. Practically everyone brings his Bible to church, and we all read out loud from the holy pages together. We do this at all of our services.

Our church is located in front of the big, downtown YMCA. Upon a day a man who was staying at the "Y" went up to the clerk at the desk and the following conversation ensued.

"I thought you told me that was a Baptist church across the street."

The clerk at the desk replied. "It *is* a Baptist church."

The visitor then said, "No, it is not a Baptist church; it is an Episcopal church."

The clerk asked him, "Why do you think it is an Episcopal church and not a Baptist church?"

The visitor replied, "Because I have been standing on the steps of the 'Y' watching the people leave after the eleven o'clock worship service and every one of the people who came out of the church carries a prayer book in his hand."

The clerk at the desk laughed and said, "Man, those are not prayer books; those are Bibles!"

This is certainly a true characterization of the congregation. We all bring our Bibles.

While I was writing this book, I had an unusual visit with a stranger who had come to our services. The city of Dallas was host to the National Conference of Nurses, and this woman was one of those nurses who had come to attend the meeting from a state on the northeastern seaboard. In her visiting with me she told me how it was and why it was that she came to our church. She said she was not a Baptist and had not intended visiting a Baptist church. But, she said, she noticed so many people carrying Bibles as they walked through the streets of Dallas that she decided to follow those people just to see where they would go. Sure enough, she said, she landed in our First Baptist Church!

Heavenly Blessings from Preaching the Book

Truly, truly, the blessings of God have been upon us in our preaching through the Bible. The power of the Holy Book to attract is one of the miracles of our modern day. If I or any man were to speak week after week, month after month, year after year, on such topics as economics, politics, literature, or social reforms or any other subject it would soon be discovered that the people would be returning in increasingly smaller numbers. Finally the attendance would be nil. Conversely, however, by preaching on the Word of God the people would come back and back and back. This is a sign from heaven that anyone can see. It is an empowering experience that anyone can share.

But not only has God blessed the congregation as I have preached the Bible. God has also wondrously and marvelously blessed me personally. I have grown in my own heart and in my own soul. In the preparation of my sermons as I study the Bible, my life has been gloriously enriched from heaven. As I look at preachers preparing their sermons, I often think of their pacing up and down the study floor, wondering what they shall preach about the following Sunday. I also pace up and down the study floor as I get ready for the preaching assignment on the coming Lord's Day. But I have an altogether different reason and purpose for my walking up and down the floor. I walk up and down the floor in an agony of spirit being afraid that I shall not have time in the span of my ministry to preach all that I want to preach and to deliver all that I want to deliver and to share all that I have seen in God's blessed Word. The Book is like an unfathomable sea. It is like the infinitude of God Himself. The more I study, the more I pray, the more I read, the more riches I find that I want to share with my people.

When I first began to preach as a teenager, I tried to spin the message out of myself like a spider weaving his web. I preached adventitiously, opportunistically. I preached about whatever fell by chance into my mind. I preached according to whatever some incident or event or saying would suggest. That is about as poor a way to prepare a sermon as could be found in all the world. I do not do such a thing now. I have a passage before me, and I ask God to reveal to me the full meaning of that Scripture. When I preach, it is always with a "Thus saith the Lord God." I am filled with a thousand marvelous, spiritual thoughts when I thus take my text and deliver God's message.

"If I Had My Ministry to Live Over Again"

If I had my ministry to live over again, I would from its very beginning preach the Bible and nothing but the Bible. I would go through book after book of the Bible. If I could not find a message in a verse, I would take a paragraph. If I could not find a message that moved my heart in a paragraph, I would take a chapter. If I could not find a message in a chapter, I would take two chapters. If I could not find a message in two chapters, I would take half a book. If I could not find a message in half a book, I would take the whole book. If I could not find a message in a whole book, I would take two or three books. I would study the passage in the Bible, however short or long it was, and I would deliver my message from that passage. I wish I had my life to live over again in order that I could seek to enrich the souls of those dear people who first heard me in my beginning ministry.

A year or so ago, in company with four other ministers, I made a journey through Northern Europe and Russia. To my sorrow and grief I saw the churches in Northern Europe, for the most part, empty and dead. To my great joy and delight I saw our Baptist churches in Russia filled to overflowing. It was an amazing sight to me. One of the things that interested me was the question of how the churches in Russia recruited their ministers and how they trained their preachers. The churches in Russia are allowed no school, seminaries, or literature, not even the printing of God's Holy Word. How then do the preachers recruit new members and how do they prepare for their task of preaching?

The answer is very plainly seen in the habits and the methods of the churches. The pastor of the church has several understudies around him. He trains and teaches those younger preachers from the pulpit itself. They have one text and that is the Bible. The preacher in the pulpit has his young Timothys to study the Word and to take turns delivering the message from the Book. This has made for a Bible-centered ministry and has trained the young preachers to love and to preach the Word of God.

It is the strength of our evangelical witness that we study God's Book and that we deliver from its pages God's message. We shall not fail in our work if we are faithful to this holy and heavenly assignment.

CHAPTER 12

The Message of Literal Truth

God's message in the Bible is plain, simple, full, comprehensive, and all-sufficient. What we need for faith, salvation, practice, we find in the Bible. We need nothing else. What the Scriptures say God says. What God says is literally true and is to be received by us as truth itself. The Scriptures enlighten us to receive Jesus, God's incarnate Son, as our divine Saviour. The Holy Spirit enlightens us to receive the sixty-six pieces of human writing in God's Book as the "inscripturated" Word of the Almighty which is able to make us wise unto salvation (2 Tim. 3:15).

Belief that the Bible is sufficient for the Christian and for the church as "a lamp unto our feet and a light unto our paths," is the fundamental persuasion of the people of God. It is even as

Article VI of the Church of England says, "Holy Scripture contains all things necessary to salvation." The Scriptures do not need to be supplemented from any other source, reason, or experience. The Bible is in itself a complete organism of truth and is sufficient for all of our needs. The Holy Spirit has provided that the church of our Lord does not lack anything in the way of doctrine or inspiration and that we may believe and preach on the ground of the written Word.

Why do we not turn to modern sources for our doctrines of God and salvation? Why, in a world that is changing so rapidly, do we still go back for our moral and spiritual guidance to what was written so long ago?

We do not do that in science. Science textbooks often are outmoded within a decade after they are written. We certainly do not do that in medicine. One would hardly submit to surgery if he were informed that the doctor was practicing medicine on the basis of what had been written fifty years ago. Why then do we do it in religion?

Because for one thing, the essence of the gospel consists of unchangeable, historical facts (1 Cor. 15:1–6). And because, for another thing, the needs of human lives do not change and God's provision for those needs does not change. Man, fundamentally, does not change. Styles change, devices change, methods change; but human nature does not change. Greed and lust are the same in every age. Sin is sin whether we see it exemplified in a Herod or in a Hitler, and the results of sin have not changed since Paul wrote in Romans 6:23, "The wages of sin is death."

The Bible that spoke to the needs of human souls centuries ago is the same Bible that speaks to the needs of human souls today. The Bible is not concerned with how fast we can travel. The Bible is concerned with where we are going. The Bible is not concerned with what we know about science; the Bible wants to know what difference truth makes in our lives. The Scriptures point to moral laws that cannot and should not be repealed. In this sense, therefore, the prophetic voices that announce God's purposes in history speak to us today. Morality is fixed and cannot be *new*. As such the Bible is the truth of the living Lord and is all sufficient for our every need.

The message of the Bible is like God Himself: the same yesterday, today, and forever. The Bible is like God Himself who is literal truth, who is infallible and who cannot be convicted of error. We are to receive therefore the Word of the Lord as literally true. By the Holy Scriptures we are to believe in literal answers to literal prayers. We are to believe in the ultimate and literal fulfilment of the literal promises made to Israel and to all of God's saints. We are to believe in the promises of our Lord in His coming again and in the eternal states of the righteous and the wicked. The whole message of the Bible is to be reverently, faithfully, and devoutly received.

Literal Promises to Be Literally Fulfilled

We are to believe and to preach that God literally answers prayer. We are encouraged to believe in a prayer-answering God. Let us read anew a few of the promises of the Lord made to His saints to encourage them to pray: Jeremiah 33:3; Luke 11:9–13; 18:1; Mark 11:22–24; John 16:23; 1 John 5:14–15. We are to believe in these promises literally and we are to intercede on the basis of their literal truth.

We are to believe and to preach that God will literally and faithfully keep His promises made to His chosen people, the children of Israel. If God breaks His promises here, if God fails here, how can we have any assurance that God will not fail in every other promise He has given? The promises the Lord has made to His people Israel are clearly expressed. Such a promise is found in Ezekiel 36:24–28 and in Amos 9:15. God surely and literally has a purpose and a program for His chosen people, Israel. The promises of God to Israel have not yet been fulfilled but in God's time and in God's sovereign grace every word He has spoken in behalf of His chosen people will be faithfully kept (Rom. 11:25–29).

The whole Bible I preach literally, as being literally true. When the words are not to be taken literally but are representative and figurative, such a fact will be clearly indicated and it will be most obvious. The context will reveal it and the Scripture passages before and after will inevitably indicate it.

Actual Body, Actual Blood?

For example, in the story of the institution of the Lord's Supper, Jesus took bread and said, "This is my body." He then took the cup and said "This is my blood." Are these to be taken literally? Is this bread the actual body of Jesus and is this cup the actual blood of Jesus? The answer is no. How am I certain of this? I can be certain of this spiritual truth because of the context in which the words are said. When Jesus uttered those declarations, He was standing before His disciples. His body was there as He spoke the words and His blood was coursing through His veins. Therefore, I know that they were not eating the actual body of Jesus nor were they drinking His actual blood. I know the fact, also, from the context which says that the Supper is a memorial and that we are eating this bread and drinking this cup in order to bring to mind the suffering and the death of our Lord. If the word is not literal but is figurative, the fact will be clearly indicated in God's Book.

It was upon this very rock that the great Reformation leaders, Martin Luther and Zwingli, struggled. When they came together to explore the possibilities of joining their forces in the mighty spiritual movement that was sweeping Christendom, they failed because they could not agree on the Lord's Supper. When Zwingli said that the words, "This is My body," and "This is My blood," meant that the bread represented the body of Christ and the fruit of the vine represented the blood of Christ, Luther asked Zwingli, "Where in the Bible can you show me that the verb, 'is,' means 'represents'?" It was then that Zwingli turned to Genesis 41:26–27 and read to Luther the interpretation of Pharaoh's dream: "The seven good kine *are* seven years; and the seven good ears *are* seven years: the dream is one." The word "are" means "represents." So said Zwingli. However, he was unable to convince Martin Luther, and the Reformation fragmented. But the truth of the Bible is always most clear and most manifest when we take the words literally unless there is clear indication that they are to be taken otherwise.

Are we, therefore, to take as literal the Biblical descriptions of heaven and of hell? My answer is, "Unless we know otherwise, yes." Both are everlasting for the same word that applies to one applies to the other. The same Book that reveals God reveals the devil; the same Book that tells of heaven tells of hell. If one is not true, we have no assurance that the other is not true. Is hell a place of fire and brimstone? Is heaven a place of gold and pearl and beautiful mansions? When I speak of these things, I ought to use the language of God. I have never been to heaven; I have never been to hell. I must trust God's revelation concerning the two places. If I substitute my speculations, I become evasive, anemic, and powerless. I cannot improve upon God's language however smart, shrewd, or erudite I may think I am. I cannot improve upon God and what God says; therefore, I must deliver this message as God has revealed it. I must speak God's language and when I do, I find that I am speaking in the power and unction of the Lord.

Literally Lost Without Christ

Is it true that people are literally and everlastingly lost without Christ? If the Bible is true, then the answer to this question is a categorical yes. We are lost without Christ and our message of salvation is the good news that in Him we can find forgiveness for our sins and reconciliation to God. But if we reject this message of amnesty and forgiveness, then we are everlastingly lost. We are shut out from God's people and from heaven and from all the glories that the Lord has prepared for those who love Him.

Nothing is more earnestly or desperately needed today than Christian conviction concerning Christ. I believe the text of Acts 4:12 in which Simon Peter, preaching the gospel of the Son of God, avowed, "Neither is there salvation in any other: for there is none other name under heaven given among men, whereby we must be saved." The Christianity of the first century was of all things missionary and converting. The commissions of Christ recorded in Matthew 28, Mark 16, Luke 24, John 20, and Acts 1, all are mandates to the disciples of the Lord to make converts of the entire human race. The obedience of the apostles to that Great Commission was a dedicated effort to convert all to the faith of Christ who would listen to their sermons. They proclaimed the gospel in Jerusalem, in Samaria, in Caesarea, in Antioch, and from Antioch God blessed the world mission efforts of the men whom He had chosen for that holy purpose, even Barnabas and Paul. The substance of the message these first emissaries of Christ proclaimed was to all alike, that we are sinners and lost, that we must repent and believe the Lord Jesus Christ in order to be saved. This was the message of John the Baptist in Matthew 3; it was the message of Jesus to Nicodemus in John 3; it was the message of Peter to Jerusalem in Acts 2; it was the message of Peter and John to the Sanhedrin in Acts 4:12. It was the message of the angel to Cornelius in Acts 10, and it was the message of Paul to the Athenians in Acts 17. The heralding of the gospel of Christ knew no limits and no compromise. Everyone, everywhere is to turn to repentance and to accept the atonement and grace of God in Christ Jesus.

These first apostles and emissaries of the cross confronted the Roman Empire with a message that they refused to dilute. Rome was of all governments most liberal, most broad-minded, and especially so in respect to provincial religions. Greek rulers such as Antiochus Epiphanes sought to coerce the Jews into worshiping Jupiter Olympus. Antiochus even dedicated the Temple at Jerusalem to his Greek god and profaned the altar with the sacrifice of a sow. But Rome was altogether different in its attitude toward the religions of the empire. In the city of Rome still stands the Pantheon, the best preserved building of antiquity. It was erected by Agrippa in 44 B.C. The word "pantheon" means "all gods." As Rome conquered one province after another, the emperor brought to the city any new god that was worshiped by the subdued people, and this god found his niche in the Pantheon. Rome was most broad-minded in its willingness to accept all religions and to worship all gods.

Why then did this liberal-minded Roman Empire persecute the Christians? What was the reason for the martyrdom of uncounted numbers of the followers of Christ? If a Christian would even take a pinch of incense and place it on the fire that burned before the image of the emperor, he would be given liberty and life. But the Christian preferred to die rather than offer even that pinch of incense before the graven image. There must have been some reason for this. What was it? The answer is very plain. The early Christians refused to the death to compromise the faith they preached. They were not willing for Jesus to be just another god in a Roman pantheon. To them Jesus was the one true Lord and there was no other way to be saved except through Him. And for that faith the early Christians sealed their testimony with their blood.

New Testament Christianity now confronts a modern world that is as liberal and broad-minded in its reception of different religions as the ancient Roman Empire. To the modern world all religions are good if they are earnestly received. A person can choose any course of worship that appeals to his or her own sensibilities, like an eclectic who picks from half a dozen different faiths. Our broad-mindedness in religious matters is a mark of our present generation. We are like the Romans whom Edward Gibbon sarcastically described in his *Decline and Fall of the Roman Empire*:

> To the people all religions were equally true; to the philosophers all religions were equally false; and to the politicians all religions were equally useful.

This is the attitude of our modern, academic world toward the faith.

Missionary attempts at conversion are not to be tolerated. The missionary is under fire from churchmen who say his day is finished. From a recent article in a national magazine I quote this paragraph:

> The era of the foreign missionary movement is definitely over. There has been a widespread assumption that the church was destined to convert the entire human race to Christianity. This must be

rejected as a valid goal because it has a Biblical foundation. I suggest that the church voluntarily dismantle our present missionary organization and structure.

This attitude is especially regnant as it considers the Jew. In the attitude of modern liberalism under no conditions is any effort to be made to preach the gospel of Christ to Israel.

Back of this liberalism is the heresy of universalism. The doctrine that everyone will be saved whether he believes in Christ or not has eaten through Christendom as termites eat through a foundation. Modern theology avows that there is no judgment, no wrath, no condemnation, no damnation. It avows that all souls are to be saved. If this be true why bother to preach the gospel since people are not lost? Christ is no Saviour if He does not save us or if we are saved already.

Truth Is Everlastingly Narrow

This compromising of the saving message of Christ is certainly not the teaching of the Bible. It is not found in the New Testament. The whole spirit and attitude of the preaching of the gospel in the New Testament is summed up in this passage of Acts 4:12, "Neither is there salvation in any other: for there is none other name under heaven given among men, whereby we must be saved." To the modern theologian this is a dogma to be decried. They declare it to be a belief that history has discredited. But truth is everlastingly mandatory, narrow, and exclusive. If the gospel presented in the New Testament is the truth of God, then there is no salvation outside of Christ.

The Three Aspects

There are three respects in which a person can be broad or in which a person can be narrow. In two of them he ought to be broad. In one of them he ought to be narrow. *A man ought to be broad in his sympathies.* Second, *a man ought to be broad in his horizons*; he ought to see truth in perspective, in relation. His conclusions ought not to be the results of ignorance and prejudice. But in the third category he ought to be narrow. In his reception of truth and especially *in his acceptance of God's truth he ought to be most narrow.*

All truth is narrow. Mathematical truth is narrow. Two plus two equals four, no more, no less. If a person does not believe that narrow truth, he will find himself in trouble with the bank and with the merchant. Mathematical truth is narrow. Scientific truth is narrow. There is no exception. Historical truth is narrow. An event happens at a certain place at a certain time in a certain way. The whole purpose of a jury and the whole purpose of court testimony is to arrive at that narrow truth. If a person were to say: "But I am liberal and broad-minded in my history. I believe that Julius Caesar or Alexander the Great or Napoleon Bonaparte could live at any time in any place; in fact, we can go visit George Washington now." The person who would say that would not be taken seriously. Historical truth is narrow. Geographical truth is narrow. What would you think of a person who would say: "I am no geographical bigot. I am broad-minded in my geography. I believe that the Gulf Stream is in the Pacific Ocean"? Such broad-mindedness is preposterous.

Ecclesiastical truth is no less narrow. In the days of Noah there was no salvation outside of the ark. In the days of Moses there was no deliverance from the judgment of God except for those who were under the blood. Likewise in our day the same truth still stands! "He that believeth on the Son hath everlasting life: and he that believeth not the Son shall not see life; but the wrath of God abideth on him" (John 3:36). If I receive Christ I can be saved; if I reject Christ I am eternally lost.

It is this plain. It is this true. It is this simple. This is the message that the minister of Christ ought to deliver from his pulpit.

CHAPTER 13

Fact or Fable in Genesis

What do I preach, believing that the Bible is literally true? I preach the truth of the revelations of God in the first book of the Bible, the book of Genesis. This, of course, is in diametrical opposition to the position taken by most modern theologians. In our present day the first eleven chapters of Genesis are reduced to myth and legend. The typical contemporary ecclesiastic looks upon the stories in Genesis as one would look upon the story of "Jason and the Golden Fleece," the exploits of Hercules, or the legends written by Homer and Virgil.

Is this the attitude of Jesus and of the apostles? It is not! Our Lord Jesus Christ endorsed the Mosaic story of the creation of Adam and Eve (Matt. 19:4–6). He verified the divine inspiration of the Genesis account of creation. These chapters are received by our Lord not as a myth but as the writings of Moses presenting the truth of God. Surely our divine Saviour would not mistake a myth for history.

Historical Revelations

The divinely inspired account of the creation of man in Genesis is also accepted by Paul who wrote under the inspiration of the Holy Spirit. Compare Romans 5:14. Read 1 Corinthians 15:21–22, 45, 47. Paul would hardly build these tremendous doctrinal arguments in Romans 5 and 1 Corinthians 15 on cleverly composed fables. He looked upon these narratives in Genesis as being historical revelations from God. Paul's inspired deductions from the coming of sin and death through the disobedience and fall of Adam, the original head of the race, form the basis for his glorious announcement of redemption, regeneration, and re-creation in the second Adam, who is the Lord Jesus Christ from heaven.

Genesis lays the foundation for the whole revelation in the Book of God. It contains an authoritative answer for the human race concerning matters of everlasting interest—the being of God, the origin of the universe, the creation of man, the origin of the soul, the introduction of sin, the promise of salvation, the division of the human race, the out-calling of Israel, the outworking of God's redemptive program. In fact, in this one inspired volume of beginnings we have the doctrinal background for all that is revealed in the Bible concerning sin, salvation, and the ultimate purposes of God for humanity.

Basic Doctrines

Let us look for a moment at some of these basic doctrines. The first would be the fact of God. It is an unusual phenomenon to be observed in the Holy Scriptures that nowhere does the Bible argue for the existence of God. The only place such a thing is mentioned or discussed is by the psalmist who said, "the fool hath said in his heart there is no God." We are, however, in the first verse of the first chapter of the first book in the Bible introduced to the living Jehovah of heaven.

The fact of God in Genesis is not given as a deduction of reason or as a philosophical generalization. It is a declaration. It is a revelation. It is a presentation and an affirmation of that primary truth which is received in the universal mind and which needs no proof. In glorious and triumphant contrast to agnosticism, with its lamentable creed that "I do not know," the Christian holds forth this incomparable announcement: "In the beginning God."

This is the affirmation of John 1:1.

It is the affirmation of Hebrews 1:1.

It is the affirmation of Colossians 1:16.

The Bible begins with the fact of God, and that beginning is found in these first verses and chapters in Genesis.

We turn now to a discussion of the doctrine of the fall of man. The foundation of all the doctrines of sin and of man lies in the first three chapters of Genesis. This Genesis story lays the groundwork for the doctrine of all human responsibility and accountability to God. Man was created in the moral image of the Almighty and, as such, is accountable to God. He is not an animal who developed from brute beasts and who in his continuing, triumphant elevation will someday rise to be an angel. No! A man is a creation of God, made in God's own image, but who fell because of sin. Only in regeneration is he to find his true place in the heavenlies with Christ. A lower anthropology always means a lower theology. If man is not a direct creation of God, if he is a mere indirect development through slow and painful processes of which no one knows what or how or when or why or where, then the mainspring of moral accountability is gone. But we are not brute beasts. We are the creation of the Almighty, made in His image and as such are morally accountable. This is fundamental to the doctrine of sin and of salvation.

We turn now to speak of the doctrine of redemption. The third chapter of Genesis is the basis of all soteriology, the doctrine of salvation. If there was no fall, then there was no condemnation, no separation, and therefore there is no need for salvation. If there is no need for salvation, there is no need for an atoning Saviour. The incarnation of Christ is a superfluity and the crucifixion a folly if there has not been a fall and a need of reconciliation. If the first Adam was not made a living soul and fell from that lofty estate, then there is no reason for the second Adam, the Lord from heaven, to restore us to our pristine glory. The rejection of the Genesis story as a myth tends to the rejection of the whole gospel of salvation. One of the chief cornerstones of the Christian faith is removed if the historical reality of Adam is abandoned. The fall of the first man forever remains as the starting point of God's salvation by grace and of the need of personal regeneration.

Genesis and the Known Fact of Science

Let us look closely as we discuss this question of Genesis and the proven facts of science. Is there a contradiction between Genesis and geology? Is there a contradiction between Genesis and anthropology? Is there a contradiction between Genesis and any other branch of knowledge? No. There is not.

If we look at the great truths embedded in Genesis, we shall find that they will always confirm what we actually know in science. For example, the revelation of God in Genesis is that man is the last of God's created works, the crown of all His workmanship. Surely there is no branch of science that would contradict that.

Again, in the book of Genesis there is revealed the great truth of the unity of the human race. There was no ancient people who believed in that and at one time science itself cast doubt upon it. But is there any branch of science that would contradict that revelation in Genesis? Humankind is a solidarity, as a tree with its roots, trunk, branches, leaves, and fruit is ultimately all one living organism. So the human race is one unit, of one blood, descendants from one created pair. In Adam our nature fell and in him all his posterity became sinful. There is a unity in the human race that is undeniable. The Bible knows but one Adam. He was not a myth or an ethnic name, but he was the progenitor of the human family. He was a man made by God, not an evolutionary development from some hairy anthropoid on some imaginary continent. The Bible knows but one species of man; it also knows but one primitive pair: Adam and Eve.

Created in God's Image

Again, there is the declaration made in Genesis that man was created in God's image. There is in him a moral sensitivity, a spiritual life not found in any other of God's created beings. Does the science of man's nature contradict that? No. All of humankind is conscious of that moral equation. Again, the book of Genesis avows that the region of Babylonia is the area of man's origin. This is not contradicted in history. Ultimate confirmations still lie outside the realm of our present archaeological and anthropological achievements, but we have every reason to believe that the Word of God is in no wise contradictory to any known, demonstrable fact.

Beside these truths which are confirmed by our modern scientific world, we are also deeply impressed by the nobility of the stories that are recorded of the beginning of the human race in the early chapters of Genesis. There is not anything comparable to these narratives in all the writings of ancient religions. There is nothing in Babylonian legend or in Egyptian mythology or in Persian tradition that begins to rival these marvelous revelations from God. We have in the Bible a history of its own kind. It does not in the least resemble the loose, incoherent, confused mythologies of other nations. The stories in Genesis are incomparably beautiful, ethical, and religious, and when we come to speak of the great ideas which these early chapters in Genesis present and which give the whole Bible its great unity, our wonder is even more increased.

The Flood

One of the narratives in Genesis, such as is found in other literatures of other nations, is the story of the Flood. But look at the accounts of this overwhelming catastrophe in other religions. The Flood narrative in Babylonian mythology is as debased as the Babylonian story of creation. It is polytheistic and has no analogy in spiritual depth to the account in Genesis. It is unthinkable to be persuaded that the Israelites borrowed their narrative from these sources. The contrast in spirit and character between the accounts would forbid any such derivation. The debased form can conceivably come from a corruption of a higher truth in God's revelation but not the reverse. These stories were revealed to the Hebrew people in God's own way of truth and purity. In our age, therefore, when critics are waxing bold and claiming finality for the assured results of their hypothetical theories and eccentricities, we as Christians may wax bolder in contending earnestly for the assured results of the revelation of God as it is found in the opening chapters of Genesis.

Sir William Dawson, the eminent Canadian scientist, declared that Scripture in all its details contradicts no received results of science but anticipates its many discoveries. The eminent American geologist, James Dwight Dana, said after examining the first chapters of Genesis, "I find it to be in perfect accord with known science." This is the verdict of our finest scientific geniuses and it is also the verdict of the man who loves and reverences the Word of God.

Genesis Is Vital

The book of Genesis is as vital to the Bible as the book of the Revelation. If the chapters of the Revelation are torn away, the consummation of all things is unknown. If the book of Genesis is destroyed, we have lost the explanation of the beginnings of all things. If we do not know the nature of the first heaven, the first earth, the first Adam, and the fall, then we cannot comprehend the glorious promise of the new heaven, the new earth, and the new man. We have lost the completed truth of God who has promised to us a paradise regained. The old creation and the old Adam but lay the groundwork for the glorious consummation in the new earth and the new Adam, who is the heir of all the goodnesses and grace of God.

This is what I believe.

This is what I preach.

CHAPTER 14

The Mighty God? Yes! Atheistic Evolution? No!

When I read Genesis 1:27, "So God created man in His own image, in the image of God created he him; male and female created he them," of what do I think? When I read Genesis 2:7, what do I think? Do I think of a simian hanging from a banyan tree by his prehensile tail? When I read Genesis 2:21–24, of what do I think? Of two hairy anthropoids, rambling through the jungle on all fours? Is this what the Bible means?

Countless precious young couples have stood before me to pledge to one another and before God a faith and a love that shall outshine the stars and outlast the tides of time. As I begin their wedding ceremony, I usually say something like this:

When God made the first man and placed him in the Garden of Eden, he said, 'It is not good for the man that he live alone,' and

143

God made for him an helpmate, the last and the crowning creation, the woman, and when Adam looked upon her he said, 'This is now bone of my bones and flesh of my flesh,' and God said, 'Therefore shall a man leave his father and his mother and cleave unto his wife and they two shall be one flesh.' For it was God Himself who performed the first marriage ceremony and it was God Himself who gave the first bride away, and there in the Garden of Eden our Lord hallowed and sanctified our first home.

When I say these words, of what am I speaking and to what do I refer? Am I speaking of anthropoids? Do I refer to apes? Am I describing simians or quadrupeds? No, a thousand times no. I am thinking of the beautiful story of Genesis 1 and 2 and of the first home built by our first parents, Adam and Eve.

The Beautiful Story in Genesis and the Bestial Theory of Evolution

How moving and how inspiring is this divinely majestic story in the Genesis account of creation! When you read what some writers, even those professedly religious, say about man and his bestial origin, your shoulders unconsciously droop, your head hangs down, your heart feels sick, your self-respect diminishes. But when you read the account in Genesis, your shoulders straighten, your chest rises, you feel proud to be that thing that is called man, and up and up goes your heart and your head.

We must everlastingly remember that when a man thinks he is a descendant of a brute, he looks downward to the brute for interpretations of himself, but when he believes he was made by the Almighty God in the Lord's own image and for a divine purpose, he looks upward for his inspiration. Man is weak enough when he looks upward, much less the drag that comes to him when he thinks he must look down to a brute level.

All we have to do to illustrate this tendency on the part of any man who believes that he comes from the anthropoid is to look at the book entitled *The Naked Ape*. Teach people that they come from animals and they will act like it. On the other hand, we have the sublime revelation in the Holy Scriptures that man was created, not evolved; that is, he did not come from some protoplasmic mud mass or sea ooze or by descent from fish, frog, fowl, horse, ape or monkey, but at once, direct, full-made did man come forth from the hand of God.

Must we believe in evolution to be academic, scientific, reasonable, modern, factual? Must we deny what the Bible says and what God says in order to come into a clearer understanding of the truth? No, by no means no; indeed, no.

The Grand Myth of Our Generation

The grand myth of our generation is evolution. The big lie of our modern era is evolution. I read the lie in the textbooks taught our children and seethe on the inside. The farfetched hypothesis is always presented as proven fact. Illustration of whole villages and races of half anthropoid, half human beings are drawn to delineate this most preposterous and unfactual myth; they are pictures based not on scientific, archaeological discoveries but on a vivid imagination, on a tooth or a piece of bone, some of which turn out to belong to animals.

The whole scheme of evolution is anything and everything but proven true. It is the cultural myth of the twentieth century. Many lies, economic, political, cultural, are being perpetrated in the world today but none more persistently than the nebulous concept of evolution. Never was a truer book written than the one by Anthony Standen, *Science Is a Sacred Cow*. And never was a teaching more belabored than the attempt on the part of these pseudoscientists to explain the universe without God.

What does evolution say? What does it teach? What does it believe? Christian people are constantly asked whether they believe the doctrine or not. This question is asked as if the word "evolution" conveyed anything specific. The myth of evolution is so entwined in the current world view that its absurdities and differences are seldom even noticed.

There are as many theories of evolution as there are evolutionists. No two evolutionists believe alike nor do they say the same thing nor does the same evolutionist even agree with himself. Far from the theories being more proved as a true explanation of our universe and of its life, it is becoming more untenable with every passing discovery. If we will only listen to the trained scientists who write in their separate fields, we will soon realize that the data on which this grand hypothesis stands are indeed slender and all of it capable of a thousand different interpretations.

The contradictory confusion among evolutionists is a menagerie to behold. You would think that a theory so profusely expounded and so profoundly fortified with every conceivable argument would be the very epitome of truth and observation. Instead we find among these evolutionists a bedlam of voices. The many different ways evolutionists have to bolster their theories and hypotheses are amazing when they are reviewed.

One of the chapters in a book that I wrote entitled *Did Man Just Happen?* is this, "The Dubious Defenses of Darwinism." The theories of the evolutionists and the so-called scientific approaches that they make in defense of their doctrines are denied so quickly after they are propounded until before I can get through writing a book about their theories they are out of date and before I can publish the volume they have changed them to something else.

The Science of Genetics

One of the illustrations of the war that truth wages against evolutionists involves the science of genetics. As an atheist and a naturalist, Sigmund Freud was compelled to adopt an explanation for the presence of the human race other than as revealed in the Bible. However, he had tremendous difficulty in bringing himself around to accepting evolution in its Darwinian version because the hypothesis involved natural selection. Freud felt that for natural selection to account for such a Godlike creature as man was too big a miracle even for a naturalist to receive.

He finally came to the conclusion that Lamarck's theory of acquired characteristics would explain the superior development of man above his brute counterparts. This theory is that if you cut off a dog's tail through enough generations, the puppies will be born without tails. Now we know that Lamarck's hypothesis is altogether untrue. It has been decisively disproven. Any characteristic or lack of it acquired by a sire is not by heredity passed on to the offspring. Heredity depends upon chromosomes and genes and not upon acquired characteristics. The acceptance of Lamarck's disproved theory has been an embarrassment to Freud's biographers ever since.

This example of Freud but illustrates the confusion and dilemma that are inherent in all evolutionary thought. We cannot but agree with the observation of one of the great paleontologists of Princeton University who said, "What we need are more competent fossils; we have plenty of confident anthropologists but not nearly enough fossils." This is so very true. What we need is more proof, more delineation, more observations, and more description of facts. Most evolutionary thinking is entirely speculative and nonscientific.

Nor has the missing link been found. A curator of the British Museum and one of her ablest paleontologists said: "In all this great museum there is not a particle of evidence of transmutation of species. Nine-tenths of the talk of evolutionists is not founded on observation but rather is wholly unsupported by facts."

Another great professor said: "Evolution is nonsense. You are as far as ever you were from establishing any connection between a man and an ape." A great gulf is fixed between the theory of evolution and the sublimity of the creation of humankind as revealed in Genesis 1:26–27.

The Astonishing Assumptions of Evolutionists

The astonishing assumptions of evolutionists are amazing to behold. Blindly and nonchalantly and almost with sophisticated indifference they spin off assumptions that are fantastic. The unbelievable persuasions of evolutionists stretch credulity to fantastic extremities. They ask us to believe that nothing created something, that out of nothing came something. This is one of the most unimaginable hypotheses ever presented, yet we are supposed to believe it. Then they continue. Out of this inert, inanimate, static something we are to believe came life of its own accord and of its own self. Then out of this ooze came human personality, human intelligence, and the consciousness of God. All of these assumptions are beyond human credulity.

They are persuaded and would have us believe that all of life and all of nature tend upward and progress forward and higher. This is denied by every observation we are capable of acknowledging and discovering in the universe. The universe itself is running down. Somewhere, sometime Someone created it and wound it up, and like a great clock it has been running down ever since.

This same principle of regression is found in all nature. It can be seen in plant life. If there are fine strains of wheat or fine strains of corn or fine strains of any other vegetation, leave it alone and soon it will run down. If there are finely developed trees bearing oranges or figs, if there are finely developed vines bearing grapes, leave them alone and they will run down. The same principle is observed everywhere in the animal world. If there are fine breeds of cattle, leave them alone and they will descend to scrags. If there are thoroughbred horses, leave them alone and they will degenerate into broomtailed ponies. This principle also applies to the human race. Man has descended, not ascended, and in some instances to the level of the Australian aborigine. Only in medicine and in hygiene have we been able to lengthen the span of life through a lessening of infant mortality and conquering infectious diseases. But by nature we are not stronger.

Order Out of Confusion?

We must insist that the attempt to ground reality in a naturalistic theory of origins simply cannot be done. It is impossible to assume in the light of current knowledge that order sprang out of confusion and that light created itself spontaneously. Mechanical nature proposed by the evolutionist, which runs on the lines of physical causation, simply cannot become the mother of free and intelligent human beings. It is sheer irrationality to believe that random chaos should have produced freedom, order, purpose, intelligence, personality.

The assumption of the spontaneous development of nothing into something and the development of that inert something into the personality of a person is about as reasonable as if an explosion in a printing plant resulted in the twenty-four volumes of the *Encyclopedia Britannica* or as likely as if one should throw alphabets into the air and keep throwing them up until they came down in the form of an Aristotelian treatise on drama. Man, made out of the dust of the ground and created on the same day with the highest group of animals, has physiological affinities with the animal creation but he was made in the image of God and is transcendentally superior to any animal. Man is a walker; the monkey is a climber. A man does a thousand things every day that an anthropoid could not do if he tried ten thousand years. Man has designing, controlling, ordering, constructive, governing faculties. Man has personality, understanding, will, conscience. Man is fitted for apprehending God and worshiping God.

The Only Possible Basis

The Genesis account of man is the only possible basis for our understanding the human soul. The revelation of fatherhood, truth, the good and the beautiful, of purity, of all the attributes of the divine intelligence is incomprehensible to a horse, a dog, or a monkey. The most civilized simian could have no affinity with such conceptions nor could such an anthropoid receive them if they were revealed.

Just what proof do these mythologists of our modern day present for the hypothesis of evolution? What they say is sometimes almost amusing. There blew into Dallas one day a pseudo-scientist who was known as a famed evolutionist. When newspaper reporters had their interview with him, they asked him, "How do you know that evolution is true; what proof have you for it?" He replied, "Evolution has been definitely and scientifically proven to be true by the example of Drosophila."

Now just what is it that Drosophila, the fruit fly, has proved along evolutionary lines? It is this.

Technicians have bombarded the genes of the Drosophila for years and years in order to speed up the possibilities of mutation. These possibilities of mutation in the life of the fly are as if the fly had lived through millions and millions and millions of generations.

What has the result been? The result has been this. They have developed all kinds and sizes and shapes of Drosophila. On the basis of these mutations this pseudoscientist said that evolution had been positively and undeniably proved. But that is not the point. Through their bombardment of the genes of Drosphila and through the mutation of his hereditary characteristics they may have produced cross-eyed Drosophila and tri-cornered Drosophila and Drosphila with and without wings, Drosophila colored pink, purple, and pea green, but the point is, he is still Drosophila. He is not a June bug or a bumblebee. The point is that with all the representations of millions and millions of generations, he is still a fruit fly. He is not something else.

Another instance of these, to me, amusing persuasions of the evolutionists is found in an article published in a daily newspaper here in Dallas, in which a geologist had taken my book, *Did Man Just Happen?*, and ridiculed it unmercifully. But when time came in his article to disprove what I had said and to illustrate his theory of evolution, all he had to present was the minute changes that had been observed by geologists in the fossilized animal life that had been discovered in the drilling of oil wells. This is some tremendous proof for so vast and far-reaching a hypothesis.

After Its Kind

It is beyond our power to get beyond the set law of God which is that everything reproduces "after its kind" (Gen. 1:11–12, 24–25). This is God's universal law of life. God has placed within the nature of every creature the ability to reproduce itself. If you plant persimmon seed, you cannot get orange trees from it. The Bible asks, "Do men gather figs from thistles?" Everything is after its kind; this is the only law that can be proved and that can be observed in all of the manifestations of life.

We may put monkeys on a lonely island for ten thousand years and yet they would never evolve into a man. No lapse of time and no environment would bring it about. Repeatedly we find the phrase, "after its kind." When God created the creatures of the land and of the sea and of the air, He placed within their power a reproductive ability to bring forth like progeny. Thus, cats begat cats, crabs always produce more crabs, oysters produce more oysters, birds propagate more birds. Every creature produces after its kind. It is not only physically impossible to produce unlike but also God has sternly commanded obedience to His creative mandate that like produces like.

Within a species there can be great variety. Mutation is always possible and is one of God's delightful secrets. We may see such an example in the dog family. We have many different kinds of dogs. There are large ones, small ones, brown ones, black ones, those with long ears, those with short tails, those with curly hair. But although there is a seemingly endless variety, yet they are all dogs. That is mutation. But if a dog should produce a hippopotamus and if a hippopotamus should produce a giraffe that would be transmutation, and transmutation the Bible forever forbids. The law of God does not allow for a half man or a half monkey or for a missing link. No living thing has ever violated that mandate of God that like produces like. There is development. There is progress from immaturity to maturity. There is the acorn growing into the tree. In the mechanical world there is the development of the automobile. In every area of life, even in the area of sinful propaganda and evil influences, there is development and progress, but there is no such thing as evolution, where one thing turns into something of another kind.

The Mandate of God

The obedience of all of life and nature to this mandate of God is endlessly illustrated. They say the strata of the rocks tell the story of countless eons. Yet it is strange that during those countless eons the trilobite never produced anything but a trilobite nor did the anemone ever produce anything but another anemone. We have in the record of the sea little tiny animals called coral. We can look upon the work of the coral as they were fossilized and embedded in ocean beds for millions and millions of years. Yet the sea coral today is exactly as the sea coral was millions of years ago. The cockroach today is the same as he was uncounted centuries ago. The amoeba of today is exactly as the amoeba in the beginning. The paramecium is exactly as he was in the beginning. Why do not these protozoa ever develop or ever evolve or ever change into anything else? Because of God's immutable law. The tumbling tumbleweed never changes into a rose bush. The rose bush never grows into an orange tree. They each produce after their kind according to the law of Almighty God.

The Secularists' Necessity for the Theory of Evolution

The blind persuasion of the evolutionists in denying the creative work of God and in substituting for it the almighty primordial cell is something for us to take into consideration when we look upon their theories. The reason evolution is believed and taught as fact is not due to the evidence for it but rather to the need for it. Any natural miracle according to the atheist, the agnostic, and the secularist is preferable to a supernatural miracle that has God as its author.

We think we free ourselves from the bondage of religion and the burden of an inerrant Bible when we turn aside from the truth of God in Genesis to accept the so-called academic freedom that is offered us in the world of evolution, but this freedom is a freedom that shuts God out and leaves man a slave to his brute ancestry. It is a freedom to know nothing, to believe nothing, to be persuaded that the whole meaning of life ultimately comes to nothing. We cannot forget or overlook the words of Paul who describes our modern world when he said that "claiming to be wise, they became fools" (Rom. 1:22, RSV).

Evolution succeeds not because it is a sound factual theory but because it can be made the basis of a humanistic faith which a sinful person can adopt in place of the regenerating gospel of the Son of God.

The Bible's Account of Creation

There has never been proposed as a substitute for the Bible account of creation any account that is as reasonable, as understandable, and as true to the observations we make concerning the nature of life. Only in this revelation is there solid rock on which to stand. All else is shifting sand. There is no other explanation beside Genesis 1:26 that can be found anywhere to give purpose to our presence in the earth. No one without this revelation has ever solved the problem of life—no one, no philosopher, no scientist, no one. It was God who put us here in order that He might accomplish a divine purpose in a divine plan. God has given to us life and the laws governing life, and the same Lord God has revealed to us the reason for our existence in the earth. These great answers to our souls' questions cannot be found anywhere else, neither in philosophy nor in science nor the speculations of men.

CHAPTER 15

The God-Man, Christ Jesus

Believing that the Bible is literally true, I preach that Jesus our Lord is all that the Scriptures say He is. Born of a virgin, God in the flesh, God, very God, offered on the cross as a literal atonement for our sins, raised from the dead by the power of the Holy Spirit, our Mediator and Intercessor in heaven, and our reigning, coming-again Lord and King. This I preach about our blessed, exalted Lord Jesus.

The Miracle of the Virgin Birth

That Jesus was miraculously born of the virgin Mary, I preach. The Biblical narratives concerning the conception of Jesus are literally and everlastingly true. Perhaps the most bitterly assailed of all the miracles in the Bible is this one of the miracle of the Incarnation. Two special objects of critical wrath can be observed through these last 150 years. One is the inspiration of the Bible and the other is the miracle of the virgin birth. For example, Matthew Arnold said, "I do not believe in the virgin birth for that would imply a miracle and miracles do not happen." Loofs, speaking for all rational critics said, "I think it the duty of truthfulness to state openly that the virgin birth arose out of fabulous tradition." In practically all quarters of liberal religion the virgin birth is openly treated as a fable. This is true not only in circles of unbelief, but also the virgin birth is discredited in many areas of the church itself. Some cast doubt upon the fact while other less antagonistic ones simply treat it as a nonessential element of the Christian religion. This is the tenor of modern critical theology.

The Tremendous Fact of Jesus Christ

In Christ Jesus we have a great fact to explain, the greatest in the universe. How are we to account for Jesus, the most stupendous personality in the history of the human race? Those who worship at the shrine of science feel obligated to make religion conform with the latest fads of research. They seek parallels to the virgin birth in natural science. They seek to find it in parthenogenesis. There are many algae, fungi, and plant lice that propagate from unfertilized spores. These pseudo-religionists seek to compare Mary and the wonder of her child to this algae or fungi or plant lice. The comparison in itself is unspeakable and unthinkable.

There are those who adduce so-called "comparable" stories in Greek and Roman mythology. But they have an impossible assignment before them. We can read those stories for ourselves and plainly see their fictional character. They are manifestly fabrications and have no theological relativity whatsoever. For example, Alexander the Great claimed to be begotten by a serpent cohabiting with his mother. It was told of Augustus Caesar that his mother lay asleep in the temple of Apollo and was visited by that god in the form of a serpent. Hercules is said to have been born of a woman with whom Jupiter lay in adulterous union. The more we would compare these fabricated, fictional, mythological, immoral narratives with the beautiful and humble story of the birth of Jesus, the more we are impressed with the colossal difference between the two. It is the difference between truth and error the difference between light and darkness, the difference between good and evil.

A Work of the Holy Spirit

The Incarnation of Christ was a work of the Holy Spirit (Luke 1:35). The initial event in the life of our Lord as the last event, the resurrection of Christ, was the work of the Holy Spirit (Rom. 1:4). The purpose of the Incarnation is clearly stated in Hebrews 10:5 and Hebrews 9:14. The Spirit of God was preparing a body in the womb of the virgin for a sacrifice on the cross to make atonement for the sin of the world. A spirit could not make that sacrifice. The sacrifice had to be made in a body. That body was fashioned for that holy purpose in the womb of Mary.

The miraculous story of the Incarnation is the record of the intervention of Almighty God in human history. The virgin birth is the external sign of Immanuel, God with us. It signalized a new age, a new blessing, a new revelation, a new relation to God. In the miracle of the virgin birth, God is beginning a new work, and this is the initial sign. As in Genesis 1:2 the Spirit hovered and brooded over the chaotic world to introduce a new creation, so in Luke 1:35, Matthew 1:16, 18, and Romans 1:4 the Holy Spirit is inaugurating a new, spiritual creation of humanity.

This intervention of God in human history in a mighty, apocalyptic demonstration of His presence and power is witnessed in the Holy Scriptures in many places. There was a heavenly and mighty intervention of God in the days of Noah. There was an intervention of God in the days of the building of the Tower of Babel. There was an intervention of God in the days when Moses heard the voice of the Almighty speaking from the burning bush. There was an intervention of God in the days of Elijah on Mount Carmel. There was an intervention of God in the days of Pentecost. There will be an ultimate and final intervention of

God in human history as recounted and prophesied in the Revelation. So there was an intervention of Almighty God in human history in the coming of Christ and in the miracle of the virgin birth.

An Apocalyptic World

The world we live in is an apocalyptic world. Second Peter 3:8 declares that one day with God is as a thousand years and a thousand years as a day. Years, centuries, millennia pass, then God suddenly and dramatically intervenes. He did so in the creation of matter and substance. God created all that there is in the universe, and thereafter the creation remains. We cannot add to or take away from anything that God created in the beginning. Ether waves, the principle of jet propulsion, the minerals and medicines and elements that we find in this world have been here from the beginning. It is only now that we are beginning to discover and to understand some of them.

Likewise, in the creation of the world of life God intervened, created life, and locked it in nature. We cannot change God's laws of the fixation of the species. Each kind produces after its kind and each species follows the genetical boundaries of its own species.

So it is in God's self-disclosure. There was an intervention of God in human history as in the days of 1 Samuel. The years and the years passed when there was no open vision. Then God spoke to Samuel. It was thus in the days of Elijah the prophet during the great apostasy in Israel. It was thus in the days of John the Baptist when the forerunner came from the presence of the Lord to break a prophetic silence of over four hundred years. Thus it was in the intervention of God in human history in the miraculous birth of Jesus the Lord.

The Incarnation is a mystery which ultimately lies beyond the veil of human comprehension or analysis. It is so incredible to some that they seek to remove it from the gospel record, but the testimony of the miraculous birth of Christ as found in the Gospels of Matthew and Luke is an integral part of those narratives. Can we trust the infallible, inerrant Word of God? Are these stories fables? The chapters in question are found in every manuscript and version of the Gospels known to exist. The versions in different languages such as Latin, Syriac, and Egyptian all carry the story of the virgin birth. The story is a piece with the whole and it is eminently appropriate. Reading the stories of the miraculous birth of Christ we feel no incongruity in passing from these narratives to the wonderful stories in the chapters that follow. The virgin birth is as natural at the beginning of the story of Christ as the resurrection is at the end.

Conceived by the Holy Spirit

Without a miracle such a person as Jesus Christ could never have existed. It is sometimes argued that a virgin birth is no aid to the explanation of Christ's sinlessness. Mary, they say, being herself sinful in nature, would convey to her son the taint of corruption. But it is overlooked that the whole fact is not expressed by saying that Jesus was born of a virgin mother. There is another great factor: the Scriptures plainly state that "He was conceived by the Holy Spirit." What happened was a divine creative miracle wrought in the production of this new humanity which secured from its earliest germinal beginnings freedom from the slightest taint of sin. The birth of Jesus was not as in ordinary births the creation of a new personality. In the birth of Christ there was a divine personality already existing entering into a new mode of existence. It was God Himself emptying Himself, who, being in the form of God is now being made in the form of a man. Miracle alone could effect such a wonder. Denial of this miracle is an attempt to rule out the supernatural in the Holy Scriptures. If the critics can succeed here they can destroy the whole building of God.

If We Eliminate the Miraculous . . .

There are eighty nine chapters in the four Gospels. If we eliminate the miraculous, we eliminate fifty-two of those eighty-nine chapters. Miracle and mystery are tokens of the presence of God. We find them everywhere in God's universe. It is no more amazing to find them in the Book of God's written Word than to find them in the book of God's created universe. These miracles we see all around us such as gravity, such as the resurrection in the spring. In fact, it can almost be truthfully said that the miracles of nature make the miracles in God's church pale in comparison.

There have been two great biological miracles wrought by the hand of God. The first one was the creation of Adam out of the dust of the ground and the succeeding great miracle of mitosis with the somatic cells fixed in their number of chromosomes, but which, halved from the ova of the female and the spermatozoa of the male, unite and recreate the original number of chromosomes. This creation of Adam and the race is the first biological miracle of Almighty God.

The second biological miracle of God is the creation of the second Adam from heaven. By a creative act God broke through the chain of human generation and produced this marvelous supernatural Being whom we call the Son of God. It is thus that we come to understand the Scriptures. The seed of the woman in Genesis 3:15 is a reference to the coming Lord from heaven. Isaiah 9:6–7 is a description of the glorious Son. Micah 5:2 describes this One who is from everlasting, and John 1:1–3,14 no less exhibit His marvelous grace and glory.

Belief in the virgin birth is of infinite value to the right apprehension of Christ's unique and sinless personality. For here, in this fact, Paul brings out, as in Romans 5:12, that He who is free from sin himself and not involved in the Adamic liabilities of our race can reverse the curse of sin and death brought in by the first Adam. It is Christ who established the reign of righteousness and eternal life through the creation of a new order of humanity.

Had Christ been naturally born, not one of these things could have been affirmed of Him. As one of Adam's race, as a fellow sinner, He would have shared in Adam's corruption and doom and would Himself have been required to be redeemed. But being sinless, miraculously born of the Holy Spirit in the womb of the virgin Mary, He is God's instrument to redeem us from the curse of sin and death. It is thus that the angels sang at His birth and thus that we read in the Holy Record the Magnificat of Mary: "And Mary said, My soul doth magnify the Lord, and my spirit hath rejoiced in God my Saviour" (Luke 1:46–47).

The Literal Atonement for Our Sins

What do I preach, declaring the message of the Lord Jesus Christ as it is literally presented to us in the infallible Word of God? I preach that the death of Christ is a literal atonement for our sins.

The most tragic of all of the stories recorded in human literature is the execution of Christ. What does it mean? Is it a dramatic play like the *Agamemnon* of Aeschylus? Is it as one of the tragedies of Shakespeare such as *Macbeth* or *King Lear*? Is it to be likened to O'Neill's *Strange Interlude*?

What is this death of Christ? Is it a historical tragedy like that of Socrates who drank the deadly hemlock or Julius Caesar who was murdered at the feet of the statue of Pompey, or Abraham Lincoln who was assassinated in Ford's Theater? What is this death of Christ?

Is it a defeat and a failure? So wrote Albert Schweitzer in his far-famed theological book entitled, *The Quest for the Historical Jesus*. The thesis of that book is that Jesus expected the kingdom of heaven to descend apocalyptically from God. When it did not come down, Jesus died, according to Albert Schweitzer, in frustration, in disillusionment, in defeat, and in despair. Is this correct?

No. The death of Christ is the atonement for our sins, an atonement toward which all time and eternity have moved. It is the redemption wrought out by the hand of God through the ages. Here is the Lamb of God slain from before the foundation of the world. This is the blood of the New Covenant shed for the remission of sin. This is the answer to Job's agonizing cry, "I have sinned, what shall I do?" This is the passover sacrifice. This is the blood of the Day of Atonement sprinkled on the mercy seat. This is the suffering servant of Isaiah by whose stripes we are healed.

This is the seed of the woman born to crush Satan's head. This is the sacrifice of the body, which was fashioned by the Holy Spirit in the womb of Mary in order that it might be offered as an atonement for our transgressions. This is the final consummation of God's plan of redemption.

When Jesus bowed his head and cried, "It is finished," that cry represented the consummation of God's plan of salvation through the ages and the ages. The anguished cries of Christ from the cross were not occasioned by a natural fear of death. Thousands of His followers have faced a death as cruel with no cry escaping from their lips but rather with a sense of victory in the commitment of their body to the cross or to the flame or to the rack. But Jesus was not dying a martyr's death; He was not dying a hero's death. He was dying for the sins of the world.

He who knew no sin was made sin for us that we might be made the righteousness of God in Him. The Lord was assuming in His own spirit and in His own body the penalty and the judgment for the mountains of sins of the whole human race.

Revelation 19:15 says "He treadeth the winepress of the fierceness and wrath of Almighty God."

Hebrews 2:9 avows, "He by the grace of God should taste death for every man."

First Peter 2:24 says, "Who His own self bare our sins in his own body on the tree."

John 1:29 introduces him to the world from the lips of John the Baptist, "Behold the Lamb of God, which taketh away the sin of the world."

It is this bearing of our sins that explains our Lord being forsaken as He hung on the cross. Sin caused this isolation. As the Passover lamb was singled out to die, shut up, penned up, isolated for four days, so the Son of God was isolated and singled out for death. Here God committed Him to death on the cross, openly, publicly, before the eyes of the whole world, and there on the cross sin and Satan thrust the dagger into the soul and body of the Son of God and thrust it up to the hilt. God made an offering of Christ for our sins (Isa. 53:10). This is God's way of dealing with sin, washing it out with His own blood. Christ received the stroke in Himself. A picture and a type of this expiation of sin and substitutionary atonement is found in Genesis 22:7–8, "God will provide Himself a lamb." All the types, rituals, sacrifices, and prophecies of the Old Testament pointed toward the atoning death of Jesus. This is the ultimate purpose of the Incarnation and the pouring out of the life of our Lord.

In His Own Blood and Body

The Memorial Supper of bread and the fruit of the vine set forth in dramatic form His remission of our sins in His own blood and body. The cry from the cross, "It is finished," referred to the work He had come to do. The preaching of the apostles was to proclaim the finished work of Christ. As Paul says in Galatians 6:14, "God forbid that I should glory, save in the cross of our Lord Jesus Christ," and, as John says in 1 John 1:7, "And the blood of Jesus Christ his Son, cleanseth us from all sin." This is the song of the redeemed in heaven: "Thou art worthy: . . . for thou wast slain, and hast redeemed us to God by thy blood" (Rev. 5:9). This is the love and mercy of God extended and exhibited to us all. The arms of the cross are outstretched wide as the wide world. There is no frontier. Wherever we stand, as far as the East goes East and the West goes West, thus is extended the love of God in Christ Jesus our Lord.

This is to be the heart and substance of my preaching. In the shadow of the cross the early apostles, martyrs, and witnesses took their stand. Every leaf, every word, every syllable of the New Testament they left behind is inspired by Christ's suffering and stained by His blood. This is the gospel of the Son of God by which we are saved (1 Cor. 15:1–4). Whatever the social implications and the political overtones of the Christian message, its heart and its soul is this: Christ died to save us from the penalty of our iniquities and to those who look in faith to Him there is an actual expiation, an actual atonement, an actual propitiation, an actual deliverance from the judgment and penalty of sin and death. *I believe in and I preach a literal atonement in Christ Jesus.*

The Literal, Physical Resurrection of Christ

I believe that He was bodily raised from the dead; it was a physical resurrection. This, as Paul states in 1 Corinthians 15 is at the very heart of the Christian message. The Book of Acts is the glorious and triumphant news announced by the apostles. Jesus has conquered sin and death, and His resurrection is a pledge that we also shall be raised from the dead. The focal point of the attack against Christianity is sometimes found in the attack against the physical resurrection of Christ. The issues at stake are so serious, the validity of the Christian message is so wrapped up in our answers, the hope of the resurrection is so dear to our hearts that we ought to examine the proofs for the literal, physical resurrection of Jesus. I would name seven.

1. There is a harmony in the resurrection of Christ with the life, words, and work of so marvelous a Saviour. *A perfect life, filled with the truth of God, could not end in a cruel shameful death* such as we read in the New Testament and there be a God in the universe. Is that all there is to life, goodness, beauty, and perfection? If death is the climax of a life so pure and godlike, we are faced with an insolvable mystery, namely, the permanent triumphant of wrong over right. Truth and justice are ultimately nothing. But this is not the way God has made the world and this is not the story of Christ. According to His words and promises He was to be raised from the dead. Whenever He mentioned His death, He also mentioned His resurrection (John 2:19–21; Matt. 16:13 ff.; 17:1 ff.; Mark 9:9). It is not without significance that the enemies of the Lord after He was crucified and buried and sealed in a tomb were careful to remember that He said that He would rise again (Matt. 27:63). Truly, the life and words of our Lord predicate a resurrection.

2. Another proof for the physical resurrection of our Lord is to be found in *the empty tomb.* He was buried with a great stone placed over the sepulchre, it was sealed with a Roman seal, and a Roman guard was set to watch the place by day and by night. Yet on the morning of the third day the body had disappeared. What happened? There are two alternatives: either it was taken by

human hands or it was raised by supernatural hands. If the body were taken by human hands, there are two alternatives: it was either taken by His friends or by His foes. Let us look at these alternatives. If His body were taken by His friends, could they have done it? If it were stolen, what of the grave clothes that were so carefully arranged and left in perfect order? If the body were stolen, it had to be done hastily because there was a guard watching. If the body were taken by His foes, would they have done it? Why do the very thing that would most likely lend itself to the support of a false rumor? How account for the silence of the Jews when they heard Peter preach a few weeks later at Pentecost? In order to contradict all that Peter said about the living Lord, what easier and more conclusive thing could they have done than to produce the dead body of Jesus? That would have silenced Peter and the apostles forever. There is no other explanation for the empty tomb except that God supernaturally raised Him from the dead.

3. We find another proof of the physical resurrection of our Lord in *the transformation of His disciples*. On Friday there was sadness and hopelessness. On Sunday there is gladness. The incredulous disciples themselves were hard to convince that a miracle so triumphant and precious had restored to them the blessed Lord Jesus. They literally believed not for joy (Luke 24:41). They were not looking for an immortalized Jesus. They had gone to the tomb to receive a corpse.

4. Another proof for the physical resurrection of Jesus can be found in *the existence of the primitive church*. Where did it come from? To the Jew, one hanged on a tree was accursed (Deut. 21:23). Yet multitudes of Jews were led to worship Him (Acts 2:41) and a great company of priests were obedient to the faith (Acts 6:7). The only explanation is the marvelous truth of the resurrection of our Lord.

5. Another proof of the resurrection of our Lord is *the witness of the apostle Paul*. He was outstanding both in spirit and intellect. Witness his letters found in the New Testament. Paul writes of the resurrection of our Lord in 1 Thessalonians and in 1 Corinthians when the many witnesses to the fact were still living and

could be examined. The personal testimony of the great apostle cannot be easily discounted.

6. Another proof for the physical resurrection of our Lord can be found in *the gospel record itself.* There is nothing comparable in human literature to the stories of the raising of Christ from the dead. Read them for yourself. In John 20 read the story of the race of Peter and John to the tomb. In John 21 read the story of the revelation of Christ to the seven disciples by the Sea of Galilee. In Luke 24 read the story of the unknown Christ as He walked with the two on the road to Emmaus. There is reality and unadorned testimony in all of these chapters.

7. Another tremendous testimony to the literal, physical resurrection of Christ is *the testimony of believers* then and through the centuries. When the Lord Jesus was raised from the dead He was recognized as the same Lord whom the disciples knew in the days of His flesh, only He was not immortalized and glorified.

Our Ever-present, Living Lord

The Lord Jesus appeared to His disciples again and again during that forty-day period. Sometimes it was without announcement. Suddenly He was there. In the garden there He was. Down a lonely road there He was. At the supper table there He was. In the upper room there He was. On the seashore there He was. On the mountainside there He was. Walking up Mount Olivet there He was. As this continued for over forty days, finally the disciples no longer needed that their eyes behold Him. They knew Him by His presence working with them. They treasured the promise in Matthew 28:20, "Behold I am with you all the days until the consummation of the age." Not a day would He be away from them to the end of the world. In prosperity and in adversity; in prison, in trial, in sickness and in health; today, tomorrow, and forever the living Lord would be with His people. Stephen saw Him when he was so bitterly assailed by those who blasphemed his name. Paul met Him on the Damascus road. John saw Him on the lonely Isle of Patmos. Thus it has been through the centuries and the ages. Christ is our living Lord.

Dr. W. R. White, one of God's great Christian statesmen, told a story of a brilliant Chinese who came to the services being conducted by the missionary. The briliant young man asked for a New Testament and was given one. Later he came back to confess Christ and in his confession made this stirring testimony:

> I took the New Testament home with me. I sat down on the floor and read it through before I did anything else. I have read the great writings of Confucius. I wanted to satisfy my hungry heart there. I knocked at the door but no answer came for Confucius was dead. I read the message of Buddhism seeking that for which my soul so profoundly longed. I knocked at the door of Buddha but no answer came for Buddha was dead. I read the Koran. My soul longed to find peace there. I knocked at the door but no answer came for Muhammad was dead. I read the writings of the greatest patriots and religious leaders of the past. I knocked but no answer came. While reading this New Testament, I found that it claimed its Author to be alive. I knocked at that door. I found the living Christ. He came into my soul. Here my hungry heart found peace, a peace for which it has longed.

This is the testimony of God's saints through the years and the ages. Christ is more alive today than in all of the years of the days of His flesh. Caesar is dead, Charlemagne is dead, Richard the Lionhearted is dead, Washington is dead, Lenin and Stalin and Karl Marx are dead. They all are dead. But Jesus is not dead! God is not dead! Jesus is alive and He has with Him the keys of hell and death (Rev. 1:18).

Christ Lives Today!

That Christ lives today, God of very God, the Saviour of the world, is a testimony of God's saints here and around the world. One of the most moving events to be read in the life of a man is the tragedy and triumph that overtook Dr. George W. Truett, my illustrious predecessor and pastor of the First Baptist Church in Dallas, Texas, for forty-seven years. In the congregation of the Dallas church was Captain J. C. Arnold of the Texas Rangers, who had become chief of police of our city. He was a humble and devoted member. Upon a day Police Chief Arnold and Pastor

Truett were quail hunting in Johnson County. Captain Arnold was walking along a few paces in front of Dr. Truett. Dr. Truett shifted his gun from one arm to the other but in so doing the trigger on the hammerless weapon was touched. The discharge struck the police chief and mortally wounded him.

All Dallas was shocked by the death of their police officer. The pastor himself was plunged into indescribable grief. He felt that he could never preach again. His hands were stained with the blood of his dear friend, blood shed as he awkwardly and carelessly handled a gun. He shut himself off from the world and in the black shadows he brooded and prayed and read his Bible, crying unto God.

Late one Saturday night, for the first time since the accident, he fell asleep. During the night there came to him a dream in which Jesus stood as visibly and realistically as some earthly friend standing by his side. He heard the Master say, "Be not afraid, you are my man from now on." Dr. Truett awoke. He awakened his wife and told her the dream. The second time he went back to sleep and the same vision and the same words were repeated. Again he told his wife what he had seen and heard. He went back to sleep and the third time the same vision appeared. The Master came and spoke to him just as he did before.

On Sunday, Dr. Truett returned to his pulpit to preach the gospel of the unsearchable riches of Christ Jesus. That Sunday morning the Methodist churches and the Presbyterian churches and the other churches dismissed their services that they might hear the great pastor. The news swept like wildfire through the city of Dallas. One spoke to the other saying: "Truett will be in his pulpit this Sunday. Truett will be preaching Christ again today."

Thus it is that Jesus our Lord is more alive today than He was two thousand years ago. He is not dead. He is alive! He lives in our hearts and He looks upon us from heaven.

I believe in the literal, physical, resurrection of Jesus. I preach it.

CHAPTER 16

This Same Jesus Is Coming Again

What do I preach, believing that the Bible is literally true? I preach that Jesus is personally, visibly, actually, truly, really coming again. I believe the promise that He made in John 14:3 will be literally fulfilled. I believe the promise of the angels in Acts 1:11, word for word, syllable for syllable, letter by letter. I believe that Jesus is coming again even as the apostle John wrote the text of the Apocalypse in Revelation 1:7, "Behold he cometh with clouds; and every eye shall see him" and even as Jude wrote of the glorious promise in verse 14, "Behold, the Lord cometh with ten thousands of his saints."

His appearance at the consummation of the age will be personal, bodily, and visible. It is Christ Jesus Himself who is coming. God is Spirit (John 4:24). The Holy Spirit is Spirit, but

Jesus is not a spirit. Jesus has a body (Luke 24:36–43). He is in our hearts only in the sense that the Spirit of Jesus, the Spirit of God, is in our hearts. He is in heaven. Stephen saw Him in heaven. Paul met Him on the Damascus road in the glory of a light that shined from heaven. John, on the Isle of Patmos, saw Him above the brightness of the meridian sun. It is Jesus coming from heaven that we are expecting. The only God there is is Jehovah God. The only God we shall ever feel is God's Holy Spirit. The only God we shall ever see is Jesus, the Lord God of heaven and earth. The exalted Lord Isaiah saw in the vision described in Isaiah 6:1–4 was Jesus for John 12:41 declares that the two are the same. John 8:58 declares that Jesus is the great "I Am" and John 14:9 declares that he who hath seen Jesus has seen the Father. God the Father and God the Saviour are One (John 10:30).

It Is Jesus We Want to See

It is Jesus that we want to see, Jesus in power, beauty, and glory. It is not enough to have a letter from Him such as the seven letters to the churches in Asia. It is not even enough to have the third Person of the Trinity, the Holy Spirit, the Spirit of Jesus, in our hearts. Our cry is the cry of the Greeks at the feast, "Sir, we would see Jesus" (John 12:21). This is what Paul calls "the blessed hope" (Titus 2:13).

But, says one, the destruction of Jerusalem was the coming of Christ. When Titus descended upon the doomed city with the shout of his Roman legions, that was the promised fulfilment of the returning Lord. No. A thousand times no. The Bible says the Lord *Himself* shall descend. Others say the occurrence of death is the second coming of Christ. Christ is coming to receive His people in death. That is the fulfillment of the promise. No. The Scripture reiterates the glorious words, *"This same* Jesus shall come." Others say the diffusion of the gospel and the gradual transformation which it effects in human civilization is the coming of the Redeemer. No. No. Still resounds the Word of God, "The Lord *Himself* shall descend." They have so spiritualized Jesus into a vague shadowy presence; they have so allegorized Him into a myth, fable, and fiction; they have so diffused Him in history; they have so dissipated Him into metaphysical suppositions; they have so confounded Him with death until we can almost hear the plea of Christ as of old He said to His disciples, "Behold my hands and my feet, that it is I myself: handle me, and see; for a spirit hath not flesh and bones, as ye see Me have" (Luke 24:39).

The answer of the Scriptures concerning the coming of the actual Lord Jesus is one of our most comforting reassurances. The Bible is replete with statements of the certainty, the literalness, the visibility of Christ returning to earth. And lest there should be any mistake, reiteration comes to endorse assertion, emphasis to enforce reiteration: "This same Jesus," "In like manner," "The Lord Himself shall descend."

"I Will Come Again," He Says

Jesus has not lost His identity nor has He so merged it with history of providence or with death that we must look in these things for His coming. "I will come again," He says, "Behold I come quickly," He avows. Who is this "I"? This "I" is identified in Revelation 22:16. When His appearing shall be ushered in, it will be that of the Man, Christ Jesus: the same holy face, the same pierced hands, the same gracious voice as at the first.

He is coming under a twofold simile. He is coming as a thief in the night and He is coming as lightning shines across the blackness of the sky (Matt. 24:27; Rev. 16:15). He is coming as a thief in the night. He is coming with unsandaled feet, softly, furtively clandestinely. He is coming to steal away His jewels, His pearl of great price, His people in the earth. He is coming for His saints, and this will include us all (1 Cor. 15:50–52). Those who have fallen into the open arms of the grave will not be forgotten. The Lord will not leave in the dust of the ground the least of His saints. There shall not be a bone left in the region of death, not a relic for the devil to gloat over. We shall *all* be changed. As Enoch was translated, as Noah was placed into the ark of safety, as Lot was taken out of Sodom and Gomorrah before judgment fell, so God will translate His saints from the earth before the days of the terrible tribulation. Two will be in a bed, one taken and the other left. Two will be grinding at a mill, one taken and the other left. Two will be working in a field, one taken and the other left. The Lord is coming as a thief in the night—suddenly, without announcement, softly, to steal away His people.

The Lord is also coming under another simile. He is coming as livid lightning cleaves the bosom of the sky. He is coming openly, visibly, triumphantly with His people. The Lord is coming with great publicity (Matt. 24:30–31; 1 Cor. 15:51–52; 1 Thess. 4:16).

He is coming in great power and glory, even this same Lord Jesus who went away from us. Christ predicts what people will say and what will happen before the time of His coming. Look at Matthew 24:4–5;23-26. Many say "why, Christ has already come." This is like the heresy Paul refers to in 2 Timothy 2:18 where he describes those who say the resurrection is already past. They avow that He came in the form of truth and metaphysical propositions promulgated during the past century. There are those who say that He came in the great revivals of England and America. There are those who say that He came in the form of a revelation to a certain woman in the practice of divine healing. We are looking for Jesus. Is that what I am to find in answer? Christ said, "Beware." If they say over there or yonder or here or some other place, do not believe them. When He comes, it will be the Lord Jesus Himself. It will be a lightning (Matt. 24:27). It will be with a shout, with the voice of the archangel, with the trump of God and with the resurrection of the dead (1 Thess. 4:16). When they say, "He has come; He is here," go out to the cemetery and see. Have the dead been raised? Have the angels appeared, has the trumpet been sounded, and has the shout that shall raise us from the dead been heard?

Truly, the Lord is coming in great power and glory. "Then shall appear the sign of the Son of man in heaven: . . . and they shall see the Son of man coming in the clouds of heaven with power and great glory" (Matt. 24:30). He is coming with a visible sign, an outward token which addresses the eye. In Luke 2:12

we have the sign of Christ's humiliation. There is the sign of the manger. He who was the mighty God and the everlasting Father became a babe wrapped in swaddling clothes and finally in manhood was crucified through weakness. In Matthew 24:30 we have the sign of Christ's glory. What is that sign? Many of the ancient fathers supposed it would be the appearance of a cross burning in glowing splendor in the clouds. Others believed that the Advent star would reappear, shining in unearthly brilliancy in the heaven. All agree that it indicates some visible, intensely glorious appearance which all eyes shall see and before which the whole earth will be astonished in deep wonder.

The Sign of the Coming of the Lord

What is this sign? The sign of the coming of our Lord? All the Scriptures say that He comes in clouds (Matt. 24:30; Rev. 1:7; 1 Thess. 4:17). He is coming with clouds moving like golden chariots beneath Him as He rides upon the wings of the wind. He is coming in clouds, with glory above the splendor of the noonday sun, a sunburst of resplendent radiance from His presence. He is coming in clouds, the insignia of power that shall fasten upon Him the astonished gaze of all humanity. These are the invariable features of the scene of Christ's coming wherever the Scriptures portray it from Daniel 7:13 to Revelation 1:7.

What is this cloud in which the Son of Man will appear? It is nothing else but the Shekinah glory in which, from the beginning, God has invariably revealed Himself to man. It is called a "cloud" because it is the nearest descriptive word known language can give it. But it is no wreath of mist or vapor. It is the garment of God's glory in which He appears to talk and to deal with us. He appeared in the cloud and in the pillar of fire at the Red Sea and through the wilderness. He appeared in the Shekinah glory, the lambent flame, burning above the mercy seat. At Sinai God talked to Moses out of the cloud. It was like devouring fire on the top of the mountain to the eyes of the children of Israel below. In the dedication of the Temple the cloud so filled the glorious edifice and sanctuary until the priests could not enter it. In the marvelous vision of Christ in Isaiah 6 the glory of God like a cloud filled the Temple.

The sign of the Son of Man coming from heaven is this: We shall see Him in the Shekinah glory of the Old Testament. At His first Advent He put off His glory (Phil. 2). At His second Advent He will put on His glory. In the first Advent He was clothed with the veil of His flesh. At the second Advent He shall be clothed with the garments of God. At the first Advent He appeared in weakness; at the second Advent He shall appear in power. These are the two signs of the coming of the Son of man. In the first sign the infant lay in a manger. God stooped down to the lowest stages of human weakness and covered with swaddling clothes the feebleness of His human flesh. But the sign of the King of Glory appearing in the heavens will be the sign of His exaltation before God. The Man, Christ Jesus, reclothing Himself with light as with a garment. Behold the man! Behold our God!

King of Kings, Lord of Lords

I believe that Jesus is literally, physically, triumphantly coming again. In the Japanese military occupation of Korea in the first part of this twentieth century, our Baptist churches and people suffered greatly. There were five thousand Korean Baptists meeting in more than forty church groups. The Japanese military became suspicious of their meetings so they called in the president of their convention, the chairman of their association of churches. They asked him exhausting questions. They asked him about the second coming of Christ. He replied, "Sir, we believe that this same Jesus will come again." The interrogator asked, "Then what?" The Korean Baptist leader replied, "then every knee shall bow and every tongue shall confess that He is Lord." The Japanese military continued, "Does that include our Emperor?" The Korean pastor bravely replied, "Yes, for our Saviour is King of kings and Lord of lords." The military asked, "Do you believe this alone or do all of you believe it?" And the leader replied, "Sir, we all believe this." They arrested all the pastors. For three or four years they remained in prison under terrible trials. This moderator died under the terrible exhaustion of the ordeal. Another pastor soon died. When finally they were liberated, two more died. They gave their lives in witness and testimony to the truth of "the blessed hope."

Christ Jesus shall surely come again. He is coming in the glory of the Father, the Son of God, God the Son. He is coming in the glory of the angels, as the Captain of the hosts of heaven. He is coming in the glory of the church, as the Bridegroom with the bride. He is coming in His own glory as the Son of God, the Son of Abraham, the Son of David, the Son of man; born of a woman, the crucified Man, the risen Man, the infinite, eternal Man, both God and man, the God-man, Christ Jesus. He is coming as the King of Israel, the King of the Jews, the King of the nations, the King of kings, the Lord God *Pantokrator*. He is coming as the Restorer of the earth, its Re-Creator, its Prince, its manifest and eternal God. Then will be fulfilled those marvelous prophecies that we read in God's immutable and inerrant Word. Then will be fulfilled Micah 4:3. Then will be fulfilled Isaiah 11:6-9. Then will be fulfilled Titus 2:13. Then will be fulfilled Revelation 22:20.

> It may be at midday, it may be at twilight, It may be, perchance, that the blackness of midnight Will burst into light in the blaze of His glory, When Jesus receives His own. "Oh joy! Oh delight! should we go without dying, No sickness, no sadness, no dread and no crying, Caught up thro' the clouds with our Lord into glory When Jesus receives His own.

CHAPTER 17

God's Word and Human Problems

Believing, as I do, the Holy Scriptures to be the veritable truth of the Lord, I find in them the answer to all human problems. The Word of God contains principles of human adjustment and emotional growth which were revealed by the Lord from heaven long before the advent of modern psychology. The human race, fundamentally, does not change. Death does not change. Sorrow does not change. Sin does not change. Judgment does not change. The tragedies, sorrows, and sins of ten thousand years ago are the same sorrows and tears we know today. The perplexities that baffled our remotest ancestors baffle us today. From philosopher to peasant the same questions are asked; they differ only in the degree of their sophistication.

As a pastor for over forty years, I have found that nothing equals the power and the help of God's Word in ministering to human necessity. The unique contribution of the Bible in counseling is beyond my ability to adequately present. The Scriptures are a veritable fountain of life and healing. To turn to the Bible as an effective aid in time of need is to open God's door for the minister who believes God's Book. The Bible has no equal in its message to the human heart. The counselor who introduces it brings into view a powerful dynamic. The one who fails to use the Bible is overlooking the most important instrument in all the world.

Practical and Relevant

God's Word is practical and relevant, designed by God to be applied directly to the problems of life, reaching people where they are. The Bible-centered counselor finds in the Word of God great truths for human adjustment, for insight into the nature of man, his motivation, his defenses, and for the ultimate resolutions of his conflicts. Such insight is not available to the unbeliever because it is spiritually discerned (1 Cor. 2:14). In the realm of psychology and psychiatry, Christian professionals attest that the Bible advances itself ahead of every generation and continues to be the most effective tool in the hand of any counselor. It is a fact that among those who are pushing back the frontiers of human knowledge, many of them are devoted servants of God who know and honor God's Word.

Since God made human beings in the first place, we cannot afford to ignore God and His Word. The Bible-believing counselor holds the only key to a meaningful philosophy of life. Neither Plato, Aristotle, or Freud has given to us the sense of meaning, destiny, and purpose that is revealed in the Word of God. The Bible-believing counselor is able to point out the message of salvation in Christ Jesus.

The Word of God produces faith. Psychologists and psychiatrists universally agree that faith is a necessary ingredient in the development of a well-integrated personality. This is how God made us. People are unsatisfied unless they have something in which to believe. The Bible-believing counselor can help people to have this basic need met, and through the Word of God they can place their trust in Christ. This personal relationship with the Saviour carries an influence through time and eternity.

Reliance on the Bible

The abounding blessing of the Bible-believing counselor is that as a therapist he can bring reliance upon the Bible as a guideline for moral and spiritual behavior. A searching soul is not left to the whims of his imagination or to the counsel of the ungodly to determine his standards. Ofttimes have I listened to people in my study at the church as they have recounted to me what godless psychiatrists have advised them to do in throwing off their inhibitions, such abominable things as to seek out adulterous affairs to relieve pent up emotions and neurotic conflicts. The Bible-believing counselor would never engage in so harmful and so unbiblical a practice. Nor do I believe that the counselors themselves who advocate such therapy would defend it in their own family circles.

Let me discuss the use of the Bible in helping people in their deepest frustrations and despair. I speak first of sin and guilt. The most disturbing element in all the world is sin. It brings discouragement and failure. The Bible has the only clear answer to the problem. No amount of rationalization or soul-pacification will cleanse the heart of a sinful person and fill his life with a sense of purity and fulness. The Christian counselor knows that many serious difficulties are caused by sin and unless the sinful roots are removed by asking God's gracious forgiveness, problems will continue to arise to plague the victim. God's Word holds the only real remedy. When sin is reckoned with, many of its resultant hurts resolve themselves. When we come face to face with our sins and confess them before God, immediately there is forgiveness from heaven and a new sense of purity, healing, and well-being in the soul. God faithfully says that if we confess our sins, He will fully forgive (1 John 1:9; Isa. 44:22; Psalm 51:1, 9; Mic. 7:19; Heb. 10:17; Jer. 31:34). When we confess our sins to God and when we believe God's Word and promise, we face the future as though our transgressions had never been committed. This is a powerful cathartic in human life.

Sharing Our Sorrows

God reveals to us how we may find strength in our pilgrimage through this evil world. The catharsis that comes from sharing our sorrows and faults with one another was not conceived in the mind of Freud. Centuries ago, James, the pastor of the church in Jerusalem, wrote, "Confess your faults one to another, and pray one for another, that ye may be healed" (Jas. 5:16). This turn to another for support, strength, help, and encouragement is not the sole property of psychology. Paul wrote, "Bear ye one another's burdens, and so fulfil the law of Christ" (Gal. 6:2). The psalmist suggested that counsel was to be sought but not from the ungodly: "Blessed is the man that walketh not in the counsel of the ungodly" (Ps. 1:1). What a tragedy it is that we have turned our backs upon the Biblical principles that lead to emotional healing and left it to the unregenerate to rediscover these basic truths. One key to the success of the first-century church over which James presided as pastor was the open confession of sin and the bearing of one another's burdens.

The Bible and the Home

Any pastor will have almost illimitable instances where he is brought into the tragedy of a broken home. The Bible, of course, does not say that we are forced to live with anybody. A home can be violently and brutally torn asunder. The divorce courts are places in which the unhappy home can be legally dissolved. But divorce is an extremity that is tragic. If it is humanly possible, the man of God ought to do everything he can to save the home. Divorce, in many instances, is not the answer. Sacrifice is. If there are children in the home it is an everlasting hurt to their hearts and to their lives to be torn between the conflicting love and devotion of the two parents.

God is not pleased when we put away our companion to whom we are faithfully and covenantly devoted in wedlock.

"The Lord hath been witness between thee and the wife of thy youth yet . . . she is thy companion, and the wife of thy covenant. And did not He make one? . . . And wherefore one? That He might seek a godly seed. Therefore take heed to your spirit, and let none deal treacherously against the wife of his youth. For the Lord, the God of Israel, saith that He hateth putting away" (Mal. 2:14–16). If one will heed the Word of God, if one will listen to the voice of the Spirit in the Bible, the home can be saved, the children can be blessed, and the whole fabric of human society can be infinitely strengthened.

If only we could get our fathers and mothers, our husbands and wives to read the Bible in the home, many of the tragedies that come to us would not materialize. The sorrow, however, is that so few people read the Bible any more.

A minister delivered a devotional message on the Bible from the local radio station. That evening, after he had spoken in the church, he was approached by a man who told him this incident. The man said he had gone home for lunch as usual that day. When he entered the room where his wife was seated, she was reading the Bible. Surprised to the point of being startled, he asked, "What's the matter, dear?" She replied: "Nothing is the matter. I just heard a broadcast about the Bible and it made me want to read it again." The man continued his story to the minister. He said, "We decided around the table at lunch that day that something was very much the matter in our home when we had so neglected Bible reading that when one of us saw the other with a Bible, he thought something must be wrong."

Indeed, something is the matter when we do not read God's Word. Without its message we lose our greatest reasons for believing in the abiding nature of God's purposes in our lives. There could be no greater enrichment of our homes or of our own hearts or of the lives of our children than to make God's Word the standard by which we shall live together.

In Our Grief and Sorrow

Another tremendous area in which one who believes the Bible can be of illimitable help to human need is to be found in the realm of bereavement and sorrow. If I have no Bible, I have no ultimate word of comfort and hope. Or if the Bible is not true I have no sure and final word. But believing the Bible, I find in its pages a balm from Gilead and the veritable touch of the Physician's hand. There is healing for our hurt in God's Word. Times without number have I read to the bereaved and the sorrowing the fourteenth chapter of John, the fifteenth chapter of 1 Corinthians, the latter part of the fourth chapter of 1 Thessalonians, the precious words of John the Seer in Revelation 21 and 22. If one believes the Bible, he has a heavenly word of hope and assurance.

In my counseling I have found that many, many people are deeply disturbed by their lack of assurance concerning their salvation. They feel that possibly they are not saved and they tremble at the thought of death and the future judgment of Almighty God. What shall we do with the soul that is in agony concerning whether or not he is saved? What can we say to one who is afraid to die and is afraid of the eternity that lies beyond? Our assurance, our comfort, and our pledge is found in the Word and promise of God (John 1:12; 5:24).

The Promises of the
Bible and Material Blessings

Among a multitude of other perplexities that have been brought to me as a pastor, let me speak of one other. Many people come to me and talk to me about what they should do before the Lord in the possessions that God has given them. What is a true stewardship of substance and property? Always in my counseling with them I tell them that I believe literally the Word of God. God promises us that He will bless us if we tithe, and I encourage them literally to believe the literal promises and to expect a literal blessing from God.

But immediately the reply is made that there is no such thing as material blessings promised from the Lord. This I reject. I believe God will bless the person who is faithful to Him in material possessions. I can defend this in a thousand different instances and in a thousand different ways. For example, the godly Christian has every opportunity to prosper because, if for no other reason, he does not squander his money in the sinful and wasteful habits of the world.

All of the money that is lost in gambling will never be lost by him. All of the money that is wasted on liquor will never be wasted by him. All of the money that is spent on cancer-producing, lethal tobacco will not be spent by him. There are one hundred sicknesses that come to others that will not come to the man who is free from the slavery of tobacco. There are blessings that come to the man who lives according to the rules of health that are absolutely unknown to those who engage in hurtful drugs. None of the losses that come to those who seek to drown their sorrows in alcohol and drugs will come to the one who believes God's Book and who finds strength and healing in God's Word. There are ten thousand things that bless the person who reads and follows God's Holy Scriptures.

In one of my pastorates one of my leading deacons spoke bitterly against tithing. One of the illustrations that he would use in the deacons' meeting and in any circle where he had opportunity to speak concerned another man in the church who had been a faithful tither but who had fallen into serious, financial difficulties. This deacon who was against tithing always pointed out that unfortunate figure as an example of how tithing did not pay.

Then an unusual thing happened. One day, at the end of my sermon, that man who had fallen into such tragic misfortune came to the front and with many, many sobs and tears told me how he had been properous in years gone by, how God had blessed him, how he had faithfully tithed, and how he had been true to God's Word. Then the man said to me that he became proud, that he turned away from the Lord, and even began to use God's tenth for his own personal advancement. It was then, he said, that he began to fall into tragic misfortune. He closed his word to me saying that that day he was coming back to God, he was reconsecrating his life to the Lord, and that he was beginning anew to give God the firstfruits of all of his increase. And from that day onward God blessed that man and restored him.

This I believe: God's Word is literally true and to the man who will literally believe it God will add inward, outward, and upward blessings.

PART III

An Appeal to My Brethren to Preach that the Bible Is Literally True

THE BIBLE—THERE IT STANDS!

Where childhood needs a standard
Or youth a beacon light,
Where sorrow sighs for comfort
Or weakness longs for might,
Bring forth the Holy Bible,
The Bible! There it stands!
Resolving all life's problems
And meeting its demands.

Though sophistry conceal it,
The Bible! There it stands!
Though Pharisees profane it,
Its influence expands;
It fills the world with fragrance
Whose sweetness never cloys,
It lifts our eyes to heaven,
It heightens human joys.

—James M. Gray*

* *Master Book of New Illustrations*, Walter Brown Knight, compiler (Grand Rapids: Wm. B. Eerdmans Publishing Co., 1956). Used by permission.

CHAPTER 18

Standing on the Authority of the Word of God

Religion is built upon authority, and without that authority faith is sheer speculation. If religion is nothing but human, fallible, probing guesswork, one person's conclusions may be about as good and acceptable as another's. Religion is absolutely washed out when it is based on philosophical conjectures. If the faith is nothing but what a person may or may not think it to be, it is nothing. If there is to be real religion, somewhere, sometime, somehow God must speak. God must disclose Himself. Has God spoken? Yes. Has God revealed Himself? Yes. Where is that spoken word? Where is that revelation? In God's infallible Book, the Bible! Upon this rock the true preacher of Christ can take his stand—and stand there in strength and in power forever.

A Universal Instinct

Plato lamented that he was adrift on a raft upon an open sea with no rudder and no star above to guide him. Yet, pagan though he was, he ventured to hope that in good time, "the gods will give us a strong boat to sail in." This was but the expression of a universal instinct. If there is a God, He must surely reveal Himself to His children. If there is a God anywhere in the universe and if we are His children, surely He would not leave us in doubt respecting the great problems which have to do with our spiritual and eternal salvation.

In the Christian faith there are only three possible sources to which we can look for a revelation of God and upon which foundation we may build our hope for heaven.

1. One is human speculation, what the critics and the philosophers say that God is.

2. The second possibility lies in the pronouncements of the hierarchy of an infallible church.

3. The third alternative is the Bible. Let us look at them one at a time.

Shall I build my faith on the shifting sand of philosophical or even theological opinion? Is my revelation of God to be found by means of the wisdom of the world? (see 1 Cor. 1:18–25). If I do I shall land in the cemetery along with all the rest of the "God is dead" theologians. Human reason is only one of our several faculties, and all these faculties have been affected by sin. No person by his own probing and thinking can find God. God is above a person's mind, and the truth of His being and personality are beyond human discovery.

Shall I build my faith, then, upon the second possibility, upon a self-declared infallible church? Is the church the seat of authority?

An Infallible Church
or an Infallible Bible

Those who avow the doctrine of the superiority of the church over the revelation of God in the Bible emphasize an untruth. The church existed before the Bible, they say, and gave birth to the Bible. This is a colossal error. We have but to review the birth and growth of the early church to see that it is.

Was the first church without a Bible? For those beginning years had they no Word of God? Indeed they had a Bible. They had the Old Testament. If someone had met the members of the first primitive church in that day and said, "You have no Bible," those members would have stared at you in undisguised amazement. They had in their hands the Holy Scriptures of God, the Old Testament.

But you ask: "What about the New Testament? The New Testament was not written at that time. How could they have had the New Testament?" It is true that they did not have our written New Testament, but they had the spoken New Testament message of salvation in Christ Jesus. God's Word was delivered by the inspired apostles from the days of Pentecost onward, and the church came into existence by believing that preexistent, spoken, oral word. The Word was before the church. The truth was before the church. The revelation and self-disclosure of God was before the church. The truth of the word created the church. First it was spoken; then it was written. As long as the apostles were at hand, the spoken word was sufficient. But as they went from place to place and finally afterwards died, it was essential to embody the Word in a retainable form. The spoken revelation came to be written in what we know as the New Testament in our Bible.

In this connection we might ask, did the church of Rome write the Epistle to the Romans? Was the church of Rome the maker of that letter? Did the church of Ephesus create the Ephesian letter? It was an inspired apostle who wrote the Epistle to the church at Rome and it was an inspired apostle who wrote the epistle to the church at Ephesus. And those epistles were Scripture from the moment they were received from the hand of the apostles. It was not the church creating the Word; it was the apostles as representing Christ who delivered first the spoken and then the written Word of God.

In a sense the church came into existence from the days of the divine Incarnation of God in Christ Jesus, for it was founded upon His Deity (Matt. 16:13–18). Jesus gathered the nucleus of the church in the days of His flesh and at Pentecost breathed into its life His own quickening Spirit. The church was born of the Word (John 1:1–15). The truth of the matter is, if you go further back you will find that the Jewish nation came into existence through the divine, self-disclosure of God. And if you go still further back, you will find that Abraham came to be a believer because of a divine call and revelation (Gen. 15:1). Yea, you can go back to Adam if you desire, and you will find that every divine institution or divine relationship presupposes a divine revelation from God which is the foundation of our religion, whether that revelation be corporate or individual. The authority of our faith in Christ lies not in a supposedly infallible church or in any other supposedly infallible organization but in an infallible Word. God's Word antedated both the Jewish nation and the Christian church.

A Conversation with a Benedictine Monk

On a train from Munich to Zurich one time, I sat in a compartment with a Catholic monk who had been brought up in Detroit but who had lived the last thirteen years of his life in Rome. He was a member of the Benedictine order and was being trained through a fifteen-year course for the office of a religious priest in his order. He had been up to see the Passion play, as I had, at Oberammergau. It was the first time in my life that I ever had opportunity to be thus so close for so long with a Roman priest, where I could speak to him at great length without being interrupted. I was eager to take advantage of the opportunity even though I was somewhat dubious about the outcome of the conversation. You see, I had just read an editorial in a famous national magazine to the effect that when you ask a Roman

Catholic about his faith, his answers are clear and lucid but when you ask a Protestant about his faith, his answers are always fuzzy. I thought, "Well, in this well-trained Benedictine monk I will be at a grievously unhappy disadvantage, but this is my one chance to try." With a trembling heart I started out.

The Pope had just delivered a tremendous address in Rome in which he announced the fact that when the first of November that year came, he would formally promulgate the dogma of the bodily assumption of Mary into heaven. The Pope at that time made a scorching, withering blast against those in the congregations of the faithful who were arguing against the doctrine. The Pope was saying that he was proposing to pronounce the dogma; and when and if he did, that, of course, would make it true and infallible. In matters of faith and morals the Pope is above imperfection or mistake. All this meant that the Roman Catholic was to believe the dogma, or else be guilty of mortal sin.

I started off with the priest by asking him how he knew that the dogma of the bodily assumption of Mary to heaven was true. He replied that it was true because the head of the church said it was true. Then he said to me, "You must have faith," and he asked me if I did not receive my religious convictions by faith. I answered him: "Yes, I received it by faith, but I have a reason. I have a proof for what I believe." He asked me, "What is your proof?" I replied: "I have the New Testament, and in that New Testament Jesus is more clearly seen on the pages of the Book than if I had shaken hands with Him and had spoken to Him face to face. Not only do I find Jesus in the pages of the New Testament but also His power is felt in my life, and I see it in the lives of others. All of this is demonstrable. I can hold the New Testament in my hands (and I held up my Greek Bible in my hand). All of the truth that is necessary for the church and all of the doctrines upon which the church is built are faithfully and infallibly recorded in this Bible."

Then I said to him, "What proof do you have for such a thing as the bodily assumption of Mary?" Not being able to answer that question any further than the avowal that it was true because the pope had said it was true, we turned from that discussion to others of like nature. And in each instance, whether we discussed the immaculate conception of Mary, her marriage to Joseph, the "Santo Bambino," or the doctrine of transubstantiation (the actual changing of the bread and wine into the real body and blood of Jesus), to my amazement he had no other foundation for his faith than the dogma promulgated by the church as it is exhibited in a so-called infallible Pope.

He finally admitted to me that he closed his eyes to all other considerations and accepted the dogmas of the church blindly. Surely, surely, if the only authority we have for our faith is in the fallible pronouncements and promulgations of a fallible church, we are indeed on a course that will finally result in the mountainous, monstrous follies and failures that we read on the pages of human history in the story of the Dark Ages.

The Bible

But there is another foundation for our faith, a rock upon which we can stand forever. That third alternative is the Bible. The Bible is our authority. If God has spoken, then, obviously, His Word is authoritative. Where the word of a king is, there is power. The edifice of my theology is built upon the following epistemological foundation: that the Scriptures are the teachings of the divinely authenticated messengers of Jesus Christ. All of its doctrines arise from God's self-disclosure to humanity.

We have no other final and ultimate authority in our religion than the Bible. God has spoken preeminently to us and has truthfully and fully revealed Himself to us through the Bible. But someone will say, "Is this not what is called bibliolatry?" Well, we shall not be afraid of words. No, this is not bibliolatry. We do not impose the Bible between ourselves and our Saviour. We use the Bible as the medium by which we come to know Christ. We know nothing of the personality of God except through His self-disclosure in Holy Scriptures. We could know nothing about Christ except through the Gospels.

The medium of our introduction to Christ is the Word of God. It is the same kind of a thing as our seeking to know the distant stars. Do we worship a telescope if we use it for that purpose? No. The telescope will be not a hindrance but a help. The Bible is the telescope by which we are enabled to see the Lord Jesus. If a boy were to receive a letter from his mother and his school friends were to say how perfectly absurd of him to trouble himself about a piece of paper like that, the lad could say: "It is not the paper; it is what is on it and from whence it comes that makes it meaningful to me. This letter represents my mother, my mother's interests, wishes, love, and so far from being a hindrance it is a very help of helps to know what my mother would have me know."

So the Scriptures do those two things. We do not worship them, but they provide truth for our acceptance and they provide material to guide our experience. They bring us face to face with the Lord Jesus Christ in order that we might see how far we have traveled either toward the truth or away from it. The Bible is our seat of authority. Do you remember the Bereans? They "were more noble than those in Thessalonica, in that they received the word with all readiness of mind, and searched the scriptures daily, whether those things were so" (Acts 17:11). Knowing the Word of God, we come to know God Himself.

The Immutable, Unchanging Word of God

The foundation of all true religion as it is in Jehovah Jesus is to be found in the immutable, unchanging, and infallible Word. The law was to be read in the presence of the people (Deut. 31:10–13). Joshua obligated the people to read the Scriptures (Josh. 1:8). Obedience to them was urged upon the people (2 Chron. 17:9). The king was to have a copy by which he was to regulate his decisions (Deut. 17:18–20). The basis of God's judgment of the kings was that Holy Word (1 Kings 11:38). The captivity of Israel and of Judah was caused by disobedience to the Word of God (Neh. 1:7–9). The Holy Bible was taught to the returning captives by the great scribe, Ezra (Neh. 8:5–8). The prophets were equally recognized as inspired messengers who delivered the immutable Word of God (2 Kings 17:13).

When we turn to the New Testament, we find that the Bible is the basis upon which the church is to build its life and upon which the ministers are to preach. Paul admonished Timothy to give attendance to reading God's Book, not only personally but also audibly to the people (1 Tim. 4:14). Paul further admonished Timothy to preach the Word (2 Tim. 3:17 to 4:3). Revelation 1:3 has a blessing for those who read and those who hear the word of God's prophet. This is the ultimate authority and basis upon which the minister stands to deliver God's message.

With God's Book in his hand the minister can proclaim with authority and power the living message of the living Lord. With great assurance he can call people to repentance and faith in Christ Jesus. By the pledge and promise of the Word of God he can speak to the people regarding the great matters of faith, life, death, and judgment to come. Upon the authority of the Word of God he can baptize converts and upon the authority of the Word of God he can build the church and deliver the true doctrines of the faith. The Bible is the only testing ground of doctrine (Isa. 8:20; John 10:35). When the minister delivers God's message in conformity with God's will, the result will always be the building up of a household of faith and the blessing of the people of the Lord.

We need never equivocate or be apologetic when we stand up to preach the message of Christ on the authority of the Word of God. The very tone of the Bible is authoritative. It might be supposed that a book dealing with spiritual truths, all of which lie beyond the purview of the physical senses, would speak with some measure of reserve or uncertainty. But it is the opposite in the Bible. There is not an "if," a "maybe," or a "hope so" in the Bible. A divine book, heavenly inspired, could not speak that way concerning truth and salvation, and if it did speak that way it would have no message for us. We want no guesses about life and death, heaven and hell. We must know and must know certainly. We want authority, and there can be no final authority with respect to these questions unless we find it in a divine revelation. Therefore, the Book of God, being God's Word, always says "Yea," "Amen," "Thus saith the Lord," and "Verily, verily I say unto you." If we put an "if" into the Decalogue we lay a charge of dynamite under the morality of humankind and nations. If you put an "if" before the story of the manger of Bethlehem you destroy the Incarnation in human flesh by a preexistent Christ. If you put an "if" by the side of the cross of Calvary you cast doubt upon the hope of the forgiveness of our sins. If you put an "if" by the side of the story of the empty tomb in Joseph's garden, our visions of life and immortality vanish into thin air. But blessed be God, there are no "ifs" in the Bible. It gives no uncertain sound. The trumpet call is clear and plain. The Bible speaks as the oracle of God.

Would I preach like Jesus? Then let me preach the Bible as He did. Would I preach like Peter? Then let me preach the Bible as he did. The example of these glorious representatives of heaven as we see them in the New Testament are brilliant as they preach from God's Word in Nazareth or at Pentecost or in the pagan city of Lystra. Possibly the most eloquent man who ever lived was the author of the Epistle to the Hebrews. Would I preach like the eloquent author of the Epistle to the Hebrews? Then let me preach the Bible. This is what he did and this is the immovable rock upon which a preacher can stand in strength and in authority forever.

CHAPTER 19

The Sublimest—or the Sorriest Way of Preaching

What is the sorriest way to preach? It is the spiritualizing, allegorizing way. What is the sublimest way to preach? It is the grammatical-historical way, the expository method. It is proclaiming the message as it is in the Holy Scriptures. True Bible preaching is kerygmatic; it consists of the proclamation of the Good News in Christ Jesus. This is the New Testament kerygma: "And . . . Apollos, . . . an eloquent man, and mighty in the scriptures . . . spake and taught diligently the things of the Lord, . . . for he mightily convinced the Jews, and that publicly, shewing by the scriptures that Jesus was Christ" (Acts 18:24–28).

The history of preaching consists primarily of the story of these two contrasting and conflicting methods of interpretation and presentation of God's Word: the method of the spiritualizer and the method of the expositor. The more ancient method would be the interpretation and proclamation of the Scriptures in their literal meaning. It is generally agreed by all students of the history of hermeneutics that the interpretation of Scripture began at the time of the return of Israel from the Babylonian Exile under Ezra as recorded in Nehemiah 8:1–8. Some of the people had forgotten their Hebrew language because of their long exile and had replaced their native tongue with Aramaic. Upon their return the original Hebrew Scriptures were for the most part unintelligible to them. It was necessary, therefore, for Ezra to explain the Scriptures to the people. It can hardly be questioned but that Ezra's interpretation was a literal interpretation of what had been written.

The Method of Literal Interpretation

The method of literal interpretation continued through the following centuries, so much so that sometimes the rabbis carried this hyperliteralism to fantastic extremes. It is certain that the prevailing method of interpretation among the Jews at the time of Christ was this literal method of presenting God's Word.

But as time went on another method of preaching developed in Alexandria, Egypt. It is called in contradistinction to the literal exposition of the Scriptures, the allegorizing or spiritualizing method. It began with a legendary Alexandrian Jew named Aristobulus and found its greatest exponent in the brilliant Philo, who was a contemporary with Christ. Philo defended the method as something new and unheard of. He accepted these two theses: that Greek philosophy was borrowed from the Old Testament, especially from the law of Moses, and that all of the tenets of Greek philosophy, especially that of Aristotle, were to be found in Moses and the prophets. Philo adopted these concepts of interpretation in order to reconcile Mosaic law and Greek philosophy. The purpose of Philo was to demonstrate the harmony between Jewish faith and classic philosophy in order to make the former acceptable to the educated Greek mind. The only way that Philo could effect this harmonization was by adopting an allegorizing method of interpreting the Scriptures.

An illustration of the preaching of Philo would go like this: There was actually no Adam and Eve; they represent the human race. There actually was no Garden of Eden; it represents the mind. There were actually no trees in a Garden of Eden; they represent our thoughts, good and bad. There actually were no four rivers that watered the garden; they represent the four cardinal Greek virtues. It was the use of this method of allegorizing and spiritualizing that characterized the interpretation of the Bible according to Philo. (This use of Genesis reminds me of the modernist today!)

The Allegorical Method

In the development of Christian theology and Christian preaching in the theological school of Alexandria the influence of Philo was dominant. It was in this school, also, that Origen developed the allegorical method of the interpretation of Christian Scriptures. He followed Philo in his spiritualizing away the letter of Scripture and substituting instead all kinds of strange and irrelevant ideas. This method of preaching suited and fitted the taste of the age, and the capable and gifted Origen was literally the exegetical oracle of the early church until his extremism brought him into disrepute.

Grammatical-Historical Method

But while the school of allegory was dominating the theological world in those early first Christian centuries, there was another method of interpretation that was being developed in Caesarea and in Antioch. This was the grammatical-historical school, which has given to us some of the greatest commentaries on the Bible in all New Testament history. The glorious exponent of this marvelous method of presenting God's Word, just as it is and just as it means, is John Chrysostom, the pastor of the church at Antioch and at Constantinople. No greater preacher has ever lived than "John the Golden Mouth." His way of interpreting the Scripture according to its literal, grammatical, and historical meaning has been a paragon of excellence for all true preachers of Christ since his day.

However, the rise of ecclesiasticism and the recognition of the authority of the church in all doctrinal matters finally destroyed this glorious preaching method of John Chrysostom. The church turned again to an allegorical presentation of the Word of God. Not what the Book says, but what the church says, became the order of the day. During the Middle Ages, from the seventh to the twelfth centuries, and during the Renaissance, from the twelfth to the sixteenth centuries, it was this principle of interpretation that was adopted in order to make the Scriptures conform to the traditions and to the doctrines of the church.

The Preaching of the Great Reformation

Then God gave to the church the great Reformation movement. It can be truly said that the reform movement in the church was activated by a return to the literal method of the preaching of the Scriptures. In this period two great names stand out as exponents of the historical-grammatical method of interpreting God's Word—Luther and Calvin. Luther said: "Every word should be allowed to stand in its natural meaning and should not be abandoned unless faith forces us to it. The literal sense of Scripture alone is the whole essence of faith and of Christian theology." Calvin said: "Let us know that the true meaning of Scripture is the natural and obvious meaning. Let us embrace and abide it resolutely. It is the first business of an interpreter to let the author say what he does say instead of attributing to him what we think he ought to say."

Thus the reformers gave a mighty impulse to the science of hermeneutics. They made the Bible an open book to all and they tore away and scattered to the wind the dense cobwebs of arbitrary tradition which had been spun around it for so many years. The post-Reformation period and the years since have been marked by the appearance of great men of God who have followed closely in the footsteps of the reformers and who preach the Bible in its literal truth and according to its true interpretation.

In preaching according to the school of John Chrysostom, Martin Luther, and John Calvin, we are following the literal method of presenting God's message as it was proclaimed by the apostles. It was not necessary for the apostles to turn aside from this method rightly to understand the Bible. They took the prophecies of the Old Testament and found in them a literal fulfillment in the birth, ministry, death, resurrection, and return of our Lord. There is no such thing as a nonliteral fulfillment of these prophecies in the New Testament. When the Old Testament is used in the New, it is used only in a literal sense.

Sometimes people will seek to justify the allegorical method of preaching by referring to Paul's use of a passage in the Old Testament regarding Sarah and Hagar. However, this is not justification for allegorical preaching on our part. Paul is explaining an allegory. The Scriptures abound in allegory, whether in types, symbols, or parables, but they do not call for an allegorical method of interpretation which would deny the literal meaning of God's Word. The allegorical method of interpretation is nothing but a springboard for the interpreter's imagination. When we speak of the types in the New Testament, we are not speaking of allegory. We are merely presenting the Scriptures in their true sense as they present the truth in God.

The Bible abounds in figurative language and these figures have in them tremendous spiritual meanings. To speak of those meanings in keeping with the figure or the type is a true method of interpretation. For example, when John the Baptist, the great forerunner pointing out our Saviour, said in John 1:29, "Behold the Lamb of God," it is clear to those who would present the message of God what John literally meant. Even though a type is used, we know exactly what John referred to when he called Jesus "the Lamb of God." Literal truth is to be preached from these types and symbols, but we are not to destroy the figures by allegorizing them in our own eccentric imaginations.

A simple rule to follow in determining what is literal and what is figurative is this: If the literal meaning of any word or expression makes good sense in its connections, it is literal. But if the literal meaning does not make good sense, it is figurative. Since the literal is the most usual signification of a word and therefore occurs much more frequently than the figurative, any term ought to be regarded as literal until there is good reason for a different understanding, and that understanding will become clear as we read the context and background of the passage in the Bible.

The Poorest Method of Preaching

Surely and truly the poorest method of preaching in the world is that of spiritualizing. When we do not use the plain, normal, literal method of interpretation, all objectivity is lost. There is no check whatsoever on the variety of interpretations which man's imagination may produce. The purpose of the allegorical method is not to interpret Scripture, but to pervert it under the guise of seeking a deeper and more spiritual meaning. Allegorizing does not interpret Scripture; it does not draw out the legitimate meaning of an author's language. Rather it foists upon it whatever the whim or fancy of an interpreter may desire. The basic authority for interpretation ceases to be the Scriptures and becomes the mind of the interpreter. Thus the interpreter can push the Scriptures to mean anything that he pleases them to mean. Thus one is left without any means by which the conclusions of the interpreter may be tested.

Spiritualizing is an open door to almost uncontrolled speculation and imagination. It takes away the authority of the Scriptures and leaves us without any basis upon which we can know the true message from God. Men today wrest the Scriptures to prove their own theories. They glibly use Scripture without any regard for its purpose or true teaching. Shakespeare said, "The devil can cite Scripture for his purpose." The Scriptures themselves bear evidence of the accuracy of Shakespeare's observation, for the devil himself tempted Christ by quoting Scripture. The only way we can be delivered from this evil of spiritualizing is to present the Scriptures exactly as they are with the exact meaning God intended for them to convey.

The Best Way to Preach

The best way to preach, therefore, is literally, grammatically, historically. A literal interpretation gives to every word the same meaning it would have in normal usage. To accept the literal meanings of words is the normal approach to the understanding of words in all languages. Symbols, figures of speech, types, allegories are all to be interpreted plainly according to this basic rule that language means what it says.

The purpose of language itself requires a literal interpretation. Language was given by God that we might communicate with one another. It follows, therefore, that the use of language is to be normal, plain, and literal, accomplishing that purpose of God for which the Lord originated it.

Now, some spiritualizing is not purposefully evil and can make for effective preaching. For example, in the story of the terrible storm in which Paul and his companions were caught as recorded in Acts 27, there is a text in verse 29 which says, "They cast four anchors out." Now a spiritualizer can preach a sermon on the four anchors that are cast out to hold us firm to the will of God. Then he could name such anchors as faith, hope, assurance, love. Such a sermon can be used of God and be blessed of God.

But I still say that it is the poorest way in the world in which to preach. It is infinitely better to deliver God's Word exactly as God intended it. We are to give each word the exact basic meaning it would have in normal, ordinary, customary usage. We are to learn the grammatical and historical background of the passage and we are to present the message as God intended it to be presented.

The Understanding and Application of Scripture

This would mean that the true preacher of God is first to find out the exact meaning of the passage and of the words. This, of course, is exegesis. We would thus seek to understand the whole expressed mind of the human writer as he was inspired to say these words by the Holy Spirit. The next step in building the sermon would be synthesis. Here the preacher would gather up all of the integrated roots of his study and of his exegesis and would present his message in keeping with the whole truth of God as it related to this passage. In this study he would harmonize the text he is using with all of God's Word.

Scripture should be interpreted by Scripture just as one part of a human teacher's message should be interpreted by appeal to the rest. Nor should Scripture ever be set against Scripture as though the Scriptures were contradicting each other. What God says in one place is to be interpreted by what God says in another place, and the whole is to be harmonized and synthesized. An article of faith in the Church of England reads, "So expound one place of Scripture that it not be repugnant to another." The expositor should do just that.

The third phase of preparation is to consider how this message can be applied to the times in which we live. God has a word for us today just as He had for the generations past, and when we declare to the people what God has said and what it means for us today, we are thus being true messengers of the infallible Word of God.

When we follow this method of a literal and actual grammatical and historical presentation of what God has written in His book, we will find a consistency in our preaching that is a jewel indeed. So much of the marginal comment in our Bibles is not true to the Word itself. For example, in a Bible that I hold here in my hand, above the heading of Isaiah 43 there is written "The Church Comforted," but when I look down below I find there is nothing about the church at all. It concerns Israel. The church is not mentioned or referred to. As someone has said, we Christians have helped ourselves to all the blessings and have left the Jews all the curses.

These passages from God's Book are to be preached exactly as they are, and the message is to be delivered as God delivered it. We are not to substitute names and eras beyond what God intended. The Jew in the Bible is always the Jew. Israel is always Israel. The church is always the church. The Kingdom of God is always the Kingdom of God. We are not to spiritualize one into the other. What God says to the Jew is not what God says to the church. The Jew is always the Jew. The church is always the church. The Kingdom of God is always the Kingdom of God.

If we take the Bible literally and preach it literally we have nothing to worry about. But if one takes the Bible and spiritualizes it, he will find himself contradicting himself over and over again as he preaches through the years. If we preach the Bible literally, it is like telling the truth. You do not have to remember what you said. But if you spiritualize, what you said about a passage yesterday may be diametrically opposite to what you make it mean today. On the other hand, if you let the passage say what it says and mean what it means, you possess a golden consistency that makes the Bible glow from beginning to end.

There is no finer way in the world to preach the gospel of Christ and the message of the Book than to preach it exactly as it is, for the Word of God is not obscure but clear. It is because of this clarity of the Scriptures that it is an ever-flowing well of knowledge and life and is able to make the simple wise unto salvation. The all-governing point of departure in our preaching is to be the Scripture itself and not some strange spiritualizing, allegorizing interpretation that we foist upon it and force into it. Let God speak and let all people hear what God has to say.

CHAPTER 20

Preaching the Bible— or the Latest Theological Sophistry

When we read the first verses of the second chapter of 1 Corinthians, we can easily see that the words were written while the apostle Paul was going through a tremendous crisis in his life. The very sound of the words indicate that. "For I *determined* not to know any thing among you, save Jesus Christ, and him crucified" (v. 2). Nor is it difficult to discover, as we read the missionary journeys of Paul in the Book of Acts, the kind of a crisis into which he had been plunged. Everywhere he had gone preaching the gospel of the Son of God, he was bitterly persecuted. In some cities he was jailed; in others he was beaten; in others he was stoned. But when he came to Athens, the learned philosophers merely laughed at his message. The Epicureans scoffed outright. The Stoics were more polite and smilingly said,

"We will hear you again on this matter." As Paul walked across the Corinthian Isthmus from Athens to Corinth, he reviewed the message that had been entrusted to his care by a vision from heaven and by a mandate from the Lord Jesus Himself. He won that victory for Christ and thus wrote these words of 1 Corinthians 2:2.

Every preacher goes through a like crisis in his ministry. Shall he stay by the gospel of the cross, preaching the Word of God as it is revealed in the Holy Scripture or shall he exchange it for the new thought, the new theology, the latest intellectual sophistry? Many so exchange it.

I have preached in churches where every song on the blood had been purged from the hymnbook. The offense of the cross had become too great. Such "butcher-shop religion," as they describe it, violates modern, sensitive, cultivated minds.

It reminds me of a story I read one time concerning an inquiry into a terrible freight train wreck. The engineer of the freight train was called before the board and asked why he did not stop when he saw the flag on the railroad track. The engineer said, "I saw the flag but it was white." A witness objected saying, "No, the flag was red." The flag was called for, and when the board of inquiry looked upon it, they found that it had been red but the color had gone out of it.

This is veritably a parable of modern-day preaching and modern-day theology. Instead of preaching the blood of the cross and the inspiration of the Word of God and the inerrant truth in Holy Scripture, many modern theologians are teaching some passing philosophical, speculative fad.

The Emptiness of Modern, Liberal Theology

What is modern, liberal theology? It is not easy to define. By the time this book is written the current theological fad will have changed. By the time this book is published it will have changed again, and by the time it is placed in your hands it may have changed yet again. But, however many shapes modern liberalism may take, there are some things that can generally be said about it. Modern liberals believe that the Bible is the fallible product of men who were inspired only in the same way that a Shakespeare or a Dante was inspired. Modern, liberal theologians look upon Jesus as a good man, but certainly not as the preexistent Son of God. Modern, liberal theologians look upon the cross as an example of self-sacrifice and philanthropic love, but in no way do they look upon the cross as an atonement for our sins. Modern, liberal theologians think that man's fundamental problem is not that he is lost in sin and depravity, but that his problem is fundamentally environmental; if we can change the order of society, we shall reach utopia and the realization of the Kingdom of God.

Passing Religious Eccentricities

Liberal theologians require that the oracles of God conform to their passing religious eccentricities, whereas true, Biblical, evangelical theologians have only one requirement: namely, that what is taught should conform to the revelation of God in the inspired Scriptures. Which group shall we follow? Which one of these ways are we to go? And which one of these messages are we to preach?

The responsibility God places upon the minister of Christ is the most significantly meaningful in all the world. The body of truth deposited with the church has been especially entrusted to the care of the minister of Christ. In the old dispensation the prophets and the schools of the prophet were charged with the duty of safeguarding the oracles of God and with teaching them. As the days passed, this responsibility was assumed by a new order known as scribes. These men were transcribers and interpreters of the sacred Scriptures. They professed to be Bible experts, able rightly to divide the word of truth. However, as the days multiplied into the years, they began to substitute for the oracles of God their own pronouncements and their own traditions. Thus it was that by the time of Christ they had come to such a sorry state that the Lord denounced them for shutting up the Kingdom of God in its fulness and truth and offering to men nothing but the husks of their own speculations. For example, the Lord said in Matthew 15:6, "Thus have ye made the commandment of God of none effect by your tradition." And again He said in Matthew 23:13, "Ye shut up the kingdom of heaven against men: for ye neither go in yourselves, neither suffer ye them that are entering to go in." And again He said in Matthew 23:24, "Ye blind guides, which strain at a gnat, and swallow a camel." And again He said in Matthew 23:33, "Ye serpents, ye generation of vipers, how can ye escape the damnation of hell?" Our Lord used all these bitter and castigating denunciations of the scribes because they had been false to the oracles of God, adding to them and subtracting from them and substituting for them their own empty interpretations and speculations.

The Sacred Truth Entrusted

The sacred truths of the message of Christ have been entrusted to the preacher of the gospel of the Son of God. But even from the early beginning there were ministers who were false to that trust. Paul was moved to warn Timothy against false teachers who creep in among the people and make shipwreck of their faith. He warned the young pastor against their specious inroads and pled with him to be faithful to the truth which had been committed to his care. Paul closed his first letter to Timothy with this injunction, "O Timothy, keep that which is committed to thy trust" (6:20). In the last letter that Paul wrote to his young son in the ministry he pled with him to preach the Word (2 Tim. 4:2). This was the last injunction before the aged apostle was cut down by a Roman sword. His thirty years of Christian experience, his twenty-five years of apostolic ministry, and his wisdom through the inspiration of the Holy Spirit all spoke through those words. It was a command from heaven itself, not to Timothy only, but to all who filled the office of the evangelist or preacher of the New Testament Word. It was even as Paul instructed Titus that a preacher must be one "holding fast the faithful word as he hath been taught, that he may be able by sound doctrine both to exhort and to convince the gainsayers" (1:9).

Are there any such false teachers and preachers in our time and in our generation? Obviously it is an open secret that there are ministers and professors of divinity without number who undermine the written Word and deny the incarnate Word. They have so fallen away from the truth of God's inspired Book that the pulpits of the land are being filled with men who look upon the Bible as they would look upon some other piece of antique literature. A divinity student was recently graduated from a world-famed, liberal seminary in America. At the end of his course of study and upon his graduation he said, "There is nothing I can absolutely affirm." In other words, he is not convinced that the Lord exists, nor does he believe that the Bible is the inspired Word of God. This is the kind of a minister who in many instances is coming forth to guide the spiritual life of our people.

Upon a day, a friend of mine went to a great northern university to study for this Ph.D. degree in pedagogy. While he was there, he made the friendship of a young student in the divinity school. When time came for this young preacher to get his degree in theology, a church in the Midwest called him to be their pastor. The young minister went to my friend who was studying for his doctor's degree in teaching and said these amazing words to him: "I am in a great quandary. I have been called to be pastor of a church in the Midwest, but it is one of those old-time, old-fashioned churches that believes the Bible is the Word of God. Now I do not believe that the Bible is the Word of God and I do not know what to do." My friend said to him, "Well, I can tell you what to do." The young theolog eagerly replied, "What?" and my friend said, "I think you ought to quit the ministry! That is exactly what I also think. If a man does not believe that the Bible is the Word of God, he has no place in any pulpit in the land. All his preachments are nothing but speculations, and if he has not the authority of God back of what he says, he has nothing to say.

The Overthrow of the Scriptures

This overthrow of the Scriptures in our modern times has been a tragic development in the Christian world. Had any Christian in any church between the end of the second century and the closing decades of the eighteenth been asked a question as to the content of the Christian religion, his answer could scarcely have failed to be to the effect that the truths of the Christian religion were contained and conveyed in the inspired Book of Holy Scripture. Even the Roman Catholic Church, in spite of its inconsistent attitude toward the Bible, declared at the Vatican Council of 1870: "Scriptures contain a revelation without error. Having been written by the inspiration of the Holy Ghost, they have God for their Author." Similar language was also used at the Council of Trent. In the whole communion of Christendom one hundred years ago the question hardly needed to be asked among Christian people as to whether the Bible is the revelation of God and an infallible guide to our lives. But today we have entered into an altogether different and sadder world. There is no disguising the fact that we live in an age when even within the church itself there is an uneasy and distrustful feeling about the Holy Scriptures. There is a hesitancy to lean upon them as an authority and to use them as weapons of precision which once they were. There is a corresponding anxiety to find some surer basis in external church authority or in some kind of a Christian experience or in some other area of consciousness in which we can find a surer and firmer basis for Christian doctrine and belief.

There is no doubt but that the onslaughts of the modern, liberal theologian have almost destroyed for many people the Bible as the inerrant, infallible Word of God. One of these liberal authors wrote, "No single sentence can be quoted from the Bible as having the authority of a distinct utterance of the all-Holy God." They say that those who now believe the biblical teaching are to be dismissed as rather pitiful remnants of medieval credulity and as prisoners of a fossilized tradition. They contend that no intelligent person can hold to a concept of verbal inspiration. They say it would require intellectual suicide to believe in biblical inerrancy. To believe the Bible, they say, is a silly idolatry and an absurd irrationality. All of such talk is most intimidating and overwhelming to a young minister.

The Impregnable Rock of Holy Scripture

However, if Christianity is anything at all, it is the religion of a Book, the Book, the Bible. Christianity is based upon the impregnable rock of Holy Scripture. The starting point of all of our doctrinal presentations must be the Word of God. Upon the foundation of the divine inspiration of the Bible stands or falls the entire edifice of the Christian faith and "if the foundations be destroyed, what can the righteous do?" (Psalm 11:3). If we surrender the truth of the verbal inspiration of the Bible, we are left like a rudderless ship on a stormy sea. We are at the mercy of every wind that blows. Deny that the Bible is the very Word of God and we have no ultimate standard of righteousness and no supreme authority for our salvation. It is impossible to overestimate what evil is wrought when the Word of God is denied. This was the beginning of the fall of the human race when Satan cast doubt upon God's Word as he said to Eve, "Yea, hath God said?"

The Most Important
Question in the World Today

The most important question for the religious world today is this: "Is the Bible the Word of God?" If the Bible is the Word of God we have an absolutely trustworthy guide for all the answers our souls desire to know. We have a starting point from whence we can proceed to the conquest of the whole realm of religious truth. We have an assurance of our salvation and of the glories of the world to come. But if the Bible is not the Word of God, if it is the mere product of man's speculation, if it is not altogether trustworthy in regard to religious and eternal truth, then we are all in a trackless wilderness not knowing where to go or where to turn.

Truly, there is no sadder or more tragic sight than to look upon a minister or a professor of divinity attacking and ridiculing the Word of God, the anchor of the human soul. There is a depth of hypocrisy about ministers attacking the Bible that is unusually heinous. We have public halls, houses of assembly, scholastic academies, and civic auditoriums where the Bible and Christianity may be assaulted without interruption. But to see a minister of the gospel mount the pulpit to find fault with the Word of God and to decry it as a revelation of the truth of heaven is of all things most sad. In our day the Bible is assailed by infidel pseudoscientists, by rash materialists, by cheap secularists, by blaspheming communists, and by all the vice of earth and all the venom of perdition. For the minister to link hands with these enemies of the Kingdom of God is unbelievable. If there ever was a time when our wobbling world needed to hear a clamant voice calling it back to the changeless verities of the Word of God, that time is now.

A World of Jumbled Confusion

Modern, liberal critics leave behind them a world of jumbled confusion. They tell us that God has revealed Himself but refuse to pin themselves down as to exactly what the revelation is. In fact, upon occasion, we find them glorying in the uncertainty of their preaching because this offers them an opportunity for the exercise of "the leap of faith." The basic thesis of their dialectical theology is that the acts of God in history cannot be detected apart from "a leap of faith" and the revealed Words of God can never be identified with any words. They avow that divine acts are beyond history and divine words are beyond language. There is a segment of neoorthodoxy that distinguishes between God's Word and the human expression of the word. The so-called Word of God can be recognized only in the area of our experience. This would mean that not even the words of Jesus are a valid external authority. Only those words of Jesus are valid which one feels to be appropriate to Jesus according to the judgment of one's own mind, which seems to mean that one's own mind becomes one's own Jesus.

They would have us believe that a miracle is not a marvelous or wondrous event that happened in history but that it is merely an interpretation which believing people gave to an event which moved them to such an expression and such an interpretation. For example, the miraculous deliverance of Israel through the waters of the sea was not a thing that actually happened. Rather, what we read in the Bible is just the empty interpretation of people who thought that it happened. It was a miracle only in their minds. The resurrection of Christ is likewise categorized as a human, fallible interpretation. Christ did not rise from the dead. The real truth is that His disciples thought that He rose from the dead, and what we have in the Bible is just the record of their cogitations. The Bible, to these men, does not contain timeless, divine truths, but it is only a purely human testimony to the response evoked by an event in their lives. Scripture, therefore, is true only to the degree in which it evokes an experience in us. What Jesus did on the cross has no meaning, according to these theologians, except what the interpreter would like to make it mean, and the interpreter, of course, could make it mean anything.

What Is Ultimate Truth?

Thus, the entire Bible becomes a book from which one may pick and choose what appeals to one's mind. Experience becomes the supreme authority. Bible teaching becomes secondary. In this way all of religion is reduced to a speculative, human experience, and there is no ultimate standard nor is there any ultimate truth. Religious experience thus becomes an object of one's own interpretation of truth and as such it can prove anything. Truly, falling back upon experience alone leaves the church and the human soul in a limbo of doubt and agonizing uncertainty. Cutting theology off from the control of the biblical text leads to its death. The theology which delights in the absence of final truth and revelation is absolutely nonsense. It cannot escape the just charge of pure meaninglessness. It cannot finally escape from the ultimate despair of materialistic, subjective existentialism.

The destructive results of the critics' work can be seen on every hand as they busy themselves seeking errors, contradictions, and historical inaccuracies in the Bible. They have torn apart God's beautiful flower. They cannot see it any more. As vivisectionists they have cut up the living body until for them and for those who believe them it has died. Though they cannot destroy the Word of God, they have destroyed for themselves and for those who listen to them its vital life. It has become a dismembered cadaver. The critical spirit not only kills the will to worship and destroys confidence in the God who revealed Himself in the Bible but it also throws the whole life into unending doubt. It loosens the foundationstones of truth; it casts a shadow upon faith; it weakens the hold upon spiritual reality. The soul of man cannot feed upon negations. It cannot eat a stone when it demands and cries for bread.

The results of all of this doubt can be seen throughout the length and breadth of the Christian church. For many today, the question of what Jesus thought about Scripture cannot be seriously faced because the evidence against biblical infallibility is so overwhelming that it is hardly relevant. Negative biblical criticism has conducted a wide campaign of brainwashing to this effect. The results of modern critical teaching in the last century have rendered untenable to those who are influenced by it the whole conception of the Bible as a verbally inspired book. No longer can we appeal to the Book with absolute certainty for infallible guidance in all matters of faith and conduct. Therefore, without an infallible guide and without an inerrant Bible, the church is lost in this modern sea of conflicting storms and currents. The fruits of modern critical theology leave the minister without any sure word to say. We have no revelation of God to help us in our hour of greatest extremity and need.

A Closer Look at Modern, Liberal Theologians

For a moment let us look further at these modern liberals. An intelligent gentleman who sat for a time under the ministry of a liberal preacher made the following observations:

> I find that so-called liberals can be the most illiberal of men. They often degenerate into religious critics and censors. They indulge in flings at the orthodox and have little to say that is positive and constructive.

This is so true. I have, myself, felt the bitter sting of these unchristian castigations. Instead of winning people to Christ and sending out missionaries and building up the household of faith, they indulge in nothing but seeking to destroy the faith of those who believe in God's Word and who love God's Son. It is safe to challenge the whole Christian world for the name of a man who stands out as a winner of souls who also does not believe in the inspiration of the Bible as it has been loved through the generations.

What they preach is sometimes an amazing thing to behold. When I was in the seminary, some of us went to hear a liberal preacher in the city. To our amazement he was preaching from Shakespeare. At the conclusion of the service we went up to him and said: "We thought that a Christian minister ought to preach the Bible, but you are preaching Shakespeare. Why?" He replied, "I preached the Bible last year and finished it. Now I am preaching Shakespeare!" The Bible was no more to him than any other book from which he might gain a starting point to lecture on the drivel that might come into his mind.

As we examine these liberals, we find that they are consumed with presuppositions and have closed minds to any other truth. They presuppose that there is nothing miraculous and nothing supernatural in the world and they assail the Bible with those definite a priori conclusions. Therefore, they are not able to judge the Bible objectively, and what they write as "assured results of critical analysis" is nothing other than an empty recounting of what they had previously concluded.

Do the Critics Agree Among Themselves?

As we look more closely at these critics, do we find agreement among them? Do these liberals agree in what they say? No, they do not. They may unanimously deny the inspiration of the Bible, the divinity of Christ, the personality of the Holy Spirit, the fall of man, and the atonement of Christ for our sins; they may deny prophecies, miracles, the resurrection of the dead, and the final judgments, yet when it comes to the pretendedly assured results of their studies, not any two of them affirm the same thing, and their numerous publications create a flood of disputable, self-contradictory, and naturally destructive hypotheses.

When we take our stand apart from the Bible, we fall into a fool's paradise of rationalism. We have lost all sense of spiritual direction and grope in an inky, murky blackness as in a fog and in a mist. When reason substitutes for the supernatural, invisible, eternal things of God, it talks as a blind man does about colors and discourses about things of which it knows nothing at all.

When the modern liberal theologians attempt to palm off their denials of the Holy Scriptures by labeling them "the findings of science" or "the concensus of scholarship," there are some people who take them seriously and are ready to throw away their Bibles. But one man, however, was not in that class. This man was Premier Winston Churchill. Let us read again what he said:

> We reject, with scorn, all those learned and labored myths that Moses was but a legendary figure upon whom the priesthood and the people hung their essential social, moral and religious ordinances.

> We believe that the most scientific view, the most up-to-date and rationalistic conception will find its fullest satisfaction in taking the Bible story *literally*, and in identifying one of the greatest human beings with the most decisive leap forward ever discernible in the human story.[1]

Amen and Amen!

---

1. Winston S. Churchill, *Amid These Storms: Thoughts and Adventures* (New York: Charles Scribner's Sons, 1932), 293.

CHAPTER 21

Faithful to Our Christian Heritage

The Old Testament prophets had a habit of calling their people back to the remembrance of their forefathers. For example, Isaiah lifted up his voice and cried, "Look unto the rock whence ye are hewn, and to the hole of the pit whence ye are digged. Look unto Abraham your father, and unto Sarah that bare you" (Isa. 51:1–2). Let us do this with regard to our Christian heritage and with regard to the reverence of our predecessors for the infallible Word of God.

Through the centuries all Christendom has been convinced that the Bible in its entirety was veritably inspired and that as such it was endowed with all of the perfections of God. In history as well as in doctrine, the church has always believed this Book was exempt from error. This view of the Bible has been consistently maintained by every branch, sect, and denomination of the Christian faith.

Such an attitude toward the Bible was formed in the days of the New Testament. Even before the New Testament Scriptures were written, the Christian churches accepted the Old Testament as their sacred book and when the New Testament Scriptures were written they placed them alongside the Old. The attitude of the church toward the Bible was simply the attitude of Christ. That is what the Lord did; namely, He received the Old Testament Scriptures as the genuinely inspired Word of God. It was only natural, therefore, that the apostles and the Christians who followed them should maintain the same regard for the Holy Scriptures as they found exemplified in their Lord.

The Centuries of Faithful Christian Witness

We have not space here to quote from the church fathers in the centuries that immediately followed the launching of the message of Christ in the world. These patristic writers, such as Irenaeus and Origen, may have differed from each other concerning the meaning and content of the Scriptures, but they never differed concerning the character and the inspired nature of the Scriptures. They believed that its authority was self-evident and that its inspiration extended even to the phraseology of the Book. These men taught both the perfection and the authority of the Bible as words actually spoken by God Himself through the Holy Spirit.

In the early confessions and creeds of the church the doctrine of the inspiration of the Bible is hardly mentioned. If it is asked why this omission, the answer is perfectly obvious. The creeds were concerned with doctrines which had been disputed in the churches, and these great councils set forth and promulgated the truth as they found it in the study of God's Word. But the inspiration of the Bible itself was never one of the disputed points of faith. Therefore, there was never any need for any pronouncement concerning it. Everybody believed God's Book was inspired, and they believed it from the beginning. The Holy Scriptures, they were persuaded, had in them the breath and spirit of God (2 Tim. 3:16). They were produced by a miracle of concurrent action between the heavenly divine Author and the human penman.

This attitude toward the Bible is reflected throughout the Middle Ages. It is true scholastics were sometimes deeply interested in the question of the status of the Bible in relation to the authority of the church, but even then when church tradition finally came to have an authority equal with the Scriptures, there was no change of views concerning the nature of Scripture itself. Throughout the Middle Ages the Bible was looked upon as a textbook of divine truth and as a Word from heaven divinely given.

In the days of the great Reformation there was no break with the historical, traditional view of Scripture even though the reformers were engaged in a death-to-death struggle with Rome. They may have quarreled with Rome concerning the accretions that were added to the Scriptures, but they did not seek to destroy the Scriptures themselves. They dethroned the church in favor of the Spirit as the Interpreter of the Holy Word of God. They exalted the Scriptures. They held them to be self-authenticating and self-interpreting.

Basing their arguments on this persuasion, they found in the Scriptures the self-sufficient judge of church traditions which Rome erroneously taught had supplanted the Book. But there was no break either on the part of the reformers or of Rome in their attitude toward the Word of God. The centuries-old view that Scripture was veritably the revelation of God Himself was held by both the reformers and by the church of Rome. At Trent, Rome reaffirmed its belief in the Bible and did so concerning the books of both Testaments with this simple sentence, "One Author, one God is the Author of both."

Ecclesiasticism Human Reason

It is not until we come to the eighteenth and nineteenth centuries that in some areas of ecclesiasticism human reason began to replace the Holy Scriptures as the final authority of faith and life. As humanism began to sweep to ascendency in the academic world, man became the judge of everything including religion. In this liberal view of Scripture a view came to be accepted which refused to identify Scripture with God's Word or to accept the Bible as a trustworthy revelation of God. It was this new humanism and this new liberal theology that created the break with the historical understanding of the nature of the Bible.

But even through these last several centuries of storm and fury over the Word of God, there were men of tremendous intellectual stature and there were believers by the thousands who laid down their lives for the truth revealed in the Book. Felix Manz was drowned in the Limmont river at Zurich, Switzerland, by the Reformed church. Balthazar Hubmeier was burned at the stake in Vienna, Austria, by the Roman Church. Both men, powerful preachers and expositors of the Word, held the open Bible in their hands and sealed their testimony with their blood.

As the years passed, the Holy Book, under the inspired guidance of God's faithful servants, found its way into the very lifestream of our people. John Bunyan, in prison for twelve years in Bedford jail for preaching the Bible, wove its message into the most glorious allegory the world has ever seen. William Carey translated the Book into languages four hundred million people of India could read.

In America the faithful Baptists promulgated their New Hampshire Confession of Faith, the first Article of which reads like this:

> We believe that the Holy Bible was written by men divinely inspired and is a perfect treasure of heavenly instruction; that it has God for its Author, salvation for its end and truth without any mixture of error for its matter; that it reveals the principles by which God will judge us; and therefore, is and shall remain to the end of the world, the true center of Christian union and the supreme standard by which all human conduct, creeds and opinion shall be tried.

The Evangelization of the American Continent

The evangelization of the American continent was wrought by men who believed and preached the Book, word for word, syllable by syllable, verse upon verse. No more eloquent passage in all Christian literature can be found than H. C. Vedder's description of the pioneer preacher who went forth to claim the Western wilderness for Christ *(A Short History of the Baptists)*.

Vedder describes how these men of God faced an unknown continent not knowing where they should find a night's lodging or their next meal, willing to suffer untold privations if only they might point some to the Lamb of God. They traveled from settlement to settlement on horseback with no road save an Indian trail or blazed trees, forded streams over which no bridges had been built, exposed to storms, frequently slept where night found them, often prostrated by fevers or wasted by malaria, but indomitable still. If they did not wander in sheepskins and goat-skins like ancient heroes of faith, they wore deerskins and home-spun took the place of sackcloth. Their dwelling was "all out o'doors."

Vedder then quotes from the diary of one of these pioneer preachers:

> Everyday I travel I have to swim through creeks or swamps and I am wet from head to feet and somedays from morning to night I am dripping with water. I have rheumatism in all my joints. What I have suffered in body and in mind my pen is not able to communicate to you but this I can say, while my body is wet with water and chilled with cold, my soul is filled with heavenly fire and I can say with St. Paul, "but none of these things move me, neither count I my life dear unto myself, so that I might finish my course with joy."

Vedder continues with his description of the pioneer preacher, who, in the wilderness like Paul, passed through perils many—perils by the way, perils from savage beasts, perils from the savage Indian, perils from dogless and degraded men hardly less savage than either beast or Indian, but God who closed the mouths of the lions was with His servant, the pioneer preacher. Many died prematurely of privation and disease in their hard life, but there is no record of one who failed in his mission.

What kind of places did these preachers possess to preach in? What kind of libraries did they own? What kind of messages did they deliver? The houses of worship in which these preachers held their services were generally God's own temples, the great out-of-doors in the woods and on the prairies. Their libraries consisted of the Bible and a hymnbook carried in their saddle bags. In their preaching they did not read polished essays from manuscripts. The preacher was a rough and ready kind of a man, not always scrupulous of the king's English, but his messages were filled with the doctrines of grace, and they were delivered with evangelistic fervor. These men, uncouth as they would seem now, founded the churches in all the new communities of the West and laid the foundations of the denominational institutions on which our present magnificient superstructures have been built. These men honored God, honored God's Word, and God honored them.

In the tradition of these pioneer preachers, and in keeping with the message they delivered, my own Baptist people down to the present day have continued their commitment to the Holy Scriptures which are able to make us wise unto salvation. In 1962, the messengers to the Southern Baptist Convention in San Francisco expressed their deepest convictions concerning the Bible in no uncertain terms. They adopted a resulution which read in part that, "We reaffirm our faith in the entire Bible as the authoritative, authentic, infallible Word of God . . . our historic position."

An Appeal to Our Ministers to Be True to the Book

Let me speak to Southern Baptists. If our preachers, evangelists, pastors, churches, and institutions are true to that expression of faith, we shall live. If we repudiate it, we shall die. God will remove our lampstand out of its place, and we shall no longer continue to be a lighthouse in a stormy sea. As theological liberalism that denies the Word of God has destroyed other churches, the same theological liberalism will destroy us. There is no exception to this judgment, whether in individual congregations or in denominational associations. Like many others we can continue to exist, having a form of godliness and denying the power thereof, but we shall be dead, spiritually dead, evangelistically dead. Our witness in power and saving grace shall have ceased.

Which way shall we go? There is no common ground between infidelity and Christianity. God Himself says so and God Himself calls us to an obedient separation.

> Be ye not unequally yoked together with unbelievers: for what fellowship hath righteousness with unrighteousness? and what communion hath light with darkness? And what concord hath Christ with Belial? or what part hath he that believeth with an infidel? And what agreement hath the temple of God with idols? for ye are the temple of the living God; as God hath said, "I will dwell in them, and walk in them; and I will be their God, and they shall be My people. Wherefore come out from among them, and be ye separate, saith the Lord, and touch not the unclean thing; and I will receive you, and will be a Father unto you, and ye shall be My sons and daughters, saith the Lord Almighty (2 Cor. 6:14–18).

Even our Lord asked us to be on one side or the other. "I know they works, that thou art neither cold nor hot: I would thou wert cold or hot. So then because thou art lukewarm, and neither cold nor hot, I will spue thee out of my mouth" (Rev. 3:15–16). And again Jesus said, "He that is not with me is against me; and he that gathereth not with me scattereth abroad" (Matt. 12:30).

In the spirit of the captain of the conquering armies of Israel, Joshua of old, I am prepared to say that as for me and my people we shall serve the Lord, stand by the Book, preach its treasures, love its words, serve its Saviour, and humbly seek to obey His mandates.

Will you?

Questions for Group Discussion and Personal Reflection

Chapter 1

1. Do you agree with Dr. Criswell's description of the Bible: "The Bible is a Book to live by and to die by. It is worthy to be received as an infallible guide to heaven. It is true and trustworthy every way. It is the veritable Word of God." Why or why not? Discuss.

2. "The Bible works." What is meant by this statement?

3. Do you agree with Dr. Criswell's example of the Auca Indians as a testimony of the Bible's power? Do you know of other examples of miraculous conversion? Discuss.

4. Consider this statement: "The testimony of transformed lives to the literal truths of the living Word spans the centuries. From Saul of Tarsus to Justin Martyr to Augustine to John Bunyan to John Newton to John Wesley to B. H. Carroll to Jerry McCauley, to the host of God's glorious witnesses today, the testimony is ever the same. There is power in the Word of God to convert." Why do you think Dr. Criswell mentions the above people as examples of the "power in the Word of God to convert"? Discuss.

5. "Scientific knowledge and the words in which that knowledge is conveyed have no power to change our character or to give us a living hope of heaven." Comtemplate this statement and discuss.

6. Read John 5:24, and then discuss the following: "The Word of God is a living message containing within itself God's own life.

7. Read Hebrews 4:12–13, James 1:23, Luke 8:11, Ephesians 6:17, 1 Peter 1:23. What do these passages say about the Bible? Can you list other passages that describe the Bible?

8. Discuss the definition of "universal." Why does Dr. Criswell say that the "appeal of the Bible is universal"? What experiences in your own life prove this statement to be true?

9. In his story of the shepherd, Dr. Criswell tells us the shepherd called the Bible "the sheep book." Out of your own experience, what would you call the Bible?

10. What is meant by this statement: "The Bible never grows old. While it is an ancient Book, yet century after century it renews its youth."

11. Consider the following: "Centuries of so-called progress and advancement have added nothing to the truths of the Scriptures that move our souls." Discuss.

12. "The Bible has been the mightiest factor in shaping the moral progress of the entire race." Do you agree? Why or why not?

13. Discuss the creativity and beauty of John Bunyan's *Pilgrim Progress*.

14. "Everywhere men of letters, eminent statemen, and men of science have testified to the value and inestimable importance of God's Holy Word." Can you name other eminent men and women today who would also testify as to the "value and inestimable importance" of the Bible?

Chapter 2

1. What does Dr. Criswell mean when he writes: "Why do I believe that the Bible is literally true? One reason is the testimony of Jesus Christ, our Lord. The teachings of Jesus are the highest authority to which a Christian can make direct appeal." Discuss.

2. Do you agree with the following statement? "If we accept the teachings of Jesus Christ, we must accept the teachings of our Lord concerning the Bible." Why?

3. What do you think of this statement? "If we accept the teaching of Jesus Christ, we must accept the whole Bible, for Jesus Christ has set His stamp of authority upon the entire Book." Why is the statement true?

4. Read the following passages of Scripture: Matthew 19:4–5; 22:29; 23:35; Mark 7:13; Luke 24:44; John 5:39; 10:35. Discuss.

5. Concerning Jesus and the Scriptures, discuss the following: "He sets His seal to its historicity and its revelation from God. He supplements it, but He never supplants it. He amplifies it, but He never nullifies it. He modifies it according to His own divine prerogative, He fulfils it according to His divine mission, but He never lessens its divine authority."

6. Read Matthew 4:4 and discuss its implications.

7. What are some of the details of Jesus' ministry and message that support the statement: "Jesus' ministry was governed down to the smallest detail by what the Bible predicted the Messiah would do and be."

8. Why is this statement true: "[Jesus] never dreamed of separating revelation from the Scriptures. Such a breach could only lead to the morass of subjectivity."

9. Read the following and discuss: John 6:63; 8:26,28,40; 12:49,50.

10. Read and retell the story of Jesus tempted by Satan in the wilderness experience (Matthew 4).

11. How did Jesus begin His public ministry?

12. Read Matthew 5:17,17. Discuss.

13. Discuss the meaning of "jot" and "tittle." Why are they significant?

14. Explain what Dr. Criswell means when he writes: "If some critic says that the Master in the days of His flesh had only partial knowledge of the whole truth and was limited, therefore, in His understanding of the Scriptures, there can certainly be no question of His partial knowledge after His resurrection."

15. Why is it "abundantly evident that the Jewish Scriptures are the veritable Word of God".

16. According to Dr. Criswell, how did Jesus "set the seal of His authority upon the New Testament," even though the New Testament wasn't written while Jesus was on earth?

17. Explain the significance and meaning of the following Scripture in John 16:12–13: "I have yet many things to say unto you, but ye cannot bear them now. Howbeit when he, the Spirit of Truth, is come, he will guide you into all truth: for He shall not speak of himself; but whatsoever he

shall hear, that shall he speak: and he will shew you things to come."

18. Discuss the following statement: "If we accept then the authority of Jesus Christ, we must accept the apostolic teachings and New Testament writings as being given by the Holy Spirit." Why is this statement true?

19. Did Jesus think of the Bible as being full of errors? Why or why not? What argument does Dr. Criswell give to support his answer?

20. Do you agree with Dr. Criswell's "threefold possibility" as follows:

   1. "That there are no errors in the Scriptures."

   2. "That the errors were there but Christ was not aware of them."

   3. "That He was aware of these errors but did not choose to tell the people of them."

21. Discuss Dr. Criswell's conclusion: "There are no errors in the Scriptures." Why is this statement profoundly important?

22. Why is the Bible "our final court of appeal?"

Chapter 3

1. Read the following portions of Scripture and discuss: Exodus 31:18; Psalm 119:152,160; Proverbs 30:5; Isaiah 40:8; 1 Peter 1:23–25.

2. What is meant by this statement: "The Word of God is its own tremendous witness to its own inspiration."

3. What is the significance of this statement? "The prophets . . . habitually introduced their message with the avowal, 'And the Word of the Lord came unto. . . .' The prophet does not regard himself as a speculative theologian;

rather, he delivers a message which he understands to have originated from heaven."

4. What does Dr. Criswell mean when he writes: "The Bible is the Word of God, not merely contains it."

5. What is the message contained in 1 Peter 1:23–25?

6. What do Hebrews 3:7 and Psalm 95:7–8 tell us about the Scriptures?

7. What do the words *graphe* and *theopneustos* imply?

8. Why did Dr. Criswell use the examples of Balaam and Caiaphas to make the point that what is written in the Bible is inspired by God Himself?

9. Why is this statement so urgently important? "Paul plainly states in this text in 2 Timothy 3:16 that *all the Scriptures* are 'God-breathed.'"

10. Explain the meaning of Dr. Criswell's "verbal theory of inspiration."

11. "The verbal theory of inspiration . . . is vehemently denied by many modern theologians," Dr. Criswell writes. "They say it is too mechanical. They say it degrades the writers to the level of machines. They say it has a tendency to make skeptics and unbelievers. . . ." Discuss this statement. List other reasons why some would deny the verbal theory of inspiration.

12. Contemplate the meaning of 1 Peter 1:10, 11: "Of which salvation the prophets have inquired and searched diligently, who prophesied of the grace that should come unto you: searching what, or what manner of time the Spirit of Christ which was in them did signify, when it testified beforehand the sufferings of Christ, and the glory that should follow."

13. Discuss the following statement: "[The prophets] were reporters of what they heard rather than formulators of that which they delivered. They were voices and echoes.

They did not originate their message. The message came from God."

14. In what way does Dr. Criswell demonstrate his point with this statement? "Moses will thus emphasize that the commandments are the work of God and the writing is the writing of God."

15. Read 2 Samuel 23:1–2. Discuss.

16. What does Dr. Criswell mean by this statement; to what does he refer? "This lifts the Bible from human hands and places it back in God's hands."

17. What is the "remarkable fact regarding the revelations of the Bible" that Dr. Criswell highlights? What are some of the examples he gives to help explain his point? In actual fulfillment, how did both lines of prophecy meet in Jesus?

18. What are some of the methods God used in originating His message?

19. Contemplate the meaning and significance of Revelation 1:1: "The Revelation of Jesus Christ, which God gave unto him, to shew unto his servants things which must shortly come to pass; and he sent and signified it by his angel unto his servant John." What point does Dr. Criswell make by using this particular verse of Scripture?

20. Why is the Bible a "miracle"?

21. What statements in this chapter speak most loudly to you? Why? Would you agree with every point Dr. Criswell makes? If not, list and discuss.

Chapter 4

1. What does Dr. Criswell mean by this statement? "The fulfilled prophecies of the Bible bespeak the omniscience of its author."

2. Why does Dr. Criswell write that Isaiah 41:21–23 records "the most remarkable challenge to be found in the Bible"?

3. What are the negative and the positive values found in this Scripture (Isaiah 41:21–23)? "Produce your cause, saith the Lord; bring forth your strong reasons, saith the King of Jacob. Let them bring them forth, and shew us what shall happen: let them shew the former things, what they be, that we may consider them, and know the latter end of them; or declare us things for to come. Shew the things that are to come hereafter, that we may know that ye are gods: yea, do good, or do evil, that we may be dismayed, and behold it together."

4. Explain why "fulfilled prophecy is a potent argument for the inspiration of the Bible."

5. Why did the writers of the books of other religions avoid foretelling the future? What are the reasons Dr. Criswell gives here?

6. Discuss this statement: "God's ability through His spokesmen to transcend the confines of human knowledge provides objective proof of His sovereignty over history."

7. What are the Old Testament methods to test a prophet?

8. What does Dr. Criswell believe to be the most remarkable chapters in the Pentateuch, and why?

9. Why have scholars called the Jews the "enigma of history"?

10. What is the argument Dr. Criswell gives "for the Word of God which no infidel can answer"? Do you agree? Why or why not?

11. Read Matthew 24:34 where the Master declares that this kind—this race, shall not pass away until all these things that pertain to the consummation of the age have been

fulfilled. Discuss and ponder the implications of this statement from Scripture.

12. What are some of the prophecies Dr. Criswell cites that have been fulfilled to the letter? Discuss them.

13. Read Matthew 11. What are the three cities whose destruction was commented upon by Jesus Himself?

14. Read 1 Timothy 4:1–2; 2 Timothy 3:1–5; 4:1–3 and discuss.

15. What are the Bible's prophecies that are "so full and complete and . . . so marvelously fulfilled," more than any other?

16. Explain what is meant by this statement: "Christ is the center of Old Testament prophecy as He is the center of New Testament history."

17. What are the two kinds of prophecies found in the Old Testament?

18. Examine and explain the following "types":

the Lamb of God

altar

sacrifice

atonement

propitiation

expiation

sin offering

How do these Old Testament descriptions of the construction and practices of the tabernacle, Levitical offerings, and worship services give us a clear picture of the meaning of Christ's death, atoning grace, and the gift of everlasting life?

19. What did you find the most perceptive point Dr. Criswell makes in this chapter? Why?

Chapter 5

1. What does Dr. Criswell mean when he writes: "No man has intelligence enough to insert a hypothetical fact into circumstances not belonging to it and make it fit perfectly and exactly"?

2. Explain this statement: "A thousand silent witnesses have been brought to life to testify to the truth of the record we find in God's Book." On what basis is this true?

3. Explain what is meant by the following: "When the faith of many was waning and many heralds of truth were tempted to speak with uncertain sounds, the very stones have cried out with a voice that only the deaf could fail to hear."

4. Discuss the significance of this statement: "Every stone that has been turned and every spade of dirt that has been lifted has been in confirmation of the truth of the Word of God."

5. How has modern archaeology confirmed the book of Genesis. What are the examples Dr. Criswell gives?

6. Concerning the "walls of Jericho," what evidence is given to support the Biblical story?

7. According to Dr. Criswell, "what has archaeology done to the book of Daniel"?

8. What have archaeologists discovered about Belshazzar? What is the significance of this find?

9. Can you name other Old Testament discoveries that have again and again proved the consistency of the Scriptures?

10. Concerning Simon Peter and the apostle Paul, how were the critics wrong?

11. What impressed you about this study in archaeology? Discuss the discoveries and how they prove the critics wrong.

Chapter 6

1. Explain the following statement: "If the destructive critics were to be taken at their word, then the Bible is full of monstrous mistakes. Its prophecies have failed, its history is not historical, its science is unscientific, its stories are myths, its facts are fables, and there is practically nothing trustworthy in it."

2. What does Dr. Criswell mean by the following: "The so-called errors of the Bible are a very slippery lot."

3. Why "is it imperative to distinguish between a difficulty not yet solved and an error"?

4. Ponder and discuss the statements made by B. H. Carroll and R. A. Torrey concerning errors in the Bible.

5. "Difficulties in the Bible are generally scientific, historical, or ethical." Do you agree? Why or why not?

6. Read Matthew 19:3–8 and discuss.

7. Read and discuss 2 Peter 3:16 in light of Dr. Criswell's comments.

8. What is meant by this statement? "When men ought to be taught to proclaim the message of Christ and the truths of the Holy Book, the time of instruction seems to be spent in pointing to inconsequentials."

9. "God speaks to us through the Scriptures, not in order to make us mathematicians or biologists or historians but in order to make us children of our heavenly Father." Do you agree? Why is this true?

10. Define the terms "lower criticism" and "higher criticism."

11. Discuss the following: "There is no contradiction in the Bible to any fact of science. The physical universe, the mystery of planetary and stellar movements, the constitution of man, the world of plant and animal life, the mystery of life itself, and the constitution of the earth in material forms and forces—all of these things that we know in science are in perfect harmony with what is presented in the Bible."

12. Read John 5:4. Discuss the argument given by Dr. Criswell concerning the difficulties we make ourselves in Scripture.

13. Read 2 Kings 18:14 and discuss Dr. Criswell's example.

14. Read Acts 5:36. Discuss in light of Dr. Criswell's example.

15. Read John 19:20, and explain the point Dr. Criswell makes.

16. Ponder the issue of faith and works and Dr. Criswell's reply.

17. Dr. Criswell writes: "'Miracle' is a signature of God. Wherever there is God, there is miracle. A Bible without miracles would be a Bible without God." Discuss this interesting point. What would your own definition of a "miracle" be?

18. How does Dr. Criswell explain the miracle of Jonah and the "great fish"?

Chapter 7

1. Discuss the following: "One of the castigations on the part of those who scoff and ridicule the Book is to the effect that the Holy Scriptures are full of moral blemishes."

2. Read Joshua 6:17 and discuss. Dr. Criswell states: "One immorality that [critics] refer to concerns God's command to exterminate the ancient Canaanites.

3. What reason is given by Dr. Criswell concerning the following: "The holy war conducted by the Israelites at the command of the Lord was truly aimed at the total annihilation of these ancient people." Are you satisfied with the argument given for this annihilation? Why or why not?

4. Ponder this statement: "The destruction of that [Canaan] religion and culture is presented in the Old Testament as a display of God's righteous anger."

5. Do you agree with this statement? "The moral degradation in which the Canaanites lived before Israel invaded the land required not a revelation of the love of God but a manifestation of His holiness and severity." Discuss.

6. "Is God a God of wrath as well as a God of love?" How does the author address this question?

7. Read Romans 3:5, 19, and 2 Thessalonians 1:5–10. Comment upon these verses.

8. As you contemplate the following, give any examples that come to mind: "There is no evidence that Jesus found difficulty in identifying the God of wrath of the Old Testament with the God whom He claimed to reveal."

9. Read Matthew 23. What would you say in reponse to the following statement: "We have but to read the words of Christ in Matthew 23 and the words of the Apocalypse to see that the true God of heaven and earth is one whose righteous dealings with men necessitate judgment upon unrighteousness."

10. Concerning the hardening of Pharoah's heart, what is your response to this statement? "It is said in criticism that if God hardened Pharaoh's heart, in consequence of this act on the part of God, then God Himself was responsible for Pharaoh's sin and that it was unjust to hold Pharaoh accountable for his rebellion and to punish him for it. If God did it, they say, then God is responsible and should be held accountable. For God to take a man who

desires to know and do God's will, harden his heart, and thus incline him not to do God's will, would indeed be an action on God's part that would be impossible to justify."

11. Study Exodus 5:1–2, and then discuss the argument Dr. Criswell makes concerning the statement above.

12. Read 2 Thessalonians 2:9–12 and Romans 1:24–26. Ponder and comment upon this statement: "If a man chooses error, God gives him up to that error. If, with a hard heart and an obstreperous will, men choose sin, then God finally gives them over to that sin with its accompanying judgment." Can you think of other biblical examples where this sequence occurred?

13. Read and ponder psalms 58–59, 69, 79, 109, and 137, and then comment on the following statement: "[Critics] say that they see in these psalms a spirit of revenge and a desire to see one's enemies crushed in a way contradictory to the teachings of our Lord."

14. Dr. Criswell writes: "The imprecatory psalms announce the fate of all the godless when final judgment comes." Are you satisfied with this argument? Do you agree? Why or why not? Discuss.

15. Read the following and then discuss Dr. Criswell's thesis given: Isaiah 13:13–18, and Revelation 18:1–24."

16. The author writes: "The critics are quick to point out another supposed moral blemish in the Bible in the story of Saul and especially in 1 Samuel 16:14 where the Bible says that 'the spirit of the Lord departed from Saul, and an evil spirit from the Lord troubled him.'" What is meant by this "evil spirit" from the Lord?

17. Comment upon this statement: "If we make right use of this spirit of unrest and depression ['evil spirit'], repentance will follow and bring us back to God and to the joy of the Holy Spirit."

18. Do you believe this statement to be true? "There are those who purport to be greatly offended by the so-called immoralities that are found in the characters of the Bible."

19. What examples does Dr. Criswell give to support his statement above? Can you think of other examples of immoralities in Biblical characters?

20. Read 1 John 2:15–17, and Romans 3:10–12. Discuss what it says about sin.

21. "The delineation of the characters that walk across the stage of Biblical history is faithful and true in every respect. God does not seek to hide away their imperfections and blemishes." Why is this fact so important? Discuss.

22. Dr. Criswell asks the following questions. Contemplate them. "Shall we expurgate the Bible? Shall we add our human embellishments to the Word of God? Shall we touch up places that we think ought to be touched up, take out things that we think ought to be taken out, and add to things that which we think ought to be added?"

23. What is meant by this statement: "A stream cannot rise higher than its source, and a book cannot lift men up beyond that moral station it itself possesses."

Chapter 8

1. "The media of the divine revelation of God to man are words." Explain what this means and why it is true.

2. Exodus 32:16, Revelation 19:9, Luke 1:70, and 1 Corinthians 2:13. What do these Scripture verses say to support Dr. Criswell's statement above?

3. "The inspiration of the Holy Scriptures, therefore, concerns not only the minds of the writers but also and more pertinently the writings themselves because the writers in

many instances did not understand what they wrote." Comment upon this statement.

4. "Divine truth demands divine revelation and infallible language." Why is this statement true?

5. What comment does Dr. Criswell give concerning Galatians 3:8? Do you agree?

6. Read Romans 9:17. What does Dr. Criswell say about this passage?

7. Do you agree with this statement? "We have no record of Jesus Christ and what He did and said except in the Bible."

8. Comment upon this strong statement made by the author: "Any rejection of the Bible is a rejection of Jesus our Lord."

9. Would you agree with this definition of "inspiration"? "When we refer to the inspiration of the Bible, we refer to the fact that the collection of words in the Holy Scriptures is veracious and conveys the divine truth effectively to the human mind."

10. Dr. Criswell writes: "They speak of the inspiration of ideas instead of the inspiration of words." In your own words, what is the difference between the "inspiration of ideas" and the "inspiration of words"?

11. Read and comment upon Matthew 24:35. Does this passage stress the importance of words? Why?

12. What does this statement mean? "Thoughts are wedded to words as necessarily as soul to body."

13. Can God give a thought to man without the words to clothe it? Dr. Criswell believes the two cannot be separated. What do you think?

14. Discuss the following: "To say that the inspiration of the Scriptures applies to their concepts and not to their

words, to declare that one part of the Bible was written with one kind or degree of inspiration and another part with another kind or degree of inspiration, is not only destitute of any foundation or support from the Scriptures themselves but is repudiated by every statement in the Bible which bears upon the subject."

15. What does the apostle Paul write in 2 Timothy 3:16? What are the implications of such a statement?

16. Ponder this statement: "Inspiration extends to the form as well as to the substance, to the words as well as to the thoughts."

17. Discuss the words of Paul as recorded in 1 Corinthians 14:37: "If any man think himself to be a prophet, or spiritual, let him acknowledge that the things that I write unto you are the commandments of the Lord."

18. Dr. Criswell writes in 1969: "The doctrine of verbal inspiration is for the most part discounted in our day." Is this still true today? Explain.

19. Discuss this statement: "If the modern contention concerning the Scriptures is correct that God inspired the deeds and not the words then a vast portion of the Bible is not revelation at all." Do you agree? Why or why not?

20. What is meant by this statement? "It is not experience that is to judge the Book but the Book that is to judge all human experiences."

21. Read Psalm 119:89, 160 and discuss.

22. A statement to contemplate: "Revelation is not an ecstatic experience, a wordless encounter with the Other; rather it is a gift of grace in which language is employed in all its rich functions to inform, to evoke, to rebuke, to summons, to bless, to heal, to save."

23. "When we speak of the inspired authors of the Bible, we refer to the inspiration of the words and not of the men." Do you agree with this statement? Why or why not?

24. What does Dr. Criswell say about the book of Ecclesiastes concerning Solomon's inspiration?

25. Consider and discuss: "The truth of inspiration concerns only the miracle by which the Spirit of God produced a document in human language which could function as a truthful instrument of God's self-revelation."

26. "Frequently we hear discussions concerning whether the Bible is the Word of God or only contains the Word of God." What is the difference between the two?

27. "The inspiration of the Bible concerns the fact that they are perfectly and infallibly recorded." Discuss, and if necessary, debate this thesis.

28. "Do we possess the exact words that were inspired of God in the Old Testament and in the New Testament?" How does the author answer his own question (above)?

29. Why is this true? "It is because of the inspiration of the infallible Word that we have the reason for our exegesis of God's Holy Scriptures."

30. "If the Bible is not inspired in its words, there would be no reason for Biblical exegesis." Do you agree? Why or why not?

31. Take a few moments and ponder this statement: "The Bible rightly read, read as a whole, read Christo-centrically, read humbly and under the guidance of the Holy Spirit will lead us to life everlasting."

Chapter 9

1. Why is the "wonder of the world the Word"?

2. Why is this statement true? "That it ever was a book and is today *the* Book of the modern world is really a literary miracle." Why is the Bible a "literary miracle"?

3. Discuss the following:

   a. There never was any order given to any man to plan the Bible.

   b. There was no concerted plan on the part of men to write the Bible.

   c. The Bible was written on two continents, in countries hundreds of miles apart.

   d. The Bible was written in three different languages: namely, Hebrew, Aramaic, and Greek.

   e. Some writers wrote hundreds of years after or before the others.

   f. The authorship of the books of the Bible extends through the slow progress of nearly sixteen centuries.

   g. The Bible was written by men upon every level of political and social life, from the king upon his throne down to the herdsmen, shepherds, fishermen, and petty politicians.

   h. The circumstances under which the Book was written were sometimes most difficult and always most varying.

   i. Not only in background and in circumstances do the authors differ who wrote the Word of God, but they also display in their writings every form of literary structure.

   j. Every part of the Bible fits every other part of the Bible.

   k. There is one ever-increasing, ever-growing, ever-developing plan pervading the whole.

4. Consider the following and discuss: "Despite the varying circumstances, conditions, authors, and workmen who produced the Bible, the Bible is not many books but one

Book. Behind its many parts there is an unmistakable organic unity. It contains one system of doctrine, one system of ethics, one plan of salvation, and one rule of faith."

5. How does Dr. Criswell illustrate the following point? "The phenomenon of the oneness of the Bible is one of the great miracles in the history of the human race."

6. In what ways is this statement true? "The more one really studies the Bible the more one is convinced that behind the many authors there is one overruling, controlling mind."

7. How does Dr. Criswell illustrate the Master-minding of the Bible to the building of a temple? Is his illustration effective? Does it make the point he intends to make? Why or why not?

8. Dr. Criswell writes: "The unity of the Bible is not superficial or peripheral but dynamic. It is not the unity of a dead thing like a stone but the unity of a living thing like a tree." In what way does a tree serve to illustrate the unity of the Bible? Can you think of other examples that could be used?

9. "There are certain conceptions that run through the entire Bible like cords on which are strung many precious pearls," writes the author. What are they? Explain and discuss each in detail.

10. What does the author mean by this clever use of words: "All history is *His-story*."

11. In what ways does the Bible present Christ throughout its pages?

12. "As we hold the Bible in our hands, we are amazed at its logical order." Discuss the logical order of the Scriptures.

Chapter 10

1. Contemplate the following: "I believe that the Bible is literally true because it partakes of the nature of God, who is eternal, who is the same yesterday, today, and forever. The Bible is not *a* book; it is *the* Book."

2. Read Psalm 119:89 and Hebrews 4:12, and discuss.

3. With what ordinary images does Dr. Criswell describe the Bible? Why is each one used? Can you think of other images to describe the Bible? Discuss them.

4. "Throughout the ages the Bible has been the central object of Satan's assault." Why do you think this is true?

5. Name several examples Dr. Criswell gives in reference to this statement: "Generations of people have arisen with a determination to annihilate the Bible, but they have never succeeded." Can you think of others who have "arisen with a determination to anihilate the Bible"?

6. What does Dr. Criswell write about the Emperor Diocletian?

7. What is the definition of *"Extincto Nomine Christianorium"*? Why is it important?

8. If time permits, research the following and discuss:

   a. the year A.D. 325

   b. the First General Council (Nicea)

   c. Constantine: who he was and what he did.

9. Discuss the implications of this statement: "Every engine of destruction that human wisdom, human science, human philosophy, human wit, human satire, human force, and human brutality could bring to bear against the Bible has been brought to bear against it. Yet the Bible still stands!"

10. Discuss Thomas Paine and his book, *Age of Reason*. What does Dr. Criswell say about it?

11. What is meant by "the attack of modern rationalism"? Why is it dangerous?

12. What does Dr. Criswell say is now the chief instrument of the destruction of the Bible?

13. What is the result of "the attempt to discredit and destroy the authenticity and authority of God's Word"?

14. Think of this: "Fifteen hundred years after Herodias wrote his history there was only one copy of it. Twelve hundred years after Plato wrote his books there was only one copy of it. But God was so careful to let us have the Bible in the exact way that he wrote it that we have thousands of ancient manuscripts of it. The Books of the Bible that we have in our present catalog are the same as they have been through all the centuries." Discuss.

15. What is the meaning of the "apocryphal books"? Discuss.

16. Read Isaiah 40:8. Why do you think this is Dr. Criswell's "favorite verse"?

Chapter 11

1. What does the Scripture found in 2 Timothy 3:16 to 4:2 say to you? "All scripture is given by inspiration of God, and is profitable for doctrine, for reproof, for correction, for instruction in righteousness: that the man of God may be perfect, thoroughly furnished unto all good works. I charge thee therefore before God, and the Lord Jesus Christ, who shall judge the quick and the dead at His appearing and His kingdom; preach the word." Discuss.

2. Do you agree with the following statement? "The text [above] avows that *all* the Scriptures are inspired of God, that *all* the Scriptures are God-breathed, that the writing

is the writing of God and contains the breath and the presence of God." Why or why not?

3. Why is the following true? "I have found that even in those sections and passages in the Bible that seem the least profitable are the seedbeds for some of the most profitable and precious sermons."

4. Why is it important for a pastor to preach the whole Word of God?

5. What impact did Dr. Criswell's expository preaching from Genesis to Revelation have on his congregation at First Baptist Church, Dallas, Texas? Discuss.

6. Ponder the following and comment upon: "To this present hour our people hunger and thirst for the Living Word of the Living God."

7. What is the "one great theme" that runs through the Bible?

8. What effect did "Bible-preaching" have upon Dr. Criswell's congregation? Why do you believe the congregation grew?

9. Discuss the following: "The power of the Holy Book to attract is one of the miracles of our modern day." Why do you think this is true? Give examples of this from your own experience.

10. Why is the Bible "like an unfathomable sea"?

11. "It is the strength of our evangelical witness that we study God's Book and that we deliver from its pages God's message. We shall not fail in our work if we are faithful to this holy and heavenly assignment." Discuss this statement.

Chapter 12

1. Do you agree with this statement? "God's message in the Bible is plain, simple, full, comprehensive, and all-sufficient.

What we need for faith, salvation, practice, we find in the Bible." Why or why not?

2. Discuss 2 Timothy 3:15.

3. Answer the following: "Why do we not turn to modern sources for our doctrines of God and salvation? Why, in a world that is changing so rapidly, do we still go back for our moral and spiritual guidance to what was written so long ago?"

4. Put 1 Cor. 15:1–6 in your own words and explain.

5. Why does Dr. Criswell make the following statement? "Styles change, devices change, methods change; but human nature does not change." Do you agree? Why or why not?

6. "Morality is fixed and cannot be *new*." Discuss.

7. Why are we to "believe in the ultimate and literal fulfilment of the literal promises made to Israel and to all of God's saints"?

8. Why are we to "believe in the promises of our Lord in His coming again and in the eternal states of the righteous and the wicked"?

9. Read the following Biblical promises and discuss: Jeremiah 33:3; Luke 11:9–13; 18:1; Mark 11:22–24; John 16:23; 1 John 5:14–15.

10. Why are we to "believe and to preach that God will literally and faithfully keep His promises made to His chosen people, the children of Israel"?

11. Dr. Criswell asks: "If God breaks His promises here, if God fails here, how can we have any assurance that God will not fail in every other promise He has given?" Discuss.

12. Read Ezekiel 36:24–28, Amos 9:15 and Romans 11:25–29. What do these verses say?

13. What is meant by this statement?: "When the words are not to be taken literally but are representative and figurative, such a fact will be clearly indicated and it will be most obvious. The context will reveal it and the Scripture passages before and after will inevitably indicate it." What are some examples cited by the author? Can you think of other examples where this proves true?

14. Why could Zwingli and Luther not agree on the Lord's Supper?

15. How does the author answer this question: "Are we, therefore, to take as literal the Biblical descriptions of heaven and of hell?" What are the Biblical descriptions of heaven and of hell?

16. Why is this statement true? "I cannot improve upon God and what God says; therefore, I must deliver this message as God has revealed it. I must speak God's language and when I do, I find that I am speaking in the power and unction of the Lord."

17. How does Dr. Criswell answer the following question?: "Is it true that people are literally and everlastingly lost without Christ?" How would you answer that same question?

18. Discuss the significance of this statement: "Nothing is more earnestly or desperately needed today than Christian conviction concerning Christ." Why is it true?

19. Comment on the commissions of Christ as recorded in Matthew 28, Mark 16, Luke 24, John 20, and Acts 1.

20. What is the message of John the Baptist in Matthew 3?

21. What is the message of Jesus to Nicodemus in John 3?

22. What is the message of Peter to Jerusalem in Acts 2?

23. What is the message of Peter and John to the Sanhedrin in Acts 4:12?

24. What is the message of the angel to Cornelius in Acts 10-11?

25. What is the message of Paul to the Athenians in Acts 17?

26. Describe the meaning and the purpose of the Roman Pantheon?

27. Ponder the author's questions: "Why did this liberal-minded Roman Empire persecute the Christians? What was the reason for the martyrdom of uncounted numbers of the followers of Christ?"

28. Do you agree with the following statement? "New Testament Christianity now confronts a modern world that is as liberal and broad-minded in its reception of different religions as the ancient Roman Empire. To the modern world all religions are good if they are earnestly received."

29. Explain the meaning of Edward Gibbon's statement in his *Decline and Fall of the Roman Empire*: "To the people all religions were equally true; to the philosophers all religions were equally false; and to the politicians all religions were equally useful."

30. Why is the "doctrine that everyone will be saved whether he believes in Christ or not" like termites eating through a foundation?

31. Concerning "the heresy of universalism," Dr. Criswell asks a significant question: "If this be true why bother to preach the gospel since people are not lost?" What would you say?

32. What does the following Scripture tell us? "Neither is there salvation in any other: for there is none other name under heaven given among men, whereby we must be saved" (Acts 4:12).

33. Why does the author say that "truth is everlastingly mandatory, narrow, and exclusive"? What examples does he give to support this statement?

34. Explain the meaning of these two points: "A man ought to be broad in his sympathies; a man ought to be broad in his horizons"?

35. Why is "all truth narrow"?

Chapter 13

1. Dr. Criswell begins his chapter this way: "What do I preach, believing that the Bible is literally true? I preach the truth of the revelations of God in the first book of the Bible, the book of Genesis. This, of course, is in diametrical opposition to the position taken by most modern theologians." Ponder this statement and discuss.

2. "In our present day the first eleven chapters of Genesis are reduced to myth and legend." Have you found this to be true? Explain.

3. In what way did Jesus endorse the Mosaic story of the creation of Adam and Eve?

4. How did Jesus verify the divine inspiration of the Genesis account of creation?

5. Does the apostle Paul accept the Genesis account of creation? What does he say?

6. How does Genesis lay the foundation for the whole revelation in the Book of God?

7. What are the affirmations found in John 1:1, Hebrews 1:1, and Colossians 1:16?

8. How does the Genesis story lay the groundwork for the doctrine of all human responsibility and accountability to God?

9. What does the author mean by this statement? "A lower anthropology always means a lower theology." Do you agree?

10. Why is this statement true? "If there was no fall, then there was no condemnation, no separation, and therefore there is no need for salvation. If there is no need for salvation, there is no need for an atoning Saviour." Discuss.

11. Why does the rejection of the Genesis story as a myth tend to the rejection of the whole gospel of salvation?

12. Dr. Criswell asks three questions. How does he answer them? "Is there a contradiction between Genesis and geology?"

    "Is there a contradiction between Genesis and anthropology?"

    "Is there a contradiction between Genesis and any other branch of knowledge?"

13. "Humankind is a solidarity, as a tree with its roots, trunk, branches, leaves, and fruit is ultimately all one living organism," writes Dr. Criswell. To what does he refer when he uses the image of the tree?

14. What does the author mean by "a moral sensitivity, a spiritual life not found in any other of God's created beings"?

15. What does the author write about the flood narrative in Genesis?

16. Why is the book of Genesis "as vital to the Bible as the book of the Revelation"?

Chapter 14

1. Did you find Dr. Criswell's argument for biblical creation as opposed to evolution convincing? In your opinion, what are the most important points he makes?

2. What does the author accomplish with his chapter beginning? "When I read Genesis 1:27, 'So God created man in His own image, in the image of God created he him; male and female created he them,' of what do I think?

When I read Genesis 2:7, what do I think? Do I think of a simian hanging from a banyan tree by his prehensile tail? When I read Genesis 2:21–24, of what do I think? Of two hairy anthropoids, rambling through the jungle on all fours? Is this what the Bible means?"

3. Ponder the author's question: "Must we believe in evolution to be academic, scientific, reasonable, modern, factual?"

4. What does Dr. Criswell mean by this: "The grand myth of our generation is evolution. The big lie of our modern era is evolution." Do you agree? Why or why not? Discuss.

5. In this chapter, did the author answer to your satisfaction these questions: "What does evolution say? What does it teach? What does it believe?"

6. Explain the example of Lamarck's theory of acquired characteristics? What does it state? What argument does the author make about Lamarck's theory?

7. "[Pseudoscientists] would have us believe that all of life and all of nature tend upward and progress forward and higher. This is denied by every observation we are capable of acknowledging and discovering in the universe. The universe itself is running down." Discuss the author's point in making this observation.

8. Why is the Genesis account of man "the only possible basis for our understanding the human soul"?

9. What conclusion has the author drawn from Drosophila, the fruit fly, and its evolutionary lines?

10. Dr. Criswell makes a significant statement: "It is beyond our power to get beyond the set law of God which is that everything reproduces "after its kind" (Gen. 1:11–12, 24–25). This is God's universal law of life." Discuss its implications.

11. "Within a species there can be great variety. Mutation is always possible and is one of God's delightful secrets." Explain what the author means by mutation.

12. What is the "secularists' necessity for the theory of evolution"?

13. Discuss the following statement: "Evolution succeeds not because it is a sound factual theory but because it can be made the basis of a humanistic faith which a sinful person can adopt in place of the regenerating gospel of the Son of God."

Chapter 15

1. Discuss the significance of this statement: "Born of a virgin, God in the flesh, God, very God, offered on the cross as a literal atonement for our sins, raised from the dead by the power of the Holy Spirit, our Mediator and Intercessor in heaven, and our reigning, coming-again Lord and King." What does it mean to you?

2. Describe the biblical narratives concerning the conception of Jesus.

3. What does Dr. Criswell mean by this statement: "Perhaps the most bitterly assailed of all the miracles in the Bible is this one of the miracle of the Incarnation?"

4. Discuss Matthew Arnold's comment: "I do not believe in the virgin birth for that would imply a miracle and miracles do not happen."

5. What does the author mean by this statement: "In practically all quarters of liberal religion the virgin birth is openly treated as a fable. This is true not only in circles of unbelief but also the virgin birth is discredited in many areas of the church itself." Why do you believe this statement is true?

6. Discuss the following: "The Incarnation of Christ was a work of the Holy Spirit (Luke 1:35)."

7. Discuss the following: "The initial event in the life of our Lord, as the last event, the resurrection of Christ, was the work of the Holy Spirit (Rom. 1:4)."

8. Read Hebrews 10:5 and Hebrews 9:14. What was the purpose of the Incarnation?

9. Why is the "miraculous story of the Incarnation the record of the intervention of Almighty God in human history"?

10. Why does the virgin birth "signal a new age, a new blessing, a new revelation, a new relation to God"?

11. Discuss the following verses of Scripture: Genesis 1:2; Luke 1:35; Matthew 1:16,18; and Romans 1:4.

12. Dr. Criswell makes this statement: "This intervention of God in human history in a mighty, apocalyptic demonstration of His presence and power is witnessed in the Holy Scriptures in many places." What examples does the author use in order to prove this statement? Discuss them.

13. Explain the significance of 2 Peter 3:8 in light of Dr. Criswell's statements.

14. Why is the Incarnation "a mystery which ultimately lies beyond the veil of human comprehension or analysis"?

15. According to the author, why is "the virgin birth as natural at the beginning of the story of Christ as the resurrection is at the end"?

16. "In the birth of Christ there was a divine personality already existing entering into a new mode of existence. It was God Himself; emptying Himself, who, being in the form of God is now being made in the form of a man." What does this statement mean?

17. What does the author say about "miracles" and "mystery"?

18. According to Dr. Criswell, what are the "two great biological miracles wrought by the hand of God"? Discuss.

19. What does the author say about the "execution" of Christ?

20. What is the thesis of the book by Albert Schweitzer, *The Quest for the Historical Jesus*, concerning Jesus' death?

21. What does the author mean by the following: "[Christ's death] is the passover sacrifice. This is the blood of the Day of Atonement sprinkled on the mercy seat"?

22. Explain the significance of this statement: "Jesus was not dying a martyr's death; He was not dying a hero's death. He was dying for the sins of the world."

23. Read Revelation 19:15; Hebrews 2:9; 1 Peter 2:24; and John 1:29. What do these Scriptures reveal?

24. Discuss: "Christ died to save us from the penalty of our iniquities and to those who look in faith to Him there is an actual expiation, an actual atonement, an actual propitiation, an actual deliverance from the judgment and penalty of sin and death."

Chapter 16

1. Why does the author believe/preach that "Jesus is personally, visibly, actually, truly, really coming again"?

2. Read John 14:3; Acts 1:11; and Revelation 1:7. Discuss.

3. Read John 4:24 and discuss the concept of "God is Spirit."

4. Read Luke 24:36–43 and discuss this concept: "Jesus has a body."

5. Read and discuss Isaiah 6:1–4; John 12:41; 8:58; 14:9; 10:30.

6. What arguments are cited by others that Jesus has already come? Name them and discuss.

7. Discuss the following: "The Bible is replete with statements of the certainty, the literalness, the visibility of Christ returning to earth."

8. Explain the meaning of Revelation 22:16.

9. Explain what Dr. Criswell means by a "twofold simile."

10. What is the "sign" of the coming of Jesus, as expressed by the author?

11. The author asks the question: "What is this cloud in which the Son of Man will appear?" How does he answer it?

12. What does the following mean: "At His first Advent He put off His glory (Phil. 2). At His second Advent He will put on His glory?"?

13. Read Micah 4:3; Isaiah 11:6–9; Titus 2:13; and Revelation 22:20. What are these prophecies that will be fulfilled? Explain.

Chapter 17

1. Explain the meaning of this observation: "The Word of God contains principles of human adjustment and emotional growth which were revealed by the Lord from heaven long before the advent of modern psychology. The human race, fundamentally, does not change." Do you agree? Why or why not?

2. How can God's Word be used in counseling?

3. The author writes: "The Bible-centered counselor finds in the Word of God great truths for human adjustment, for insight into the nature of man, his motivation, his defenses, and for the ultimate resolutions of his conflicts."

Why does Dr. Criswell write that "such insight is not available to the unbeliever"?

4. Discuss the following: "Neither Plato, Aristotle, nor Freud has given to us the sense of meaning, destiny, and purpose that is revealed in the Word of God." Why is this true?

5. Why is faith a "necessary ingredient in the development of a well-integrated personality"?

6. Dr. Criswell writes: "The most disturbing element in all the world is sin. It brings discouragement and failure. The Bible has the only clear answer to the problem." What is the Bible's answer to the problem of sin?

7. Read 1 John 1:9; Isaiah 44:22; Psalm 51:1,9; Micah 7:19; Hebrews 10:17; and Jeremiah 31:34. What do they say?

8. Ponder the meaning of the following Scripture: "Confess your faults one to another, and pray one for another, that ye may be healed" (Jas. 5:16).

9. Describe the emotional despair that divorce can bring to a family? What does the Bible say about divorce?

10. What reasons are given in favor of reading the Bible in the home?

11. Do you believe that the Bible suggests material blessings for those who honor the Word? Why or why not? What does the author say about this?

12. What would you add to this chapter if you were its writer? What primary point does this chapter make?

Chapter 18

1. Contemplate this statement: "Religion is built upon authority, and without that authority faith is sheer speculation."

2. What are the three possible sources in the Christian faith to which we can look for a revelation of God and upon which foundation we may build our hope for heaven? Name them and discuss each.

3. What is "human speculation"?

4. What is the "hierarchy of an infallible church?

5. Why is the third alternative the Bible?

6. What does the author refer to when he speaks of the "God is dead" theologians?

7. Did the church exist before the Bible, as some say? Why or why not? What answer does Dr. Criswell give?

8. Ponder and discuss the following statement: "God's Word was delivered by the inspired apostles from the days of Pentecost onward, and the church came into existence by believing that preexistent, spoken, oral word. The Word was before the church. The truth was before the church. The revelation and self-disclosure of God was before the church. The truth of the word created the church."

9. Read Matthew 16:13–18 and discuss.

10. Read John 1:1–15 and discuss.

11. What was the significance of the discussion that Dr. Criswell had on a train to Zurich with a Benedictine monk?

12. Ponder the importance of this statement: "We have no other final and ultimate authority in our religion than the Bible. God has spoken preeminently to us and has truthfully and fully revealed Himself to us through the Bible."

13. What does the author mean by "bibliolatry"?

14. Why does the author use the examples of a telescope and a letter to explain the medium of the Word of God?

15. If time allows, read and discuss the following Scriptures: Deuteronomy 31:10–13; Joshua 1:8; 2 Chronicles 17:9; Deuteronomy 17:18–20; 1 Kings 11:38; Nehemiah 1:7–9; Nehemiah 8:5–8; and 2 Kings 17:13.

16. If time allows, discuss the following Scriptures from the New Testament: 1 Timothy 4:14; 2 Timothy 3:17—4:3; and Revelation 1:3.

Chapter 19

1. What does Dr. Criswell say is the "sorriest way to preach"? Do you agree? Why or why not?

2. What does he say is the "sublimest way to preach"? Do you agree or disagree? Why or why not?

3. What does the author mean by "the spiritualizing, allegorizing way" to preach?

4. What does he mean by "the grammatical-historical way, the expository method"?

5. What does Dr. Criswell mean when he writes: "True Bible preaching is kerygmatic"?

6. Do you agree that "the history of preaching consists primarily of the story of these two contrasting and conflicting methods of interpretation and presentation of God's Word: the method of the spiritualizer and the method of the expositor"? Why or why not?

7. What does the author say about Aristobulus, Aristotle, Philo, and Origen?

8. Why is John Chrysostom, the pastor of the church at Antioch and at Constantinople, referred to as "John the Golden Mouth"?

9. What destroyed the "glorious preaching method of John Chrysostom"?

10. Discuss the following comment made by Martin Luther: "Every word should be allowed to stand in its natural meaning and should not be abandoned unless faith forces us to it. The literal sense of Scripture alone is the whole essence of faith and of Christian theology."

11. Discuss the following comment made by John Calvin: "Let us know that the true meaning of Scripture is the natural and obvious meaning. Let us embrace and abide it resolutely. It is the first business of an interpreter to let the author say what he does say instead of attributing to him what we think he ought to say."

12. What did the reformers do?

13. What is an allegory?

14. What is meant by figurative language?

15. What does Dr. Criswell write that John the Baptist meant when he proclaimed in John 1:29, "Behold the Lamb of God"?

16. "A simple rule to follow in determining what is literal and what is figurative is this: If the literal meaning of any word or expression makes good sense in its connections, it is literal. But if the literal meaning does not make good sense, it is figurative." Do you agree or disagree? Why or why not?

17. Ponder this statement: "When we do not use the plain, normal, literal method of interpretation, all objectivity is lost." Do you agree?

18. What is meant by the word "exegesis"?

19. Explain this statement: "So expound one place of Scripture that it not be repugnant to another."

20. What does the author mean by this unusual statement: "As someone has said, we Christians have helped ourselves to all the blessings and have left the Jews all the curses"?

21. "If we take the Bible literally and preach it literally we have nothing to worry about. But if we take the Bible and spiritualize it, a man will find himself contradicting himself over and over again as he preaches through the years." Contemplate and explain. Do you agree? Why or why not?

Chapter 20

1. Discuss the crises the apostle Paul endured for the sake of the gospel of Jesus Christ.

2. Read 1 Corinthians 2:2 and ponder Paul's statement.

3. What does the author refer to when he writes this sentence: "Such 'butcher-shop religion,' as they describe it, violates modern, sensitive, cultivated minds."

4. How does Dr. Criswell answer this question in which he poses: "What is modern, liberal theology"?

5. Contemplate and discuss: "Modern, liberal theologians look upon the cross as an example of self-sacrifice and philanthropic love, but in no way do they look upon the cross as an atonement for our sins."

6. Ponder the following and discuss: "Modern, liberal theologians think that man's fundamental problem is not that he is lost in sin and depravity but that his problem is fundamentally environmental; if we can change the order of society, we shall reach utopia and the realization of the kingdom of God."

7. Read Matthew 15:6, 23:13, and 23:33. What did Christ say about "the scribes because they had been false to the oracles of God"?

8. What was Paul's warning to Timothy? Why was it significant?

9. The author asks the question: "Are there any such false teachers and preachers in our time and in our generation?" How does he answer his question?

10. What does the author say about this statement: "This overthrow of the Scriptures in our modern times has been a tragic development in the Christian world."? Discuss.

11. Discuss the significance of this statement made by the Roman Catholic Church at the Vatican Council of 1870: "Scriptures contain a revelation without error. Having been written by the inspiration of the Holy Ghost, they have God for their Author."

12. Do you agree with this statement: "There is no doubt but that the onslaughts of the modern, liberal theologian have almost destroyed for many people the Bible as the inerrant, infallible Word of God."? What are some of these "onslaughts" the author refers to?

13. What does the author refer to when he writes about the "pitiful remnants of medieval credulity and . . . prisoners of a fossilized tradition"?

14. What does Dr. Criswell say is the "most important question in the world today"? Do you agree?

15. What does the author mean by "a leap of faith"?

16. What is meant by this statement: "The destructive results of the critics' work can be seen on every hand as they busy themselves seeking errors, contradictions, and historical inaccuracies in the Bible. They have torn apart God's beautiful flower. They cannot see it any more."? Discuss.

17. What does Dr. Criswell define as a "modern, liberal theologian"?

18. Ponder the following: "When the modern liberal theologians attempt to palm off their denials of the Holy Scriptures by labeling them 'the findings of science' or 'the

consensus of scholarship,' there are some people who take them seriously and are ready to throw away their Bibles."

19. Explain in your own words the quote made by Prime Minister Winston Churchill.

Chapter 21

1. How did the Old Testament prophets call their people back to the remembrance of their forefathers?

2. Ponder the following: "Through the centuries all Christendom has been convinced that the Bible in its entirety was veritably inspired and that as such it was endowed with all of the perfections of God."

3. How did Jesus receive the Old Testament Scriptures in His lifetime on earth?

4. Dr. Criswell writes: "In the early confessions and creeds of the church the doctrine of the inspiration of the Bible is hardly mentioned." Why this omission?

5. What was the attitude of the Bible in the Middle Ages?

6. What was the attitude of the Bible during the Reformation?

7. Ponder: "At Trent, Rome reaffirmed its belief in the Bible and did so concerning the books of both Testaments with this simple sentence, 'One Author, one God is the Author of both.'" What is the significance of this statement?

8. What happened in the eighteenth and nineteenth centuries that "began to replace the Holy Scriptures as the final authority of faith and life"?

9. What did humanism do to the attitude of the Scriptures?

10. If time permits, research the lives and beliefs of the following men: Felix Manz, Balthazar Hubmeier, and John Bunyan.

11. As an extra project, study the life and mission of the "Father of Modern Missions," William Carey.

12. Explain and discuss the first article of the New Hampshire Confession of Faith: "We believe that the Holy Bible was written by men divinely inspired and is a perfect treasure of heavenly instruction; that it has God for its author, salvation for its end and truth without any mixture of error for its matter; that it reveals the principles by which God will judge us; and therefore, is and shall remain to the end of the world, the true center of Christian union and the supreme standard by which all human conduct, creeds and opinion shall be tried." What does this article mean to you? Why is it so important?

13. Discuss the evangelization of the American continent. How did it come about?

14. As an extra project, read H. C. Vedder's description of the pioneer preacher who went forth to claim the Western wilderness for Christ (*A Short History of the Baptists*). Report and discuss.

15. What kind of life did the pioneer preachers endure for the sake of preaching the Word of God?

16. Discuss the significance of the 1962 Southern Baptist Convention's resolution made in San Francisco: "We reaffirm our faith in the entire Bible as the authoritative, authentic, infallible Word of God . . . our historic position."

17. What is the author's final appeal to Southern Baptists?

18. Scripture for discussion: "Be ye not unequally yoked together with unbelievers: for what fellowship hath righteousness with unrighteousness? and what communion hath light with darkness? And what concord hath Christ with Belial? or what part hath he that believeth with an infidel? And what agreement hath the temple of God with idols? for ye are the temple of the living God; as God hath

said, I will dwell in them, and walk in them; and I will be their God, and they shall be my people. Wherefore come out from among them, and be ye separate, saith the Lord, and touch not the unclean thing; and I will receive you, and will be a Father unto you, and ye shall be my sons and daughters, saith the Lord Almighty" (2 Cor. 6:14–18).

19. Scripture for discussion: "I know thy works, that thou art neither cold nor hot: I would thou wert cold or hot. So then because thou art lukewarm, and neither cold nor hot, I will spue thee out of my mouth" (Rev. 3:15–16).

20. Scripture for discussion: "He that is not with me is against me; and he that gathereth not with me scattereth abroad" (Matt. 12:30).

21. What was your opinion of this book? What are Dr. Criswell's significant statements that made an impression on you during your reading of *Why I Preach That The Bible Is Literally True?* With what statements did you agree? With what statements did you not agree?

Index